Critical Acclaim for

The Profit Impact of Business Intelligence

Over the last decade, the Wal-Mart factor has placed tremendous pressure on margins for the major food and beverage manufacturers served by McCormick's Global Industrial Group. This means that we, too, are under pressure to reduce supply chain costs while continuing to provide world-class service. The ideas in The Profit Impact of Business Intelligence *were central to our deployment of business intelligence applications that allowed us to manage revenue delivery and reduce costs.*

– Kevin McCaughey, Vice President
Strategic Planning, McCormick & Company
Global Industrial Group

While we are the leader in our market, Principal Financial Group operates in an increasingly competitive environment, and one performance management approach we are taking is to leverage business intelligence to better serve our customers and to optimize our cost structure in relation to the services our customers value most. We have used the BI Pathway Method and the strategies described in The Profit Impact of Business Intelligence *to align our BI program with our critical success factors and to drive our BI development efforts.*

– Terry Lillis, Chief Financial Officer
Retirement and Investor Services
The Principal Financial Group

This is a "must read" book for anyone who wants to achieve real business intelligence. Strategic alignment is a critical element of BI success and understanding business requirements is essential. The BI Pathway Method and the proven practices described in The Profit Impact of Business Intelligence advance the discipline of BI by focusing on business value built upon a strong foundation of technology best practices. With this book, Steve and Nancy Williams take a big step toward putting the business back into BI.

– David L. Wells, Director of Education
TDWI: The Data Warehousing Institute

Clearly, Nancy and Steve Williams understand the "business" in business intelligence. This book is a must for business leaders who require that their BI programs drive real business value. The focus on strategy, the key critical success factor for BI, is outstanding.

– Barbara Wixom, PhD, Associate Professor, Director, MS-MIT
University of Virginia – McIntire School of Commerce

The

Profit Impact

of

Business
Intelligence

Steve Williams

Nancy Williams

AMSTERDAM • BOSTON • HEIDELBERG • LONDON
NEW YORK • OXFORD • PARIS • SAN DIEGO
SAN FRANCISCO • SINGAPORE • SYDNEY • TOKYO

ELSEVIER   Morgan Kaufmann Publishers is an imprint of Elsevier   MORGAN KAUFMANN PUBLISHERS

Publisher	Diane Cerra
Publishing Services Manager	George Morrison
Production Editor	Dawnmarie Simpson
Assistant Editor	Asma Palmeiro
Cover Design	Eric DeCicco
Text Design	Alisa Andreola
Composition	Integra Software Services, Pvt., Ltd.
Technical Illustration	Graphic World Publishing Services
Copyeditor	Graphic World Publishing Services
Proofreader	Graphic World Publishing Services
Indexer	Graphic World Publishing Services
Interior printer	The Maple-Vail Book Manufacturing Group
Cover printer	Phoenix Color Corporation

Morgan Kaufmann Publishers is an imprint of Elsevier.
500 Sansome Street, Suite 400, San Francisco, CA 94111

This book is printed on acid-free paper.

Library of Congress Cataloging-in-Publication Data
Williams, Steve.
The profit impact of business intelligence/Steve Williams, Nancy Williams.
      p.   cm.
   Includes bibliographical references and index.
   ISBN-13: 978-0-12-372499-1
   ISBN-10: 0-12-372499-6
1. Business intelligence.   2. Profit.   I. Williams, Nancy.   II. Title.
HD38.7. W54 2007
658.4′7—dc22

                                                            2006025719

ISBN 13: 978-0-12-372499-1
ISBN 10: 0-12-372499-6

For information on all Morgan Kaufmann publications, visit our
Web site at www.mkp.com or www.books.elsevier.com

Printed in the United States of America
08   09   10   5   4   3   2

Working together to grow
libraries in developing countries

www.elsevier.com | www.bookaid.org | www.sabre.org

ELSEVIER   **BOOK AID** International   **Sabre Foundation**

Contents

Preface

Since founding DecisionPath Consulting in 1999, Nancy and I have had the privilege of working with great clients and colleagues. We have always approached our engagements in the spirit of partnership: we bring our general business knowledge, enthusiasm, and expertise in business intelligence and data warehousing, and our clients afford us an opportunity to help them succeed. In the process of achieving those successes, we've observed a variety of challenges that can derail even the most promising BI opportunities. Simply put, most of these challenges are *business* challenges.

This experience has led us to conclude that if companies are going to fully realize the profit potential of business intelligence (BI), there needs to be a better understanding of BI in the executive and managerial ranks. That is the reason for this book.

At the enterprise level, BI has demonstrated its ability to improve profits by tens or hundreds of millions of dollars annually, depending on the size of the company. Accordingly, BI should be a key tool for managing and improving performance—and profits—at just about any company in just about any industry. It should certainly rank alongside of management tools and techniques such as Strategic Planning, Benchmarking, Pay-for-Performance, Outsourcing, Customer Segmentation, Reengineering, Balanced Scorecard, and Total Quality Management.

That being said, many large companies tend to see BI as primarily a technology play. Thus, they fail to focus on the business challenges of leveraging business information and analytical techniques to drive better performance and improved profits. Some of the typical business challenges we have seen include:

- Misalignment between business strategies, core business processes that drive performance, and the BI program or initiative
- Lack of clarity about how BI will be used *by the business* to improve profits
- Insufficient leadership to drive changes to how the company uses information and analytical tools to drive results
- Insufficient recognition by IT management that BI needs to be managed differently than transactional systems
- Weak business sponsorship and lack of accountability for the BI program or initiative
- Under-investment in developing BI and data warehousing core competencies

In addition to observing these business challenges first-hand in many different companies, we also hear these themes echoed by the BI professionals we meet when we teach at industry conferences. On the flip side, we serve as judges for TDWI's annual best practices competition: a key aspect of winning companies is their ability to overcome such challenges. More broadly, by improving business performance, BI helps companies compete successfully in an increasingly global economy, which protects local jobs, economies, and communities.

Given the mission of building a better understanding of BI in the executive and managerial ranks, we have written *The Profit Impact of Business Intelligence* from a perspective that blends general management and technology strategy thinking. By doing so, we hope to engage an audience that includes business and IT leaders and managers as well as BI and data warehousing project managers, architects, and analysts. We also believe that the book can be a source of readings for undergraduate and graduate-level MIS courses. The general organization of the book is as follows:

Part 1: Identifying and Leveraging BI-Driven Profit Opportunities

Our goal in Part 1 is to pique your interest in BI and point out in general terms what it takes to leverage BI for improved profits. In Chapter 1, we provide examples of how well-known companies in a range of industries use BI to improve profits, and we describe the prerequisites for ensuring the targeted ROI. In Chapter 2, we describe and illustrate a proven, straightforward method for identifying how your company can exploit BI for improved business performance. In Chapter 3, we point our some of the key barriers—or risks—that must be overcome to capture the full payoff of your investment in BI. In our view, the chapters that compose Part 1 should be of interest to the broad audience the book hopes to engage.

Part 2: Creating the BI Asset

Our goal in Part 2 is to provide a business and technical overview of what it takes to design, build, deploy, and leverage a BI environment—the BI Asset. In Chapter 4, we describe our BI Pathway Method, which is a complete strategic approach to the business and technical activities that must be accomplished to inject BI into your business and use it to drive business performance. The treatment in Chapter 4 is at a high level, and we would refer readers interested in a more detailed treatment to our full-day course for more of the "how-to" of the BI Pathway Method. In Chapter 5 we discuss the leadership and general management challenges of using BI to drive increased profits, which are business challenges that go beyond the sometimes complex technical challenges of building the data warehouse and the BI applications. In Chapter 6, we discuss how BI fits in the broader IT environment, which is important because IT policies and procedures optimized for day-to-day transaction processing systems are sometimes barriers to BI success. In our view, parts of Chapter 4 may be too technical for business executives and managers, and parts of Chapter 5 may be too business-oriented for the more technically inclined members of the BI team.

Part 3: Leveraging BI for Profit Improvement

One key goal in Part 3 is to delve more deeply into the different ways companies have used BI to drive increased profits, which we do in Chapter 7. In Chapter 8, we discuss common mistakes companies make with BI initiatives, and in Chapter 9 we take a look ahead to what companies can achieve with BI if they really embrace it and use the technologies to push the envelope of business performance management. In our view, the chapters in Part 3 should be of interest to the broad audience the book hopes to engage.

Appendices

Appendix A provides a glossary of common BI terms, including terms used in this book.

Appendix B builds on the material in Chapter 3 by providing the BI Readiness Assessment instrument that DecisionPath Consulting uses to assist companies in identifying potential barriers to success. With the assessment instrument, you can find out today where your strengths and weaknesses, assets and risks are for implementing BI. That information helps you plan a BI program that is primed for success, whether defined in terms of increased profit, better service, higher product quality, or other key success factors. Visit www.decisionpath.com to take an online version of the BI Readiness Assessment to see how your organization stacks up.

Special Features

Throughout the book, we have made liberal use of graphics, tip boxes, pitfall warnings, and checklists to help spotlight the key points you may want to remember. We hope you will find these helpful.

Acknowledgments

After a couple of decades in business, it becomes difficult to recall all the specific influences on one's thinking, which makes it a challenge to properly acknowledge everyone who has influenced this book. That being said, we would certainly be remiss if we failed to mention how much we have learned from our opportunities to work with major organizations in a range of industries. Companies such as McCormick, Marriott, Legg Mason, and Principal Financial Group are each leaders in their industries, and we have gotten to see a range of challenges to BI success. Many of the business-driven methods and perspectives shared in the book are a direct result of what we have learned as we worked with these clients to overcome their specific challenges.

Our thinking has also been influenced by our colleagues at DecisionPath Consulting. As we have employed the BI Pathway Method on client engagements, our colleagues have proved to be a steady source of improvement ideas and innovative uses of tools to support project execution. The result is a better method, proven in practice, and readily taught to new BI teams. Among our colleagues, Dr. Jim Thomann warrants special recognition for his contribution to the development of the BI Pathway Method, the technical portions of which are based on data warehousing fundamentals that Jim has been teaching at TDWI conferences for years.

We have also enjoyed learning from our colleagues in the business intelligence and data warehousing industry. Most notably, we are indebted to Dave Wells at TDWI for his encouragement, insight, and constructive feedback as we developed the BI Pathway Method. Many of the data warehousing fundamentals that serve as the technical foundation of the BI Pathway have been taught in TDWI courses that Dave developed. We have also benefited from the lively conversations we've had with the leading practitioners who serve as faculty at TDWI conferences and who serve as fellow judges for TDWI best practices competitions.

Another source of the learning that is reflected in *The Profit Impact of Business Intelligence* is—perhaps ironically—our work with the U.S. Social Security Administration (SSA). While we speak in terms of "profit" and "business performance" throughout the book, public sector managers are increasingly embracing business performance management techniques, and SSA is a leader in this regard. Our work with Skip Hardy at the Social Security Administration has allowed us to see this in action, and, in the process, it has enriched our understanding of the complex tradeoffs involved in establishing a responsive BI environment in a world dominated by mission-critical transaction processing systems.

As to the book itself, it has been a challenge to juggle our commitments to our clients, our responsibilities as executives at DecisionPath Consulting, and the demands of writing a book. That challenge has been made much more manageable by our colleague Scott Palmer, whose experience as an author of technical books has enabled him to "show us the ropes." Scott's knowledge of the process and the publishing industry was instrumental to keeping us on schedule. The book has also benefited tremendously from the comments of our reviewers—Barron Penner of Principal Financial Group, Sid Adelman of Sid Adelman & Associates, Wayne Eckerson of TDWI, and Barb Wixom of the McIntire School at the University of Virginia. Last, but certainly not least, our editors at Elsevier—Diane Cerra and Asma Palmeiro—have provided excellent comments and suggestions throughout the project.

Thanks to everyone!

Chapter 1

The Business Value of Business Intelligence

"The social responsibility of business is to increase its profits."
—Milton Friedman, Nobel laureate economist

The past decade has witnessed an arms race in American business: a wholesale deployment of information technology (IT) to the point at which some experts estimate that half of capital spending by business is invested in IT. The growth of companies such as SAP, Oracle, Microsoft, IBM, Cisco, Dell, and Siebel—and their consulting company partners—attests to the magnitude of this race.

Most of that investment has been in what amounts to better plumbing, better systems for managing day-to-day operations, and more frequent and voluminous reports. There is little debate that these investments are necessary to operate many modern business enterprises. That said, our experience working with and talking to business and IT leaders at major companies in a variety of industries suggests that these companies are still data-rich but information-poor. In other words, these enterprises lack the kind of actionable information and analytical tools needed to improve profits and performance.

Business intelligence (BI) is a response to this need. It is the next logical progression in management thinking about IT. The goal of our book is to show you how to follow the lead of companies who have capitalized on the potential of BI to improve profit and performance. While many major companies have implemented data warehouses, very few have used them to achieve BI. In many companies, data warehousing (DW) efforts have largely been limited to producing more reports, with a vague understanding of how this information will benefit the organization. However, other companies have gone beyond this and demonstrate the true potential of BI. For example,

- Western Digital, a manufacturer of computer hard disk drives with annual sales of more than $3 billion, uses BI to better manage its inventory, supply chains, product lifecycles, and customer relationships. BI enabled the company to reduce operating costs by 50%.

- Capital One, a global financial services firm with more than 50 million customer accounts, uses BI to analyze and improve the profitability of its product lines as well as the effectiveness of its business processes and marketing programs.
- Continental Airlines, a U.S. airline company that was near bankruptcy in the 1990s, invested $30 million in BI to improve its business processes and customer service. In the following six years, Continental reaped a staggering $500 million return on its BI investment for a return on investment (ROI) of more than 1,000%.
- CompUSA, a major retailer of computer equipment and software, uses BI to analyze its sales trends. The company earned an ROI of more than $6 million in the first phase of the project.

Done right, BI has tremendous proven potential to improve profits and performance. Done wrong, it's a waste of time and money. The bottom line? *Make sure that you do it right.* This book gets you started.

But what is BI? In this chapter, we provide a practical working definition of BI and examples of how well-known companies in a variety of industries use it to improve their performance. This will stimulate your thinking about how you can use BI in your own business.

1.1   What Is Business Intelligence?

Let's start with what BI *isn't*. BI is not:

- **A single product.** Although many excellent products can help you implement BI, BI is not a product that can be bought and installed to solve all your problems "out of the box."
- **A technology.** Although DW tools and technologies such as relational databases ETL tools, BI user interface tools, and servers are typically used to support BI applications, BI is not just a technology.
- **A methodology.** Although a powerful methodology (such as the our BI Pathway) is essential for success with BI, you need to combine that methodology with appropriate technological solutions and organizational changes.

If that's what BI is *not*, then what *is* it? BI combines products, technology, and methods to organize key information that management needs to improve profit and performance. More broadly, we think of BI as *business information and business analyses within the context of key business processes that lead to decisions and actions* and that result in improved business performance. In particular, BI means leveraging information assets within key business processes to achieve improved business performance. It involves business information and analysis that are

- Used within a context of key business processes
- Support decisions and actions
- Lead to improved business performance

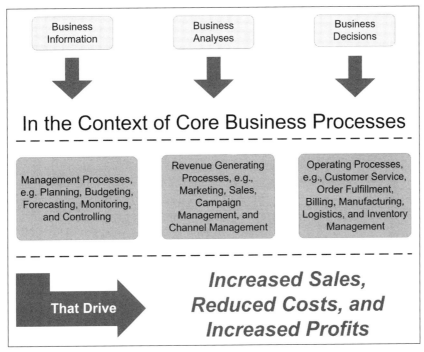

FIGURE 1-1 What business intelligence means in practice.

For business, the primary focus is to increase revenues and/or reduce costs, thereby improving performance and increasing profits. For the public sector, the primary focus is service to citizens, coping with budget constraints, and using resources wisely in support of an agency's mission. Figure 1-1 illustrates this definition.

1.2   Business Intelligence in Action

To illustrate this practical working definition of BI, consider how the hotel and casino operator Harrah's Entertainment uses BI to improve revenue and profit through customer relationship management.

Harrah's runs not only its flagship hotel and casino in Las Vegas, Nevada, but more than two dozen casinos in a dozen other states. Its BI investment enabled Harrah's to enjoy 16 consecutive quarters of revenue growth. In 2002, it earned a $235 million profit on more than $4 billion in revenue (Loveman, 2003). That was a startling improvement from Harrah's solid but not spectacular performance only a few years earlier.

Harrah's invested in BI to help it win and consolidate the loyalty of its best customers. Its first effort was the "Total Gold" program, which was modeled on airline frequent-flyer programs. However, Total Gold was too similar to the customer-loyalty programs offered by other casinos to give Harrah's a killer edge, but it did prove to be a rich resource of data for Harrah's subsequent BI efforts. In particular, the Total Gold data warehouse provided valuable *business information* about Harrah's customers:

- Total Gold cardholders were spending only 36% of their gaming dollars in Harrah's casinos. Harrah's wanted that percentage to increase.
- Twenty-six percent of Harrah's casino customers generated 82% of its revenues.
- Those "high value" customers were not the people Harrah's expected. Instead of high-rollers wearing cowboy boots stepping out of limousines, the customers who brought in the most revenue were dentists, schoolteachers, office workers, and the like. They didn't spend huge amounts of money in any one visit, but—week in, week out, month after month—they stopped at Harrah's after work, in the evenings, or on weekends to relax in the casino or have a meal.

That business information, combined with *business analysis*, enabled Harrah's both to know who its most valuable customers were and to offer them personalized service. Harrah's evolved Total Gold into the "Total Rewards" program, which divided its gaming customers into three levels of service (gold, platinum, and diamond) based on their long-term revenue value to the company.

In addition to identifying its most valuable customers, Harrah's also used BI to analyze what those customers wanted and what measures might win their loyalty. Diamond-level card holders would seldom if ever have to wait in line for anything, whether to check into the hotel, get their cars parked, or be seated in one of Harrah's restaurants. If they called to reserve a room, they might qualify for special low rates based on predictions from BI about their probable value as casino customers. Platinum-level card holders received a slightly lower level of service, while gold-level card holders were essentially "flying coach." Harrah's succeeded in structuring its services to motivate customers to try to qualify for higher-level Total Rewards cards.

BI from the data warehouse even provided insight about how Harrah's should arrange the floor plans in its casinos and how to make slot machines look more attractive. Real-time analytics enabled on-the-spot personalized service for valued customers, such as an instant grant of $100 credit to a loyal customer who'd hit a losing streak. All these factors helped motivate customers to come to Harrah's and stay there to spend their gaming dollars. And this program would not have been possible without BI techniques applied to data warehouse information.

> **Tip**
>
> BI investments are wasted unless they are connected to specific *business goals, analyses, decisions, and actions* that result in improved performance.

The combination of *business information* and *business analysis* is used by Harrah's and many other successful organizations to make more structured and repeatable *business decisions* about the features and targeted recipients of direct marketing offers. Because motivating and retaining its most valuable casino customers is a key driver of profits, Harrah's has refined its customer relationship management process, a *core business process*. The process explicitly embeds the use of the above-described business information and business analyses so that *business decisions* about whom to target with what measures are fact-based, analytically rigorous, and repeatable. These decisions are implemented through *actions* from Harrah's front door to its casinos, restaurants, rooms, and telephone services. Those actions have improved Harrah's business performance, resulting in increased profit.

The above example defines BI from a business perspective, not from a technical perspective, because BI is primarily about *profit*. That's not a technical term and it's not about bits and bytes; it's about your bottom line. And it's what you should expect from BI. It may also have occurred to you that *BI needs to be highly specific to your industry and to how your company competes in that industry*. Measures such as "Revpar" and "stays" are specific to the hotel industry and have no meaning in, say, the freight industry, in which measures such as "revenue per ton-mile" are the norm. More broadly, to get the most out of BI, you must adapt it to each specific company and situation. The kinds *of business information, business analyses, and business decisions that BI must deliver or enable, and the way that BI creates business value must be specifically determined for each company. That's the only way to get the best possible return on your BI investment.* Given this, we see that business information and business analyses are components of BI that can be combined in a wide variety of ways to create the right BI approach for your organization. Table 1-1 shows examples.

1.3   The Origins of Business Intelligence

Now that we have a better understanding of what BI is, let's take a brief look at its origins. This examination will help show where BI fits with other parts of the IT portfolio, such as enterprise transactional applications like enterprise requirements planning (ERP), and will help differentiate BI uses from other IT uses. It's also important to understand that enabling BI technologies are mature, low-risk technologies that have been used successfully by major companies for more than a decade.

Although recently the term BI has become one of the new IT buzzwords, the organizational quest for BI is not new. Approaches to BI have evolved over decades of technological innovation and management experience with IT. Two early examples of BI are

- **Decision support systems (DSSs):** Since the 1970s and 1980s, businesses have used business information and structured business analysis to tackle complex business decisions. Examples include *revenue optimization models* in asset-intensive businesses such as the airline industry, the hotel industry, and the logistics industry, as well as *logistics network optimization* techniques used in industries that face complex distribution challenges. DSSs range from sophisticated, customized analytical tools running on mainframe computers to spreadsheet-based products running on personal computers. DSSs vary enormously in price and sophistication and are application-specific. Accordingly, they have not systematically addressed integration and delivery of business information and business analyses to support the range of BI opportunities available to companies today.

Table 1-1

Combining business information with business analysis for BI

Business Information Examples	Business Analysis Examples	Business Actions and Outcomes
Business Intelligence (BI) Related to Customers		
Historical information on percentage of customer orders filled to customer request date	Historical views of customer service performance analysis	Adjust business processes to provide high level of service to most profitable customers to ensure retention, thereby increasing profitability
Historical information on percentage of customer orders filled to customer promise date	High-value customer service analysis	
	Forecasted customer retention analysis	Adjust service level provided to less valuable customers to reduce cost of service
Individual customer order delivery history information	Customer satisfaction analysis	
	Lost customer analysis	Adjust business processes to take immediate actions to intervene when highly valued customers have complaints to head off highly valued customer attrition
Customer value information (derived from historical sales and profitability information, customer demographics, external data)	Customer complaint analysis	
Customer satisfaction survey information		Address areas of high customer dissatisfaction to ensure customer retention
Lost customers		Analyze information pertaining to lost customers to better understand root causes and to take actions to minimize future lost revenues due to lost customers
New customers		
Customer complaints		
		Analyze patterns of customer complaints to address areas of dissatisfaction with products or services, thereby improving overall quality to retain current customers and attract new customers
BI Related to Sales and Marketing		
Prior years' sales by SKU (stock keeping unit), business unit, geographical unit, and so forth	Sales trend analysis	Optimize sales and marketing efforts based on revenue and profit potential, thereby increasing profits
	Historical revenue and profit analysis by customer, by product	

Table 1-1

Combining business information with business analysis for BI—Cont'd

Business Information Examples	Business Analysis Examples	Business Actions and Outcomes
Company customer demographics	Revenue and profit analysis by sales force organization	Evaluate and adjust campaigns based on effectiveness in increasing revenues and attracting new customers
External industry information on customer demographics	Revenue and profit analysis by product/service	
Historical sales information by product/service	Historical and current sales and market share analysis by product/service	Create focused campaigns based on knowledge of customer base
Historical market share information	Share of wallet analysis	Optimize sales force tactics based on knowledge of competitor sales and customer base
External industry information on market share	Campaign effectiveness analysis	
External industry sales information	Forecast vs. actual sales analysis by sales force organization, by product, by time	Increase average revenue per customer based on knowledge of customer purchase behavior
Historical campaign performance information	Historical product sales analysis	Identify and rectify sales force performance problems to meet forecasted sales projections
Sales by region, sales territory	Backorder and lost sales analysis	
Forecasted vs. actual sales	Backorder analysis	
Sales force performance information	Lost sales analysis	Identify and rectify manufacturing/supplier problems that resulted in backorders or lost sales
Number of backorders by product by time		
Number of lost sales by product by time		Identify and rectify product/service quality problems

BI Related to Finance

Historical budget/forecast/actual revenue/expense/profit information	Budget analysis	Improve quality of budgets/forecasts based on historical budget vs. actual analysis
	Accounts receivable aging analysis	
Prior years' expenses by business unit, core process, general ledger accounting, and so forth	Customer receivable aging analysis	Analyze areas of expenses that may be reduced by improving supplier contract terms
	Uncollected funds analysis	
Accounts receivable aging information	Revenue analysis	Analyze areas of expenses that may be reduced by correcting product quality problems
	Expense analysis	

(Continued)

Table 1-1

Combining business information with business analysis for BI—Cont'd

Business Information Examples	Business Analysis Examples	Business Actions and Outcomes
Purchase information by supplier, material	Unbilled sales analysis	Analyze areas of expenses that may be reduced by correcting product defect problems
Expenses due to product quality problems	Pricing/profitability analysis	Identify areas of problems related to accounts receivables processing and problems based on customer payment history; adjust policies and business processes to improve receivables performance to reduce the cost of working capital and avoid future uncollected revenues to achieve improved financial performance
Customer accounts receivable information		
Uncollected accounts receivable information		
Monthly, historical revenue		
Monthly, historical expenses		
Accounts payable analysis		
Sales vs. invoices		
Prior years' unit or service cost information by product, service line, and so forth		Ensure that all sales are invoiced so that all revenue is captured

Supply Chain Analysis

Current inventory status Forecasted sales by product by time	Material requirements planning analysis	Optimize plant operational performance and order fulfillment based on current and historical order and sales demand information
Actual/pending orders by product by time	Manufacturing schedule analysis	
Inventory levels by product by time	Supplier analysis/scorecard	Use supplier scorecard information to determine optimal supplier mix
Historical summary information on materials purchased by supplier	Supplier cost analysis	
Historical contract pricing information for materials by supplier	Supplier performance analysis	Use defect analysis information to determine root cause of defects; adjust suppliers or manufacturing processes to remedy problems to avoid returned goods and lost sales
Current number of qualified suppliers per material item	Delivery commitment analysis (capable to promise)	
Pricing information for qualified suppliers	Material requirements planning analysis, manufacturing schedule analysis	
Order history information by supplier	Defect analysis	Ensure availability of materials and plant capacity to reduce/avoid backorders and lost sales
Returns/defects by supplier	Preventative maintenance analysis	

Table 1-1

Combining business information with business analysis for BI—Cont'd

Business Information Examples	Business Analysis Examples	Business Actions and Outcomes
Current/pending product/service sales analysis		Utilize supplier purchase information to negotiate volume discounts to reduce cost of goods
Current plant capacity utilization status		Use machine downtime analysis to improve preventative maintenance to eliminate backorders/ lost sales due to plant inefficiencies
Current supplier order delivery status		
Current inventory item location in warehouse		
Plant location vs. customer location		
Product defect information		
Machine downtime history		

- **Executive information systems (EISs):** These were an early attempt to deliver the business information and business analyses to support management planning and control activities. Principally used on mainframes and designed only for use by upper management, these systems were expensive and inflexible. As BI applications and high-performance ITs have come to market, EIS applications have been replaced and extended by BI applications such as scorecards, dashboards, performance management, and other "analytical applications." These applications combine business information and business analyses to provide custom-built and/or packaged BI solutions.

Both of these examples illustrate the desire of executives, managers, analysts, and knowledge workers to harness information to improve profits and performance. Both can also be seen as steps along an evolutionary path.

In the context of discussing information challenges for the 21st century, Peter Drucker observed that ". . . information technology so far has been a producer of data rather than a producer of information" (Drucker, 2001). This view comports with capital investment trends of the past 15 years. In the 1990s, much investment in IT was focused on the following:

- Enterprise applications such as ERP, supply chain management (SCM), and customer relationship management (CRM)
- Functional applications such as warehouse management systems and human resources information systems
- Connectivity between trading partners via the Internet and via more traditional means such as electronic data interchange (EDI)

Collectively, these kinds of IT can be considered *transactional IT*, with business benefits such as transactional efficiency, internal process integration, back-office process automation, transactional status visibility, and reduced information sharing costs. The primary motivation for many of these investments was better control over more efficient day-to-day operations. For example, ERP systems allow companies to track order status, inventory, and customer service in real-time. SCM systems provide supply chain planning functions, and CRM systems provide sales pipeline management and call center management tools.

As the 1990s unfolded, we also saw the emergence of *data warehousing (DW)*, which is a means of harnessing the blizzard of data generated by transactional IT systems. Many of the early adopters of DW were in transaction-intensive businesses (such as financial services, insurance, and telecommunications) in which marketing managers tried to make sense of data about millions of customer transactions. Early efforts in DW were focused on conquering the IT challenges associated with loading, integrating, and storing large quantities of data. Although some organizations recognized the potential that DW approaches held for obtaining new insights into their business that would provide competitive advantage, many organizations limited their DW efforts to supporting better and faster reporting and to answering ad hoc requests for information by business users. After years of making substantial annual investments in DW programs, many organizations began to question the business value of DW investments. The introduction of BI as a new focus in the industry over the past several years is largely an answer to this quest. Vendors have also introduced new BI applications (such as activity-based costing, supply chain analytics, customer analytics, scorecards and dashboards) in response to business demands to have better information to analyze and measure business performance.

DW is a key enabler of BI. It became feasible and economical as a result of rapidly declining data storage and processing costs, special-purpose data integration tools, innovations in the way that data can be organized in databases, and innovations in the way data can be converted to information and presented to information consumers within a business. For the first time, it was technically possible to bring together data about the thousands or millions of daily transactions of a business and turn it into useful information. As the 1990s came to a close, enterprise applications had already been widely adopted by major organizations. Innovators were beginning to look at how to leverage IT for purposes such as strategic enterprise management, managing customer profitability, improving supply chain and/or operations performance, improving "front-office" business processes such as sales force management and campaign management, and improving indirect business processes such as budgeting and business planning. Many of the technical challenges had been overcome in DW, creating the opportunity to expand the use of DW to new parts of the enterprise and to industries that had lagged in adoption.

As was often the case with IT, technological advances spawned advances in management thinking about how to leverage the technological advances to create business value. At the turn of the 21st century, the principal limitations of DW, from the point of view of delivering business value, were that:

- Many DW projects did not systematically analyze how business information, business analyses, and structured business decisions could be inserted into the core business processes that had an impact on profit and performance
- Many DW projects did not systematically address the business process changes required to capture the business value of BI
- Many DW projects did not use sufficiently rigorous requirements analysis techniques

This is *not* to say that traditional approaches were deficient for designing, building, and deploying data warehouses. Rather, the problem was simply that such approaches did not design ROI into the process, which sometimes resulted in DW investments that did not pay off in improved profit or organizational performance.

> **Tip**
>
> To get the maximum return on your BI investment, design ROI into your BI program from the very beginning.

Historically, many DW and BI initiatives have been driven by IT, and much of the focus within the industry has been on the technical aspects of delivering information to the BI user community. Now that many of the technical challenges and trade-offs are well understood, attention has now shifted to expanding the ways in which BI can be used to deliver business value and to enhancing BI development methods to ensure that BI investments pay off. Well-known companies in a wide range of industries have already realized some of the promise of BI, and the underlying methods and technologies for delivering business value are well established. For example, Avnet, Barclays, BellSouth, Ford, Hewlett-Packard (HP), Nationwide, and Sears have established BI programs that have been used to drive revenues, reduce costs, or both.

1.4 Business Intelligence Today

Peter Drucker (2001) has observed that over the past century, businesses have continually reengineered direct labor and asset productivity to the point that many industries are approaching diminishing returns. Accordingly, American businesses must look to other means to compete, and BI is bringing a powerful new tool to businesses. With an effectively executed BI program, businesses can compete by being better than the competition at leveraging information to improve profits and performance. An executive vice president at Wachovia Bank, for example, has stated that "Wachovia's competitive position depends upon our ability to use information faster and smarter than our competition" (Davenport et al., 2001). This line of thinking—that BI can confer a competitive advantage–represents a paradigm shift in how information is used in business. To make this shift, businesses need to rethink how they use information in general and BI in particular.

Whereas the DW and BI industry has historically focused on the technical challenges, technical methods, and project management methods required to deploy DW and BI successfully, a key recent innovation is the use of *business-centric BI methods*. These methods are designed to help companies fully leverage the profit potential of BI. Business-centric BI methods—which extend the technical methods of BI pioneers such as William Inmon, Ralph Kimball, and Claudia Imhoff—*design ROI into BI initiatives from the outset and systematically drive the use of BI into the core business processes and decisions that determine business results.* The BI Pathway method discussed in this book is an example of business-centric BI methods.

Business-centric BI methods go beyond traditional approaches by putting rigor into defining the *business value capture mechanism* for each BI project. This includes determining and specifying—in advance—how business processes and key decision processes must change in order to leverage BI investments, which are managed as a portfolio. This also includes using process reengineering and process improvement techniques to ensure that BI projects actually deliver the intended ROI.

When using business-centric methods, the BI team no longer throws the BI application "over the wall" after users have been trained, hoping that the business organization will understand what changes are needed and how to make them. Rather, BI team responsibilities are extended to include helping the business organization execute the changes to the business processes and decision processes that drive business results. Business-centric methods recognize that the missing link in many DW and BI efforts is the lack of clarity in the value proposition and/or the lack of business process change to capture the business value of BI.

The availability and affordability of business-centric methods for designing and developing BI means that a cohesive BI system that drives profits and performance is well within the means of any business enterprise.

1.5   Using Business Intelligence to Capture Business Value

In economic terms, the business value of an investment (an asset) is the net present value of the after-tax cash flows associated with the investment. For example, the business value of an investment in a manufacturing plant is the sum of the incremental after-tax cash flows associated with the sale of the products produced at the plant. Similarly, an investment in BI creates an asset that must be used to generate incremental after-tax cash flow. Accordingly, BI investments should be subjected to a rigorous assessment of how the investment will result in increased revenues, reduced costs, or both.

Although there are hundreds of ways to express business benefits, no business value is associated with an investment unless the benefits achieved result in increased after-tax cash flows. Again, *there is no business value associated with an investment unless the benefits achieved connect to strategic goals.* For business, the focus is on primarily increased after-tax cash flows; for government agencies, improved performance and service to citizens. These principles apply to investments in factories, equipment, *and* BI.

For example, it is common for BI vendor value propositions to emphasize business benefits such as agility, responsiveness, customer intimacy, information sharing, flexibility, and collaboration. But investing in BI to achieve such business benefits may actually destroy business value unless those attributes can be defined in operational terms and realized through business processes that affect revenues or costs. For example, a $2 million investment in a BI application must result in incremental after-tax cash flow of at least $2 million or the organization will suffer a reduction in assets.

To illustrate this point, many companies use BI to improve customer segmentation, customer acquisition, and customer retention. These improvements can be linked to reduced customer acquisition costs, increased revenues, and increased customer lifetime value, which translate to increased after-tax cash flows. However, a BI investment that improves demand forecasting will not deliver business value unless the forecasts are actually incorporated into operational business processes that then deliver reduced inventory, reduced order expediting costs, or some other tangible economic benefit. In other words, the business benefit "improved forecasting" is useless unless it is somehow converted into incremental after-tax cash flow.

Looked at more broadly, the quest for delivering business value via BI can be seen as a matter of determining how an organization can use BI to

- Improve management processes (such as planning, controlling, measuring, monitoring, and/or changing) so that management can increase revenues, reduce costs, or both
- Improve operational processes (such as fraud detection, sales campaign execution, customer order processing, purchasing, and/or accounts payable processing) so that the business can increase revenues, reduce costs, or both

In other words, the business value of BI lies in its use within management processes that affect operational processes that drive revenue or reduce costs, and/or in its use within those operational processes themselves. Let's illustrate this point with a couple of examples.

Just like Harrah's, many companies these days aspire to use customer relationship management strategies that distinguish among customers based on their value. In retail banking, a customer with loans, large savings accounts, a checking account with large balances, and credit card balances who uses online banking is much more valuable than a customer with only a low-balance checking account who comes into a branch frequently. Clearly, the bank would not want to lose the former customer, whereas it might be willing to lose the latter. For the bank to implement a customer relationship management strategy based on the difference in customer value, it first needs BI applications that allow the bank to know which customers are highly valuable, which are valuable, which are less valuable, and which are not valuable. But that knowledge alone is not enough to ensure that the bank does not lose highly valuable customers. It must also have management processes and operational processes that take account of the differences in customer value and treat the highly valuable customers preferentially. For example, the bank might waive a late fee on a loan payment for the valuable customer but not for the less valuable customer.

The strategy of treating customers differently depending on their value as customers is also used in SCM. The central idea is to design and optimize supply chain business processes to provide superior service to those customers who drive the bulk of one's profit. To do this, a manufacturer needs a BI application that allows it to know who its most profitable customers are. As with the bank, however, this knowledge is of little use unless it can be translated into business rules for manufacturing schedules that recognize that orders for the most valuable customers should be serviced ahead of those from marginal customers.

Because capturing the business value of BI depends on being able to use BI in a way that has an operational impact, organizations must look beyond the initial rollout of BI applications (Figure 1-2).

As shown in Figure 1-2, capturing the business value of BI requires organizations to go well beyond the technical implementation of a BI environment. Specifically, organizations must engage in effective process engineering and change management in order to capture business value from BI. The implication of this requirement is that BI methodologies must be extended to include these additional preconditions, as shown in Figure 1-3.

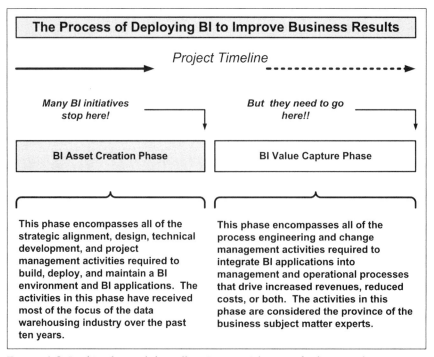

FIGURE 1-2 Looking beyond the rollout is essential to get the best result.

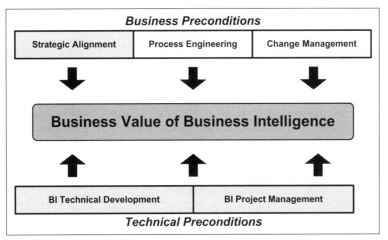

FIGURE 1-3 Business and technical preconditions for delivering business value through business intelligence.

Of the preconditions shown in Figure 1-3, those in light gray boxes are generally well understood, based on DW industry experience over the past decade. The other two preconditions, process engineering and change management, are not as well understood for BI applications. They currently stand as barriers to capturing the business value of BI. Let us examine this idea with an example.

In a typical large company, much of the information routinely available to managers comes in the form of static reports and from ad hoc information gathering and analysis. A general manager who receives a monthly profit and loss statement may notice that revenue is less than budgeted, in which case he or she will most likely assign a staff analyst, middle manager, or functional manager to figure out the factors contributing to the variance. The specific form of the analysis, the manner in which it is done, and the information sources from which the analyst draws are likely to be ad hoc and idiosyncratic. Most likely, the analyst will do the best he or she can with the information and time available, with little opportunity for extensive scenario analysis and assessment of alternative courses of action.

Imagine now that the company invests in a BI application for revenue management. The application is capable of looking at revenue trends by customer, by geographic region, by product, and by salesperson. Further, it is rolled out company-wide, with online training available to any potential business user who may want to use the application. For some reason, however, revenues continue to decline and analysis of application use shows that only a handful of potential users regularly use the application. The chief financial officer (CFO) initiates a project review to find out why the projected incremental revenues have not materialized. It is discovered that there was no plan for how the BI application would be used within the user community and no plan for introducing and ensuring the efficacy of the changes required to capture the business value of the investment. This is particularly vexing to the CFO, given that a subject matter expert (SME) was part of the application development team.

To avoid the above scenario, we recommend using a structured approach to business value capture. In the sections that follow, we will look at strategic alignment, process engineering, and change management as key interrelated preconditions for capturing business value.

1.6   How Do We Achieve Strategic Alignment?

As DW matured in the 1990s, a considerable body of expertise developed around the task of aligning the use of BI with organizational strategies. Essentially, it is a matter of

- Understanding the strategic drivers of the competitive environment (private industry) or organizational environment (government and nonprofit) and related business goals
- Determining the business questions that must be answered in order to plan, budget, control, monitor, measure, assess, and/or improve organizational performance in relation to the strategic goals
- Identifying the tools, methods, and analytical frameworks that can be used to support execution of key business processes and management of organizational performance
- Following well-established technical procedures for identifying, acquiring, integrating, staging, and delivering the data and information managers need

Although this alignment process is straightforward in concept, a wide variety of challenges must be overcome, as with any endeavor in IT. For example, working with business users of BI to determine their business questions (information requirements) is still an art despite the existence of structured requirements gathering methods. Business users are sometimes be so focused on daily challenges that they have difficulty envisioning how BI can be leveraged to improve organizational performance. On the technical side, a wide array of choices must be made with respect to architecture, methodology, tools, technologies, and processes—choices that impact project risk, total cost of ownership, and ultimately the magnitude of the "investment" portion of ROI. There is also the challenge of incorporating sufficient architectural flexibility to respond to new BI needs as strategic drivers evolve.

Although the above-described challenges of strategic alignment are significant, a substantial body of knowledge exists describing how to go about meeting those challenges, and the methods used to achieve strategic alignment are effective and widely adopted. That said, strategic alignment, although necessary for achieving business value, is not sufficient in and of itself. The reason, as we've seen, is that the availability of strategically aligned BI does not guarantee it will be used to improve the results of critical business processes that determine the revenues and costs of the business. We must also engage in process engineering and change management.

Tip
The keys to strategic alignment are worth repeating:

1. Understand your organization's strategic drivers and goals.
2. Determine the business questions you need BI to answer in order to achieve those goals.
3. Identify tools, methods, and analytical frameworks to inform decisions and measure performance.
4. Deliver the information your organization needs to take actions that improve performance and support your goals.

1.7 The Need for Process Engineering

Many different types of processes are used to run a business. There are strategic, tactical, and operational planning processes. There are financial, operational, marketing, product development, and human resources management processes. There are performance monitoring and measurement processes, quality management processes, and continuous improvement processes. There are supply chain and customer relationship management processes. All of these processes involve the use of information, analytical frameworks, and tools to support the many decisions managers have to make. In other words, these processes require BI approaches in order to be optimized. The economic and technological advances over the past decade, in IT generally and DW specifically, have opened a new frontier for the use of BI to deliver business value.

In our view, the key challenge in using BI to capture business value lies in the way that information and analytical frameworks used within organizations have largely depended on individual initiative and ad hoc choices. At a broader level, the use of business information to conduct business analysis is often an idiosyncratic, ad hoc practice that varies by industry and by company within each industry. For example, revenue optimization models are a staple of asset-intensive, high fixed-cost industries such as the lodging industry and the airline industry, but they are not widely adopted in discrete manufacturing industries. Within industries, the information and analytical frameworks used varies by company positioning within the industry. Although enterprise applications such as ERP, SCM, and CRM provide structure, automation, and process standardization for managing day-to-day transactions, organizational efforts to utilize BI approaches are more unstructured, more ad hoc, and less widely adopted, For example,

- Use of optimization tools for strategic, tactical, and operational supply chain planning has increased over the past decade but is still not widely practiced and has stalled over the past 3 years.
- Many major companies are still in the early stages of adopting techniques such as collaborative filtering and clustering to improve sales campaign performance.

- Use of scorecards and dashboards in the context of strategic enterprise management is still in its early days.
- Use of data mining for fraud detection is still celebrated as an innovative practice.
- Event monitoring and business performance management products are in the early stages of adoption.

Although DW has been around for a decade now, most organizations are still in the early stages of exploitation of the potential of BI, and this presents both opportunities and risks. The opportunity, simply stated, is that effective use of BI can deliver incremental profit and superior performance. The risk is that organizations will not do the process engineering and change management needed for using BI to capture business value. To capture business value, it is our professional judgment that organizations will benefit from a rigorous process engineering approach. This entails looking beyond vendor value propositions regarding packaged analytics, "BI for the masses," and "BI best practices" to determine specifically, with economic and process engineering rigor, how adoption of BI will result in incremental revenues or incremental cost reductions. To illustrate this concept, let's examine the simple hypothetical BI application shown in Figure 1-4.

Assume that Company A manufactures a semi-custom product and competes on cost. Given that cost is the key basis of competition, Company A has developed a BI application that is used to monitor productivity. This application is strategically aligned because productivity improvement is critical to cost reduction. We can see from Figure 1-4 that actual productivity is less than planned productivity, so our BI application has delivered useful information. That said, we can also see from the questions posed that having useful information is not the same as exploiting that information. Unless there are specific management processes for using that information in a timely manner, having the BI application will not result in business

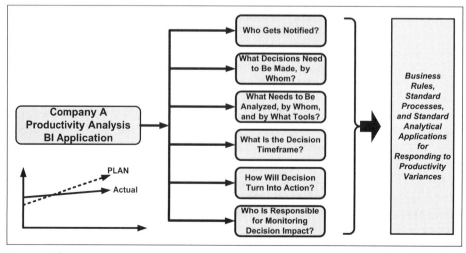

FIGURE 1-4 Process engineering to capture business value.

value creation. Process engineering focuses on providing answers to the questions posed in Figure 1-4, and those answers can be captured as the foundation for business rules, standard processes, and standard analytical applications for responding to productivity variances.

This approach can be used for all planned BI applications and will allow organizations to move from ad hoc responses for recurring business conditions to effective repeatable responses that capture the business value of BI. From this simple example, we can generalize that the business value of BI lies in its effective use within management processes and/or operational processes that drive revenue or reduce costs. Accordingly, process engineering is the critical link between building and delivering BI applications that are strategically aligned and capturing the business value those BI applications are supposed to deliver. Although this proposition is hardly novel or remarkable, we believe that BI industry experience shows that the importance of process engineering has been overlooked or undervalued. BI has been viewed foremost as a technological tool, neglecting the fact that it must be embedded in specific business processes in order to deliver its full value.

We further believe that process engineering is especially important as we stand at the frontier of expanded use of BI—with its potential for altering competitive landscapes. Vendors are offering a wide range of innovative products with value propositions that are appealing as general propositions, especially to organizations that are prone to looking for quick fixes. Although we are bullish on some of these products when used appropriately, we remain convinced that organizations must be rigorous about determining how the use of these products can deliver business value in their specific contexts, and process engineering is essential to that determination.

1.8 Process Engineering in Practice

We have the privilege of serving each year as judges for the annual Best Practices in Data Warehousing Awards. The competition is conducted by The Data Warehousing Institute (TDWI), the leading membership association of IT and business professionals involved in DW and BI. One of us recently served on the panel of judges for the advanced analytics best practices category. Eight nominees were in that category, including leading companies in a variety of industries. Although all of the nominees had achieved a high degree of strategic alignment with their BI applications, what distinguished the leaders in the eyes of the judges was the degree to which they had integrated BI with value-driving business processes. For example, the category winner, Lands' End, used a process engineering approach that included developing a corporate metric model and mind maps that anticipated the specific ways that inventory managers would use metrics to improve business performance. Another category leader, a leading automobile manufacturer, developed a closed-loop inventory management process that used BI to reduce inventory and cycle time. Viewed from the perspective shown in Figure 1-4, these companies captured business value by attending to process engineering and change management, thus satisfying key business preconditions for success.

When using process engineering to determine exactly how BI will be used to increase revenue or reduce costs, remember that the process should be tailored to the situation because the degree of process change associated with a BI investment varies from one situation to another. At one end of the spectrum, a BI application may simply deliver higher-quality information on a timelier basis. An example would be a BI application that provides managerial accounting information, such as historical product costs, to a company's budgeting process. The typical budget process makes numerous assumptions using information that budget analysts have squirreled away in numerous spreadsheets. A new BI application would provide an integrated view of product costs that could be used across the budget department, but the budget process itself might not change much, other than being easier to obtain information for making budget assumptions.

At the other end of the spectrum, a BI application may involve totally new information, analytical routines, and management processes. An example drawn from our experience involved a BI application used by a $2.5 billion consumer products manufacturer for sales and operations planning. In this case, the manufacturer lacked sales trend information that could be used for demand forecasting and did not have a sales and operations planning process. For cost improvement reasons, the manufacturer determined that it needed such a process. From a management processes reengineering perspective, there was no "as-is" state, and the implementation of the BI application involved providing managers with new information, presented with new tools, for use within a new management process.

Given the potential differences in the scope of management process change, the scope of the management process engineering must be fitted to the task at hand.

1.9 The Need for Change Management

Process engineering identifies how BI applications will be used within the context of key management and operational processes that drive increased revenue and/or reduced costs. It provides a map of which processes must change and how they must change in order to create business value with BI applications. Thus, it lays the foundation for change management because process changes drive changes in individual and organizational behavior.

Change management is a generic discipline with principles that are generally understood and have been widely applied for decades to a variety of organizational change processes, including business process changes induced by IT investments in enterprise applications such as ERP. That said, change management as it applies to BI initiatives has not yet been developed into a systematic body of knowledge. A number of BI project failures can be attributed to ineffective change management.

In our view, these failures point to a shared problem in the BI industry: that of overstating the ease with which BI applications can be deployed and accepted within organizations. These overstatements—whether by ERP vendors with packaged data warehouses, by BI vendors with packaged analytics, by consultants, or by IT organizations themselves—have a tendency to produce situations in which the adoption risk associated with BI applications is systematically understated. The result is that change management activities are ignored or under-funded.

One of the primary change management challenges for BI applications is that most organizations use information and analytical frameworks within management processes in an unstructured, ad hoc manner and that the degree of support for such processes has, until recently, been very limited. The advent of collaboration capabilities within BI products presents a tremendous opportunity, but the application of business rules thinking and workflow technologies has been largely focused on repetitive, routine tasks such as processing invoices or purchase requisitions. Given that the targeted user community for many BI applications consists of executives, managers, and business analysts, the challenge of introducing structure in the use of information and analytical tools in any given case could be substantial. In effect, the use of BI within the executive and management ranks of companies is highly unstructured—especially compared with the use of transactional IT systems such as ERP, which is highly structured and standardized. To capture the business value of BI initiatives aimed at management processes, organizations will have to apply scientific management and process control thinking to "white collar" activities, a substantial change.

1.10 Business Value Analysis of Business Intelligence Initiatives

At this point in the discussion, we have examined strategic alignment, management process engineering, and change management as key preconditions for ensuring that BI investments result in business value (positive after-tax cash flows). We have argued that analytical rigor, process analysis, and empirical methods should be used in a structured manner to determine how BI can be used to deliver increased revenues and/or reduced costs. We believe there is no shortcut for rigorous up-front business value analysis of how investments in BI will deliver business value. Although traditional ROI analysis is certainly a key component of business value analysis, we recommend taking a broader analytical perspective, consisting of the following:

- **BI opportunity analysis.** Combines environmental analysis, industry analysis, and business strategy review with a comprehensive assessment of how BI can be used to enable critical strategies and support key business processes to increase revenue and reduce costs
- **BI readiness assessment.** Applies readiness assessment instruments such as those provided with TDWI's Fundamentals of Data Warehousing course to assess organizational, business, and technical readiness to deliver information to feed BI applications and frameworks; extends BI readiness assessments by using BI maturity assessment to evaluate organizational management and decision-making cultures, capacity for change, and change management capabilities as they affect the use of BI and structured analytical methods

- **Process engineering.** Determines and specifies exactly how BI applications will be used in the context of the management and/or operational processes to plan, control, measure, manage, and improve the business processes of the organization that drive revenue and costs
- **ROI analysis.** Uses investment cost estimates and discounted cash flow analysis to estimate the net present value of after-tax cash flows that will result from the investment in a BI initiative; uses other conventional approaches, such as cost-benefit or payback, if required by organizational capital budgeting process
- **Change analysis.** Extends the results of process engineering by assessing the degree of process change required, the degree of individual change required, the skills required by new management processes, and the training required for various types of users

Business value analysis is the foundation of the business case for capital budgeting purposes, but it has a broader purpose as well. Specifically, the process engineering and change analysis activities identify the key business activities that must be successfully performed if the BI investment is to capture business value. For example, revised management and/or operational processes must be defined, the community of BI users must be trained in these processes and in the use of BI within the processes, and mechanisms for evaluating the progress of the change process must be implemented. In other words, process engineering and change analysis lay the foundation for managing for business value delivery.

1.11   Managing for Business Value Delivery

As with any capital project, capturing the business value projected for the investment requires effective management. Fortunately, the DW industry has developed an extensive body of knowledge about the technical development and project management preconditions for project success. In fact, our view is that with the maturing of DW tools and technologies over the past decade, technical impediments to success are no longer the central issue. Rather, we believe the more substantial challenge lies in meeting the business preconditions, particularly the needs for identifying opportunities for leveraging BI, process engineering, and change management.

Tip

Stay focused on your business needs and goals. Don't fall victim to vendor "out-of-the-box" solutions that don't directly support your business goals.

To this point in the discussion, the perspective we've advanced is that analytical rigor, process analysis, and empirical methods should be used in a structured manner to determine how BI can be used to deliver increased revenues and/or reduced costs. Competing with this perspective is a marketing message to which executives are frequently exposed: that BI products provide "out-of-the-box" solutions that can be implemented in very short timeframes to deliver substantial business benefits. Experience suggests that business executives often respond to value propositions that use business language to make what are essentially emotional appeals to executives' aspirations (beat the competition/make money) and insecurities (fear of failure). This is not to say that the BI products in the market cannot be used to deliver business value, because history has shown that they can—*if* they are used intelligently. Rather, it is to say that executives need to guard against these emotional appeals, because these appeals can cause an organization to underestimate the degree of process engineering and change management required for capturing the business value of BI investments, and when this happens, the organization does not manage for business value capture. It thus increases its chances of failure.

To overcome this risk, organizations need to focus like a laser on the key value capture activities—process engineering and change management. The BI project cannot stop when the BI application is deployed. In fact, we can consider the point of deployment to be like "halftime" in a sporting event. To ensure that business value is captured, the team must continue to perform at a high level. This is not to say that the players in the game will stay static. Once the BI asset has been built, the onus for business value capture falls on the business side, which is often not commonly discussed and understood. In fact, there is a strong case for this responsibility residing with the business, rather than with IT. Empirical studies suggest that IT investments deliver greater value when the responsibility for business value capture resides on the business side. This is also a cultural issue: those organizations with effective IT/business partnerships achieve better results.

Ultimately, capturing the business value of BI is a strategic challenge and opportunity, and we have seen that the potential for BI is substantial. With appropriate rigor and a willingness to manage for business value, there is no reason that organizations cannot capture the business value of BI, regardless of how it might be defined in their specific circumstances.

1.12 Key Points to Remember

- BI is about turning information into action and action into improved performance.
- Technical initiatives focused only on data have tended to fall short in supporting business goals and improving performance.
- Two key barriers to BI-driven performance improvement are lack of business vision into how BI can drive performance and lack of *will* to drive the process changes that BI requires.
- Business leadership, executive sponsorship, and an effective business/IT partnership are critical to success.

1.13 Think Tank

1.13.1 Seven Questions to Ask About Your Organization's BI Needs

1. What business information do we need?
2. For what business analyses?

3. In support of what key business decisions?
4. That impact which core processes?
5. To deliver how much business value?
6. Via what changes to people, processes, and technology?
7. And what are our competitors doing with BI?

1.13.2 Quiz: What Might BI Mean for Your Company?

1. How much could you improve your business results if you had all the business information and analytical tools you feel you need?
2. How would your business processes need to change to leverage BI?
3. Which core business processes present the best BI opportunities?
4. How could BI improve your company's ability to serve its customers?
5. How could BI help you to leverage the value of IT investments you've already made?

Chapter 2

Identifying and Prioritizing Business Intelligence-Driven Opportunities for Your Organization

"...not many executives are information-literate. They know how to get data. But most still have to learn how to use data. Few executives yet know how to ask: What information do I need to do my job? When do I need it? In what form? And from whom should I be getting it? Fewer still ask: What new tasks can I tackle now that I get all these data? Which old tasks should I abandon? Which tasks should I do differently? Practically no one asks 'What information do I owe? To whom? When? In what form?'"

—Peter F. Drucker, from "Be Data-Literate: Know What to Know"

In Chapter 1, we defined business intelligence (BI) and illustrated how it can be used to improve profits and business performance. The focus of this chapter is how you can use BI in your own organization. And as Peter Drucker has suggested above, you might have an uphill battle in getting busy business executives to focus on the business value of information. Helping you get their attention is one of the reasons for this book.

Our own experience confirms Drucker's observations from over a decade ago. Although BI has made a lot of progress, much more work needs to be done before we can say that BI has come into its own as a competitive weapon, profit improvement strategy, and performance management tool. We further believe that the use of BI will be suboptimal until all levels of executives, managers, analysts, and knowledge workers in a given company have a common, internally and externally consistent perspective about how to use BI in their company. In short, BI needs to become ingrained in company cultures.

This implies that business needs a systematic way of addressing the challenge Drucker articulated—a challenge we hear echoed with great frequency by BI business sponsors, project managers, and architects from major companies in a wide range of industries. When we are instructors at conferences sponsored by The Data

Warehousing Institute (TDWI), the premier industry association of information technology (IT) professionals involved with BI and data warehousing (DW), we always hear about the challenges of getting executives and managers to see the potential of BI and engage with the BI team to identify specific BI-driven profit opportunities for their companies. Empirical evidence dovetails with our own experience: companies that use IT most effectively have much higher levels of executive and management engagement than companies that don't (Kempis and Ringbeck, 1998).

In response to these challenges, we have developed a business-driven BI opportunity analysis framework that systematically identifies BI opportunities and prioritizes those opportunities based on business impact and risk. The BI opportunity analysis—which we have successfully applied at the enterprise, division, and functional or departmental levels—takes a structured approach to answering the following key questions about potential BI opportunities:

- What business information do we need?
- For what business analyses?
- In support of what key business decisions?
- That affect what core business processes?
- To deliver how much business value?
- Via what changes to people, processes, and technology?

Once you have identified the key BI-driven profit opportunities for your company, you can then apply BI portfolio management techniques to assess business and technical tradeoffs and establish priorities. Our clients have used the BI opportunity analysis framework not only to begin new BI initiatives but also to redirect and re-energize ongoing BI initiatives that haven't delivered the goods.

2.1 Business Intelligence Opportunity Analysis Overview

The principal methods of BI opportunity analysis are to identify and prioritize opportunities to use business information, business analyses, and structured decisions. The principal objectives are to increase revenues and/or reduce costs, thereby increasing profits and creating business value. To accomplish those objectives, a structured approach that aligns two key factors with each other is needed:

- Business drivers, business strategies, goals and objectives, and the core business processes that drive profits
- BI applications that will improve the effectiveness of those core business processes

Figure 2-1 shows an overview of the BI opportunity analysis approach.

As indicated by the arrows cascading down the left side of Figure 2-1, BI opportunity analysis is a top-down, sequential analysis of the key business factors that you must understand before you can identify opportunities to use BI to create business value. The right side of Figure 2-1 shows that the following need to be understood: (1) the business context in which a company operates, (2) how the

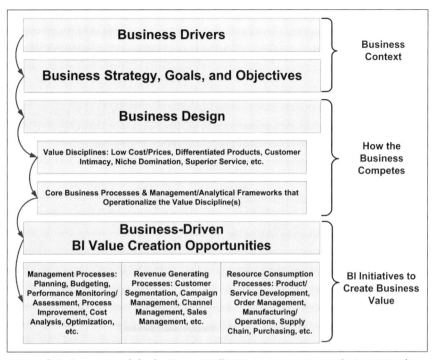

FIGURE 2-1 Overview of the business intelligence opportunity analysis approach.

company competes, and (3) how the company could use BI to compete more effectively and thereby create business value. The main flow of the opportunity analysis is from strategic to operational. It's based on the value creation fundamentals explored in Chapter 1—that is, on the idea that to earn a return on investment (ROI) in BI, you must use BI to make a difference in one or more core processes that affect profit and performance. A bottom-up variant of this model can be used to determine how the information and associated BI applications that have been proposed by business users can be used to further organizational performance. The case study below demonstrates the BI opportunity analysis approach.

> **Tip**
>
> You need a structured approach to defining BI opportunities. The BI Pathway provides one such approach.

2.2 Case Study: McCormick Opportunity Analysis

McCormick is a $2 billion manufacturer of commonly known food and beverage ingredients. Based solely on publicly available information, this section shows you step by step how McCormick might analyze its BI opportunities and applied that analysis to improve its profits and operating effectiveness.

McCormick sells ingredients to food and beverage processors, which in turn sell them to food and beverage retailers. The food industry is a mature, fragmented, international industry that is undergoing substantial structural changes typical of industry evolution. Changes in the food and beverage retailing industry affect the food and beverage processing industry (McCormick's customers), and the resulting changes to the food and beverage processing industry affect McCormick's business. From a BI strategy perspective, we are most interested in changes that affect McCormick's customers and how they make money. The nature and extent of those changes may create opportunities for McCormick to use BI to its strategic and competitive advantage.

2.2.1 Evolution of McCormick's Relevant Industries

Three key industries were relevant to McCormick's BI planning: the food and beverage *retail* industry, the food and beverage *processing* industry, and the food and beverage *ingredients* industry.

The food and beverage *retail* industry has historically been fragmented and regional. By 1999, however, it had become increasingly concentrated and global. In the United States, the top 10 supermarket players generated 33% of industry sales in 1995, but by 1999 that figure stood at 45%, not counting Wal-Mart's 12% market share. By 2004, the industry structure had the top 10 players holding between 55% and 70% of the market. Overall, the industry is a mature, consolidating, slow-growth industry with intense competition based on price, which means food and beverage processors receive pressure from the retailers to reduce prices, improve supply chain effectiveness, and differentiate themselves on more than just brand image. It is typical that mature industries spawn more aggressive competition based on cost and service, and that is certainly the model that Wal-Mart has used effectively in the consumer packaged goods industry. It is also typical that profits in the mature industry often fall, sometimes permanently.

The food and beverage *processing* industry is affected by trends at the retail level. The McCormick company's primary interest is in identifying the major trends and their likely impact on the bases of competition in its ingredients businesses. This will suggest potential areas where McCormick can leverage BI.

The balance of power between food retailers and food processors shifted from 1995 to 2005 in favor of the retailers, which continues to put pressure on pricing and profits. The food processing companies most threatened by retailer consolidation are those with lower-ranking brands. In addition, slow domestic economic growth has intensified competition, motivated global expansion, and driven business process reengineering projects seeking improved margins. Many industry leaders spent the mid-90s engaged in cost-cutting initiatives and backward integration into the ingredients industry, and such initiatives have returned as much benefit as they are likely to in the short term. Thus, the food and beverage processing industry is consolidating, which increases buyer power in relation to McCormick and its competitors. Looking forward, McCormick can continue to expect pricing pressures and demands for increased efficiency as its customers seek to maintain their own profitability in the face of slow growth and retailer consolidation.

The food and beverage *ingredients* industry is similar in structure to that of the related downstream industries: mature, slow growth, fragmented, and increasingly global. Faced with increasing customer power owing to concentration and supplier consolidation programs, price pressures due to customer industry dynamics, and the threat of backward integration, ingredients industry firms are themselves merging in an attempt to maintain some balance of power. Although the overall growth rate of the ingredient industry is low, opportunities for growth in excess of the industry average are present. Industry players segment the market into what might be called macro-categories, for example, beverages, baked goods, dairy, candy/confection, and snack foods. These macro-categories have different growth rates, different leading brands, and different rates of new product development, all of which contribute to different opportunity profiles and growth potential.

Consistent with this overall environment, McCormick has successfully executed a strategy that is at once focused, differentiated, and based on cost leadership. McCormick is *focused* because it is only in the ingredients business. It is *differentiated* because its customer-based product development paradigm was at one time a singular position in the industry, and because it offers a broader product line than its competitors. The McCormick strategy is also based on *cost leadership* because it consistently focuses on margin improvement, global sourcing, and supply chain management (SCM) as means to achieve low-cost producer status.

> **Tip**
>
> When you're planning for BI, pay careful attention to the strategic business drivers in your industry and to how your organization competes in the marketplace. These insights will provide vital guidance in helping you identify high-value BI opportunities.

2.2.2 Summary of Food Industry Drivers and Trends

Given the multiple levels of consolidation in the industry, each customer relationship takes on increased importance. At the same time, it's also imperative to improve costs, pricing, customer selection, and customer revenue management. This suggests that growth and profitability could be enhanced by effective use of BI that supports those objectives. It also suggests that customer-focused business strategies and operating policies will be at least as important as, and probably more important than, they have traditionally been. Accordingly, BI capabilities that promote top-caliber customer service and make it easy to do business with McCormick are also important. A summary of the food industry drivers and trends is shown in Figure 2-2.

2.2.3 Application of the Business Intelligence Opportunity Analysis Framework at McCormick

Working with the publicly available facts described above, the BI opportunity analysis framework can be applied to systematically identify specific opportunities to use BI to improve profits at McCormick. Both top-down and bottom-up BI opportunity analysis techniques can be used. Although top-down techniques begin with a strategic view and work down into an operational view, many business users are more comfortable discussing operational priorities. In this case, bottom-up techniques are used to discuss BI in relation to business processes, and determine how it

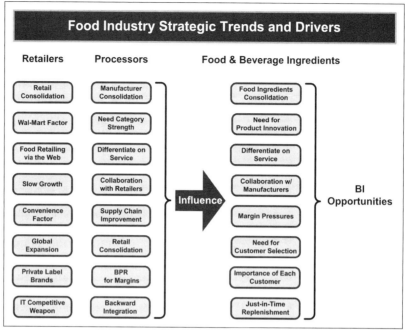

FIGURE 2-2 A summary of food industry drivers and trends relevant to business intelligence.

can be used to support business strategies and the achievement organizational goals and objectives. The analytical results, abbreviated for sake of illustration, might look like this:

Business Drivers

- Consolidation
- Wal-Mart factor
- Increased pricing pressures
- Slow growth
- Global expansion
- IT as a competitive weapon

McCormick Business Strategies, Goals, and Objectives

Tip
To assess the potential business value of a BI opportunity, it is important to understand how it contributes to supporting one or more business goals.

- Retain/increase revenue and market share through developing a broad line of differentiated products and services
- Reduce costs and improve service through strengthening supply chain collaboration and improving sales forecasting

- Improve profits by utilizing customer segmentation approaches to identify the most profitable customers and retain these customers by providing high-quality, differentiated service and support
- Preserve margins by refining pricing strategy to determine the potential short-term and long-term cost/benefit of adjusting prices for different customers and segments; make pricing decisions based on cost/benefit analysis

McCormick Business Design

Value Disciplines

- Customer knowledge
- Consumer-focused product development
- Leveraged IT
- Continuous process improvement
- Niche focus

Tip
Understanding how your business is designed and how it competes in the marketplace will provide additional insights as to where BI opportunities that provide potential bottom-line impact exist.

Core Business Processes

- Product development
- Customer service
- Supply chain management (SCM)
- Manufacturing
- Financial planning and control

McCormick Business-Driven Business Intelligence Value Creation Opportunities

Based on McCormick's industry environment, business drivers, strategies, goals, and business design, the following BI opportunities can be idenitified. Each would help McCormick improve profit and performance.

- **Product development BI.** Examples include sales trends by consumer end product categories such as beverages and baked goods, sales trends by McCormick customer and by McCormick ingredient product, and gross margin and volume trends for McCormick products.
- **Customer service BI.** Examples include customer profitability trends by customer and by consumer end-product category, such as dairy products and baked goods, and customer-specific order history, including order line volumes, frequency of orders, frequency of order changes, and order fulfillment metrics.
- **SCM BI.** Examples include demand history by McCormick product and by customer, supplier scorecards for McCormick suppliers, inventory levels by McCormick product and by customer, and performance metrics such as order-to-cash cycle time, order-to-ship cycle time, and percentage of perfect orders.
- **Manufacturing BI.** Examples include batch yield history by McCormick product and plant, batch cost history by McCormick product and plant, quality trends by McCormick product and plant, and batch setup and changeover time trends by McCormick product and plant.

- **Financial planning and control BI.** Examples include forecast versus actual order volume, prices, and mix by McCormick product and by customer; forecast versus actual revenues by McCormick region, product, customer, and salesperson; and forecast versus actual gross margin by McCormick product and plant.

> **Tip**
>
> Use both top-down and bottom-up techniques for identifying BI opportunities. The top-down techniques let you start with the strategic picture, and the bottom-up techniques can yield valuable input from business users who are more concerned with operational priorities and specific business processes.

By systematically working through the BI opportunity analysis framework, we have identified specific BI opportunities for McCormick. By investing in one or more of these BI opportunities, McCormick would have better business information and analytical tools to inform key business decisions that drive increased profits. For example, industry consolidation puts pressure on profit margins. McCormick has chosen to respond to this challenge by adopting a strategy of supply chain collaboration, which seeks to drive costs down by using IT and business process improvements to improve operational efficiency. Toward that end, having SCM BI and customer service BI would allow McCormick manage the key variables and processes that determine supply chain costs, time, asset utilization, service, and quality—all of which contribute to the ability to maintain or improve gross margins in the face of margin pressures.

The McCormick BI opportunity analysis case study illustrates how your company could go about identifying actionable BI opportunities. The process does not stop there, however, as you then need to *prioritize those opportunities based on business impact, risk, and project interdependencies.* The next part of this BI opportunity analysis overview describes a straightforward method for prioritizing your BI opportunities.

Figure 2-3 shows the continuation of the BI opportunity analysis from the point of having identified opportunities of business-driven BI value creation to the point of having used a portfolio of BI opportunities to create a BI opportunity map. The BI opportunity map is a conceptual framework aimed at prioritizing BI opportunities based on what amounts to a *risk-reward tradeoff.* The opportunity map should not be thought of as a deterministic model, although opportunities are present to use multi-factor quantitative and/or qualitative analyses to support project placement on the business impact scale and/or the risk scale. Rather, the BI opportunity map serves as a basis for risk-reward tradeoff discussions between the business and IT leaders and managers who collectively have to sponsor, execute, and leverage the contemplated BI investments so that business value is created. To illustrate the use of the BI opportunity map, let's continue our analysis of the McCormick case.

> **Tip**
>
> The BI opportunity map is an important communications vehicle. Representing your opportunities and challenges *visually* can stimulate your creative thinking and suggest approaches that you might not otherwise have considered.

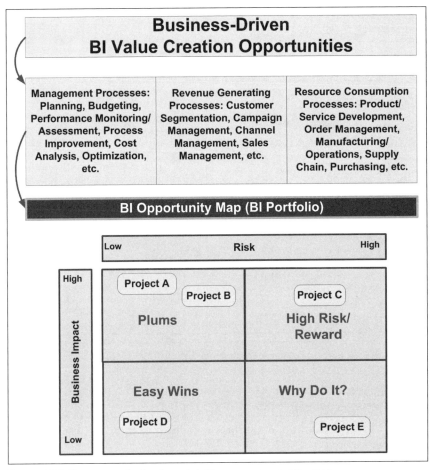

FIGURE 2-3 Structure of a business intelligence opportunity map.

For sake of illustration, to represent BI projects we will use the five categories of BI that we identified for McCormick. In actual practice, there might well be more than five projects, but for our purposes five will suffice. There are several ways to go about creating the BI opportunity map, one of which is to have one person array the projects within the opportunity map quadrants as the starting point for discussions with knowledgeable business and IT leaders and managers. If this approach is used, the initial BI opportunity map for McCormick might look like Figure 2-4.

The logic for the project placements is as follows:

- All projects were judged to have a very positive business impact owing to strong alignment with company strategies and core business processes. Manufacturing BI was considered to have relatively less business impact because supply chain costs are a much higher proportion of total finished goods costs than are manufacturing costs. Financial planning and control BI was felt to provide lagging indicators,

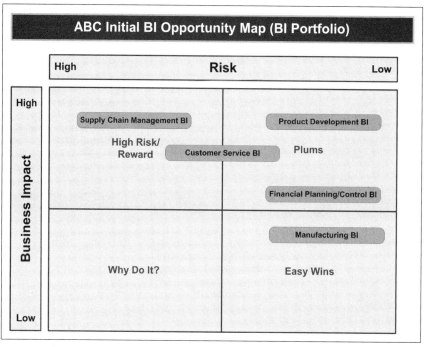

FIGURE 2-4 Filling in the business intelligence opportunity map.

whereas product development BI, SCM BI, and customer service BI were judged to have more direct impacts on McCormick's ability to execute its business strategies and value disciplines.

- The projects were judged to have different risk characteristics based on the relative technical difficulty of acquiring and integrating the data needed to delivery the information from the source systems that contain the data, the availability and quality of the underlying data needed to deliver the information, and a number of organizational readiness factors.

Tip

Your BI opportunities will yield the most value for the least cost if you prioritize them carefully. Prioritization requires understanding both the potential business impact and the technical and organizational risks that exist. If you haven't prioritized your opportunities, then you might try low-value, high-difficulty opportunities first and miss out on the "plums" that would deliver high value for very little effort.

Business and IT leaders and managers can use the initial BI opportunity map as the starting point for discussions addressing the underlying assumptions of the initial project placements, and then they can potentially adjust those placements, as illustrated by Figure 2-5.

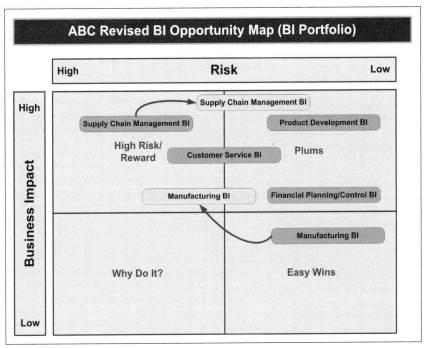

FIGURE 2-5 Revising the business intelligence opportunity map.

In the example above, the discussion of risk-reward tradeoffs resulted in a group consensus that

- Manufacturing BI had greater business impact and greater risk than originally perceived, as indicated by the manufacturing BI box
- SCM BI had greater business impact and less risk than originally perceived, as indicated by the SCM BI box

Based on these discussions and the relative placement of the projects within the BI opportunity map, McCormick might then prioritize its BI opportunities as follows:

1. SCM BI
2. Product development BI
3. Customer service BI
4. Financial planning and control BI
5. Manufacturing BI

These priorities would then establish the order in which the specific BI development projects would be undertaken.

2.2.4 Business Intelligence Opportunity Analysis Summary

The first part of this chapter has introduced a business-driven BI opportunity analysis framework that you can use to identify and prioritize the BI-driven profit opportunities for your company. We used the McCormick case study to illustrate the practical application of this approach in a specific industry, although we have used the approach in a wide variety of industries. In the McCormick case, we applied the BI opportunity analysis at an enterprise level; in other, real-world contexts, we have applied it at the strategic business unit level and functional/departmental level. As with any analytical framework or method, it is important to note that the method is only a way to organize the analysis. The quality of the outcome depends on the quality of analysis, thinking, and discussion about the specific BI opportunities, their business impacts, and the risks and rewards of investing in the specific BI opportunities. In that vein, the next part of this chapter will discuss some practical considerations for successfully using BI opportunity analysis to set the stage for using BI to improve profits and performance.

2.3 Business Intelligence Opportunity Analysis: Practical Considerations

The BI opportunity analysis framework encompasses a mix of analyses and processes: some are relatively straightforward, and others are more art than science. There are also differences among the contexts in which the opportunity analysis might be conducted. In one case, you might do an enterprise BI opportunity analysis for a company that is just getting started with BI. In another case, you might do a BI opportunity analysis for a division or function that has experience with BI but has not achieved the ROI it sought. Also, different companies and different divisions within companies have varying appetites for structured analytical approaches such as opportunity analysis. Some will embrace the approach fully, bringing their best thinkers to the task, whereas others will circumscribe the analysis and simply use it to validate their gut feelings. Because of these practical differences, and because of the potential impact on ROI, it is important to identify some key practical considerations that affect the cost and quality of the BI opportunity analysis.

> **Tip**
>
> Although there are definite advantages in doing BI opportunity analysis at the enterprise level, you can do it at lower levels (division, unit, function, etc.) based on the scope of the BI initiative. It is still important, however, to analyze and understand business drivers, value disciplines, and core processes to provide the business context needed to find the highest value opportunities.

2.3.1 Art Versus Science in Business Intelligence Opportunity Analysis

If we review the top-down analytical flow that makes up the BI opportunity analysis, we see that three of the factors we seek to understand are: (1) business drivers; (2) business strategy, goals, and objectives, and (3) business design, which includes value disciplines and core business processes. Our experience has been that developing a suitable understanding of these factors is straightforward, particularly for public companies but also for large private companies. In addition to the wide range of industry and company information that is in the public domain and often available via the Internet, a few hours of discussion with company leaders and managers will generally allow the BI opportunity analysis team to capture sufficient information about business drivers, strategies, value drivers, and core processes to serve as inputs for the process of identifying business-driven BI value creation opportunities. However, the process of identifying how BI can be used within core processes to impact profit is where art comes into play.

The process of identifying business-driven BI value creation opportunities requires knowledge of a company's core business processes and knowledge of how BI has been used in different contexts to improve profits. Sometimes both knowledge sets exist in a given company. If your company is not in that position, then using an outside facilitator with broad knowledge of business and BI may be in order. Under either scenario, the central task is to imagine how the core business processes could be improved by leveraging business information, business analyses, and potentially structured business decisions.

One way to stimulate business thinking about the possibilities is to read BI case studies. Such case studies are available from TDWI (www.tdwi.org) and other sources. Another way to stimulate the imagination is to use generic analytical frameworks. For example, in their seminal article "How Information Gives You Competitive Advantage," Michael Porter and Victor Millar (1985) apply the value chain construct at the single-company level to examine points at which information can be used as a source of competitive advantage. Figure 2-6 below illustrates the value chain for a single firm.

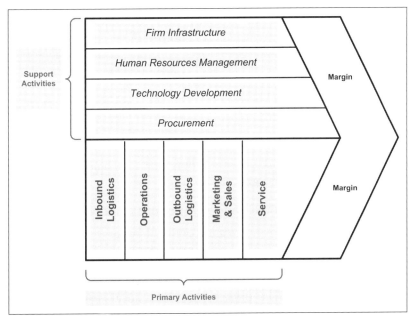

FIGURE 2-6 The value chain for a single firm.

Many companies have applied *transactional IT*—such as packaged enterprise requirements planning (ERP), customer relationship management (CRM), and SCM applications—at points in the value chain as a means of gaining transactional efficiency. The same value chain approach can be used to organize thinking about BI opportunities. For example, you could brainstorm about how to use business information and associated business analyses to improve the cost-effectiveness of inbound and outbound logistics.

Another generic framework for thinking about ways that BI could drive increased profits is provided by Thomas Davenport and James Short (1990) in their book *The New Industrial Engineering: Information Technology and Business Process Redesign*. Their framework describes various IT capabilities and how they can benefit an organization. We have adapted the framework to our purposes here, adding columns to describe how BI can be used to capture the generic business benefit and to provide relevant BI examples. The adapted framework is shown in Table 2-1.

In seeking to identify BI-driven profit opportunities, the framework provided by Table 2-1 can be used to structure a brainstorming session with business executives, managers, and front-line knowledge workers.

> **Tip**
>
> Whatever framework you use, it should help your organization develop a structured way of thinking about your business and BI opportunities.

Depending on the scope of the BI opportunity analysis, a number of other generic frameworks can be used to stimulate thinking about how BI could improve your profits. In the SCM world, there is the supply chain operations reference (SCOR) model (available at www.supply-chain.org), which details planning and operational "best practices" and associated performance metrics. At the strategic level, the use of "balanced scorecards" has spread over the past five years. If your company uses a balanced scorecard, it can be a good stimulus for thinking about the use of BI—both to report results and to improve the underlying processes that drive results. In the business process improvement arena, a wide range of published process performance metrics can be used as a starting point for BI opportunity analysis.

In short, numerous generic frameworks can stimulate thinking about how BI can improve the results at your company. There are enterprise management frameworks, functional management frameworks, business process management frameworks, value chain frameworks, and so forth. The art, we believe, lies in picking suitable frameworks to fit the scope of the BI opportunity analysis and in bringing the right business and IT leaders and managers into the conversation.

2.3.2 Quality of Business Intelligence Opportunity Analysis

The BI opportunity analysis and the creation of the BI opportunity map set the stage for a sequence of investments in BI. The premise is that making the investments will generate incremental profit in excess of the amounts invested. Two general factors determine whether the premise holds true. One factor is whether the prerequisites for leveraging BI have been met: those prerequisites are the subject of Chapter 3. The other more immediate factor is whether the BI opportunity analysis has correctly

Table 2-1

Information technology (IT) capabilities and their potential benefits for business and business intelligence (BI)

IT Capability	Generic Business Impact/Benefit	Application to BI	BI Examples
Transactional efficiency	Transform unstructured processes into structured, repeatable transactions	Can transform unstructured decision processes into structured, repeatable processes for well-characterized and recurring decision situations	Revenue optimization models used in airline and hotel industries; supply chain and logistics network optimization models used in manufacturing, distribution, and service industries
Automation of manual processes	Replace or reduce human labor in a process	Can replace time-consuming, ad hoc, and idiosyncratic manual information gathering and analysis with ready-to-use structured information and analyses	Activity-based costing/management; sales and operations planning; customer segmentation; budgeting; variance analysis; performance reporting; productivity analysis
Application of analytical techniques	Bring complex analytical methods to bear within processes	Can deliver robust analytical capabilities to a wide range of users while requiring only a short learning curve	Executive scorecards and dashboards; credit scoring and fraud detection applications; sales campaign management analytics; sales forecasting; customer segmentation
Delivery of information	Bring vast amounts of detailed information into a process	Can harness the blizzard of transactional information companies gather and use it to detect revenue-generation and cost-reduction opportunities	Data mining and pattern recognition; supply chain analytics; operations analytics; revenue trend analysis; retail category management applications
Tracking	Allows detailed tracking of status, inputs, and outputs of a task or process	Can replace manually intensive, spreadsheet-based tracking systems with automated systems	Cascading scorecards; dashboards; supplier scorecards; inventory management

identified BI investments that, if properly leveraged, will generate incremental profit in excess of the amounts invested. This speaks to the quality of the BI opportunity analysis, and there can be a lot at stake. For example,

- Brother International, a manufacturer of printers and computer peripherals, invested $1 million in BI and earned a 120% return on its investment in only 18 months.
- Southwest Airlines, a U.S. commercial airline company with 427 aircraft and more than 2,900 flights each day, implemented BI to analyze flight problems and improve the safety of its customers.
- Absa Bank, a major financial services company, invested $32 million in BI over the course of six years, earning a self-reported $57 million ROI.
- A major bank invested $78 million in BI over the course of 13 years, earning a self-reported $423 million ROI.
- A major electronics manufacturer invested $3 million in BI over the course of three years, earning a self-reported $26 million ROI.

In our experience, the low end of BI annual investments by major companies in a variety of industries falls between $1 million and $5 million for departmental or functional BI investments. At the enterprise BI level, annual investments of $5 million or more are typical, as illustrated by the examples above. Given the magnitudes of these investments, it is critical that the BI opportunity analysis be conducted with appropriate quality and rigor. That means drilling down and closely examining each potential BI investment identified by the BI opportunity analysis. How, *exactly*, will BI be used to improve profits?

More and more attention has been paid recently to this question. Experience suggests that this is because not all BI projects have been successful from a business perspective. For every success story, dozens of companies had investments in BI that did not pay off. This track record suggests that basic methods need to evolve in order to better capture the business value of BI.

> **Pitfall**
>
> Many companies fail to do a careful BI opportunity analysis. As a result, they fail to identify their highest-value BI opportunities and end up wasting money on lower-priority efforts.

As noted in Chapter 1, DW—a key enabler of BI—has historically focused on the technical challenges, technical methods, and project management methods required to deploy data warehouses and BI. However, an important recent innovation is in the methods used fully to leverage the potential of BI. Business-centric BI methods (the subject of Chapter 4) extend the technical methods of BI pioneers such as Inmon, Kimball, and Imhoff by designing ROI into BI initiatives from the outset and by systematically driving the use of BI into the core business processes and decisions that determine business results. Business-centric methods go beyond traditional approaches by putting rigor into defining the *business value capture mechanism* for each BI project. This includes determining and specifying a priori how business processes and key decision processes must change in order to leverage BI investments.

A key element of business-centric BI methods is the BI opportunity analysis and the creation of the BI opportunity map. As discussed earlier, the BI opportunity analysis identifies potential opportunities for using BI to improve profits. Those opportunities are then arrayed within the four quadrants of the BI opportunity map according to their business impact and associated risk. To score potential BI opportunities effectively on the business impact scale, the BI opportunity analysis team must rigorously examine the business value capture mechanism for each identified opportunity.

Ideally, this entails developing "as-is" and "to-be" process models as a means of understanding how a given process works today, how it would work when the targeted BI is brought to bear, and how it would generate the incremental revenue and/or reduced costs from the BI-driven process change. In actual practice, we find that many very successful companies do not have readily available process metrics for the as-is state, for example, process costs, process cycle times, and process effectiveness measures. That said, we find that experienced business leaders and managers have a deep understanding of their businesses, and they can intuitively judge whether a given investment in BI would have a suitable business impact. Accordingly, when sufficient analytical rigor is used, a good understanding of the business value capture mechanism for a given potential BI investment is developed. The key, in our view, is effectively engaging business executives and managers so that the quality of the BI opportunity analysis and the BI opportunity map is good enough to justify multi-million dollar investment decisions.

2.3.3 Risk-Reward Tradeoffs and the Business Intelligence Opportunity Map

As we discussed earlier, the BI opportunity map is a tool for promoting informed discussion of the risks and rewards associated within given BI opportunities. The rewards side of the equation is expressed on the business impact scale of the BI opportunity map, and the anticipated rewards (business impact) should reflect a rigorous understanding the business value capture mechanism for each opportunity. The risk side of the equation is expressed on the risk scale of the BI opportunity map, and *BI risk analysis* is needed to effectively place any given BI opportunity on the risk scale. An effective BI risk analysis will go beyond technical risks, although they are certainly important to consider.

Many BI initiatives have been entirely successful from a technical perspective and yet were failures because they did not deliver the expected business value. Accordingly, the business risks and the technical risks associated with the proposed BI investments on the BI opportunity map must be evaluated. To address this requirement, we have developed a *BI readiness assessment* framework (available at www.decisionpath.com/readiness.htm), which can be used to gauge a company's prerequisites to leverage BI successfully and thus create incremental profits. Lack of readiness means risk, and thus you can use the BI readiness assessment as a tool for identifying key BI risks of a given BI investment and/or a portfolio of BI investments. The critical prerequisites for successfully leveraging BI investments are as follows:

- **Strategic alignment.** The BI investment must be used within a core business process that makes a difference in profits.
- **Business and IT partnership.** IT cannot design and deliver BI without active and consistent business involvement, and business must bear responsibility for the process changes required to leverage BI investments.
- **Continuous process improvement culture.** Some companies embrace change and process improvement, and as a result, they are well positioned to leverage BI-driven process changes that impact profits.
- **Culture that supports the use of information and analytical tools.** Some companies and industries are heavier users of information and analytical tools, and as a result, they are well positioned to leverage BI-driven process changes that impact profits.
- **Decision process engineering culture.** Some companies are more structured in their decision style, which creates opportunities to insert BI into decision processes that already exist versus having to create structured decision processes from scratch in order to leverage a given BI investment.
- **BI and DW technical readiness.** A lot of technical pitfalls can adversely impact BI ROI if the company does not have appropriate experience with the technical aspects of BI and DW.
- **BI portfolio management.** Companies that manage BI as a portfolio have the opportunity to leverage BI infrastructure investments and technical experience across specific BI investments, thereby reducing costs and technical risk.

> **Pitfall**
>
> It's not enough to focus on technical success. Unless you can integrate your BI efforts into the processes, culture, and IT infrastructure of your organization, BI won't deliver the business value that it should. A structured BI readiness assessment is essential to make BI an all-around success.

Chapter 3 will discuss BI readiness in greater detail, so we offer only this summary of prerequisites—and potentially risks—at this point. By using this structured approach, you are better positioned to understand the risks of specific BI opportunities and thus to place them more accurately on the risk scale of the BI opportunity map. If you also have an accurate assessment of the business impact of the BI opportunities, you will be in an excellent position to make effective risk-reward tradeoffs and thereby to establish a realistic foundation for leveraging BI to increase profits.

2.3.4 Business Intelligence Opportunity Analysis: Summary

We started this chapter by posing a challenge to business leaders and managers. Quoting Peter Drucker, we in essence asked readers to consider whether they really know what information they need to do their jobs. Having had a variety of experiences with a variety of executives and managers, we have concluded that better, more structured approaches to determining BI opportunities are needed, and we developed the BI opportunity analysis framework systematically to identify BI opportunities and prioritize them based on business impact and risk. BI opportunity analysis is part of a broader business-centric BI method that seeks to ensure that BI investments deliver business value. To accomplish that goal, it explicitly considers the business value capture mechanism (business impact) of each BI project at the outset, it manages BI risks, and it manages the process changes required to deliver the promised business value. BI opportunity analysis establishes a solid foundation for successful BI investments.

2.4 Key Points to Remember

- BI opportunity analysis and the BI opportunity map lay the foundation for successfully leveraging BI to increase profits; therefore, the quality of analysis affects the quality of the foundation, with substantial implications for ROI.
- BI opportunity analysis involves a marriage of company-specific business knowledge and broad knowledge of BI uses. It is important to engage your company's best thinkers in the process.
- BI opportunity analysis involves imagination about how core business processes could be improved by using BI. It's imagining how you would run your business based on *having* the information you need instead of *not having* it.
- A careful assessment of BI risks is essential to have a realistic foundation for BI success. BI risks can be managed if they are known in advance.

2.5 Think Tank

2.5.1 Seven Questions to Ask About Your Company's Business Intelligence Opportunities

1. What are the major business drivers in our industry?
2. What are our strategies for coping with those drivers?
3. How do we create value for our customers?
4. Through what core processes do we deliver value for our customers?
5. How could we use better business information and better analytical tools to improve our core processes?
6. What kinds of analyses would we like to do that we cannot do today for lack of business information and appropriate analytical tools?
7. How are our competitors using BI to increase revenues and/or reduce costs?

2.5.2 Quiz: How Prepared Are We to Leverage Business Intelligence?

1. How effective are we at process improvement?
2. Is our culture open to the use of information and analytical tools within key processes and/or for key decisions?
3. How effectively do business executives and managers work with our IT project teams?
4. Do we have the technical experience to deliver successful BI projects?
5. Is our decision style amenable to structured, visible decision processes informed by business information and business analyses?

Chapter 3

Business Intelligence Readiness: Prerequisites for Leveraging Business Intelligence to Improve Profits

"...successful organizations can be distinguished by their ability to leverage IT capabilities to transform their businesses (structures, processes, and roles) to obtain powerful sources of competitive advantage in the marketplace."
—John Henderson and N. Venkatraman, Center for Information Systems Research, Sloan School of Management, Massachusetts Institute of Technology, November 1990

Historically, many data warehousing (DW) and business intelligence (BI) initiatives have been driven by information technology (IT). The BI industry has focused mainly on the technical aspects of delivering information to the BI user community. Now, however, we have arrived at a point where many of the technical challenges and tradeoffs are well understood. As a result, attention has shifted away from the technology per se and toward expanding the ways BI can be used to deliver business value, as well as toward enhancing BI development methods to ensure that BI investments pay off.

In Chapter 2, we briefly introduced the concept of *business-centric BI methods*, which design return on investment (ROI) into planned BI applications at the outset and then re-engineer relevant business processes to ensure that the organization actually captures its planned ROI. We also discussed BI opportunity analysis and the BI opportunity map in detail, and we introduced the BI readiness assessment. All of these are key components of business-centric BI methods—a comprehensive view of which is the focus of Chapter 4.

Our focus here in Chapter 3 is on BI readiness as a prerequisite for BI success and as a key BI risk analysis tool. As part of the more rigorous business-centric BI methods, BI readiness assessments are used at the front end of BI projects to determine the degree to which a given company is prepared to make the changes that are necessary to capture the full business value of BI.

A well-conceived BI readiness assessment builds on traditional DW readiness assessments by examining a range of organizational attributes that are correlated with the readiness to exploit BI for improved profits. Examining these key readiness factors "up front" focuses the attention of business sponsors and business users on *business value capture mechanisms*—that is, on the manner in which relevant organizational behaviors and business processes must *change* in order to exploit newly available business information and business analysis tools. BI readiness assessments also identify specific areas of implementation risk so these risks can be managed and mitigated, thus improving the probability of BI success. Used effectively, the information gained from a BI readiness assessment helps the BI team design ROI into BI applications and reduce the business risk that BI applications will turn out to be shelf-ware.

3.1 Business Intelligence Readiness Overview

As we discussed in Chapters 1 and 2, the business value of BI lies in its ability to improve the effectiveness of the core business processes that drive profits. Simply put, an investment in BI must return increased revenues and/or reduced costs that exceed the amount invested or business value will actually be lost. The increased attention being paid to the ROI of BI reflects industry experience over the past decade wherein many DW initiatives, and the BI applications they supported, were not successful when measured against the business value yardstick.

To overcome this problem, we need to better understand where the business value of BI is and then identify and manage the preconditions for capturing the business value.

As seen in Chapter 2, using BI opportunity analysis and the BI opportunity map delivers a richer and more rigorous understanding of the business value capture mechanism(s) for a given BI project or for all of the opportunities within the BI portfolio. These techniques are used to achieve strategic alignment among (1) business strategies, goals, and objectives; (2) the key business processes employed to meet the goals and objectives; and (3) the BI initiatives that are designed to improve the effectiveness of the key business processes. These efforts lay the groundwork for a successful BI investment by establishing a business-driven roadmap for profitable BI investments. By way of reminder, Figure 3-1 shows the BI opportunity analysis flow.

Using BI opportunity analysis and the BI opportunity map fundamentally changes the front-end analysis for BI and DW by adding rigor to the determination of how the BI investment or investments are going to increase your company's profits. These methods also change the back-end delivery process by using business process reengineering techniques to ensure that the deployed BI applications are embedded in relevant business and/or management processes that deliver business value.

FIGURE 3-1 Business-centric analysis of using business intelligence to create business value.

To reach the final destination–that is, deployed BI applications that deliver ROI–we also need to manage those business and IT factors that will either support or impede project success: that's where the BI readiness assessment comes into play. Based on our consulting experience with Fortune 1,000 companies and government agencies, and on our experience as judges for the BI/DW Best Practices competitions, we have identified factors correlated with an organization's ability to leverage BI to improve business performance and deliver business value. Figure 3-2 shows those factors.

After an organization determines where it stands in relation to these BI readiness factors, the organization can leverage strengths, manage risks, launch initiatives to improve readiness, develop competencies in embedding BI into core processes, and manage the process of capturing business value on specific BI projects. A BI readiness assessment can thus be seen as a BI risk analysis tool and as an implementation tool that, with a modest investment of effort, can greatly enhance the probability of a strong payoff for a BI investment.

Tip

Readiness assessment is crucial because it serves two important goals. First, it identifies "gaps," areas *where* you are not ready to proceed with your BI efforts. By identifying your BI readiness gaps, you can avoid wasting time and resources in areas where lack of preparation would make success difficult and failure probable. Second, readiness assessment shows you *what* you need to close the gaps and implement BI with a high probability of success.

Strategic Alignment	Organizations that strategically align BI to support business goals are well positioned to identify and fund high-impact BI projects that have ROI potential
Continuous Process Improvement Culture	Organizations that have embraced continuous process improvement are more adept at process change, a prerequisite for BI-driven value capture
Culture Around Use of Information and Analytics	Organizations accustomed to using information, analytical frameworks, and quantitative analyses are more adept at adopting BI to create value
BI Portfolio Management	Organizations where major functions have assessed BI opportunities have the opportunity to manage BI as a portfolio and thereby optimize BI ROI
Decision Process Engineering Culture	Organizations that have experience with structured decision processes based on standard, fact-based frameworks are more adept using BI to create value
BI & DW Technical Readiness	Effective technical execution of DW/BI initiatives requires proven methods for managing, designing, developing, and deploying BI that creates value
Business: IT Partnership	Using BI to create business value requires continuous business leadership and involvement and a strong partnership between business and IT

FIGURE 3-2 Impact of business intelligence readiness factors on its return on investment.

3.2 Business Intelligence Readiness, Business Risk, and Traditional Development Methods

A BI readiness assessment is a tool designed to help overcome the limitations of traditional development methods. Because it is business-centric, we are less concerned with the technical issues of DW and BI deployment—even though technical architecture, data architecture, technology choices, and appropriate methods will always be critical to project success. Instead, the *business risk* associated with BI investments is important: that's the risk that the business will not successfully identify key BI opportunities and/or capitalize on a given deployed BI application, and thus the investment will not pay off.

This is different from traditional development approaches, which make the leap of faith that the combination of sponsor support (funding, commitment, participation, political support, and testimonials), subject matter expert (SME) involvement, and sound technical and management methods will result in a successful BI project. We believe that industry experience shows a clear need to move beyond this traditional perspective in order for organizations to realize the business value of BI. Two recent cases, disguised to protect the proprietary interests of the organizations involved, will illustrate this point.

3.2.1 Manufacturing Company Example

Company A is a $4.5 billion manufacturer of consumer and industrial products. At the time of the project (2000/2001), its consumer products group had deployed a data mart with an online analytical processing (OLAP) application used for managing revenue and profit to meet Wall Street's expectations. Company A's industrial products group determined that a similar BI application would allow it to do a better job of managing revenues and profits. Funding was obtained. The group used a traditional development method to design, develop, and deploy the BI application. It held facilitated sessions with SMEs to determine the business questions the BI application would need to answer. Several business users were involved throughout the project, and the group provided training after the data mart was completed. Although the BI application was ultimately successful, there were several bumps in the road that the company could have avoided via a comprehensive BI readiness assessment. Specifically,

> **Tip**
>
> "Data mart," "OLAP," and other BI technical terms are explained in Appendix A at the end of this book.

- **Continuous process improvement** was not part of the culture of the sales organization, the intended user of the BI application. Because users were not accustomed to change and innovation, the user community had trouble adjusting to the change from static, canned reports delivered monthly to high-powered, flexible business analysis capabilities. This was a problem *even though users from the sales organization had been involved throughout the design, development, and training design processes.*
- **The culture around use of information and analytical applications** did not support adoption of the new BI application. The sales force was composed mainly of older technophobes who made their living by knowing the products and nurturing relationships with buyers. Used to static reports, they had little interest in using analytical applications, even though the applications contained information that could be used to improve the effectiveness of their sales calls. As a workaround, assistants developed report views that were similar to their legacy static reports from the BI application and e-mailed them to the sales force.
- **The culture around decision making** was strictly ad hoc and idiosyncratic, which did not allow for structured uses of the new BI application within key sales and sales management processes. Instead, each salesperson was free to interpret the new sales report views individually and use, or not use, the application as he or she saw fit.
- **The business/IT partnership was less than ideal**, which led to a 50% project surcharge from IT to the business after development was complete but before the BI application was put into production. This caused resentment and blaming, which further hindered deployment of BI applications within the company.

Had the company started by conducting a BI readiness assessment, it could have anticipated and better managed many of the obstacles that got in the way of realizing the full value of the BI investment. The design and deployment of the BI application and the tool used to deliver it would certainly have been different. Further, a richer understanding of the culture around information use, decision making, and the use of analytical applications would have allowed Company A to identify and manage

---

Pitfall

Some people take culture and cooperation less seriously because these items are not about technology and cannot easily be quantified. However, such "soft" factors are just as crucial to your BI success as metrics and technologies. You ignore them at your peril.

---

the organizational change needed to fully leverage the new BI application. In addition to training, a more proactive business process re-engineering effort in conjunction with behavioral incentives to make use of the sales analysis information would have improved the outcome.

3.2.2 Disability Insurance Company Example

Company B is an $8 billion company that faces substantial business challenges over the next decade. Those challenges come largely from increases in claims by the aging baby-boom generation, whose members are entering their disability-prone years. Other challenges come from heightened customer service expectations associated with the ever-growing number of business transactions that can be accomplished via the Internet. Accordingly, Company B needs to optimize claims processing productivity and improve service delivery. These challenges are operationally complex owing to the variable nature of disability claims and the need to apply both medical and vocational expertise to make accurate claims decisions. Accordingly, the company has embarked on a BI program aimed at providing all levels of operations management with more timely and relevant business information, as well as with appropriate analytical tools so that managers can consistently improve productivity and service. Toward these ends, the company is specifically managing the BI readiness factors described in Figure 3-2. It has funded a major project to ensure that it captures the business value of its investments in BI. In terms of BI readiness,

- **The company funded a comprehensive project to ensure strategic alignment** among its strategies, goals, and objectives; its key service delivery processes; and the BI applications required for making those processes more productive while improving service.
- **The company has a record of continuous process improvement** and a culture that supports the goal of operational excellence. The company embraces the use of IT to improve operational processes, it has come to realize the business value of BI, and it has budgeted funds for business process re-engineering to capitalize on its BI investments.
- **The company recognizes that it will have to change the culture** within its operating units to embrace the use of enhanced information, modern analytical tools, and advanced optimization models. The good news is that managers across the company have a strong desire to use BI to serve customers better and operate more productively.
- **The company formally assessed its BI and DW technical readiness** so that it could enhance its overall capabilities for delivering high-quality business information. That information is necessary to feed the full spectrum of BI applications that

are required to run the company productively and with high levels of customer service.

- **The company employs effective IT governance mechanisms that promote an effective business/IT partnership.** Those mechanisms include executive-level and working-level steering committees, regular off-site planning meetings, and Web-based status communication mechanisms. The business units are actively engaged in all aspects of the program and are prepared to manage the changes required to capitalize on the BI investments.

Tip

The essence of Company B's advantage in BI is managerial, not technological. By aligning its BI program with strategic objectives and processes, by planning for cultural change, by assessing its BI readiness, and by using effective IT governance mechanisms, Company B ensures that it will get the most from its BI investment almost regardless of the specific BI technologies it chooses to implement.

The situation at Company B is different from that at Company A because Company B has embraced business-centric BI methods that explicitly consider and manage the business risk associated with BI investments. By assessing BI readiness at the front end, Company B has positioned itself to manage process changes and implementation risks so as to ensure that the BI applications deliver business value. In other words, Company B has increased the odds that its BI applications will pay off. BI readiness assessments go beyond traditional development methods by explicitly assessing the risk that the business will not successfully capitalize on a given deployed BI application.

3.3 Business Intelligence Readiness Factors

To ensure a return on an investment in BI, those factors that make a difference in whether or not the investment pays off have to be identified and managed. From a technical perspective, an established body of knowledge around DW can be employed to ensure that fundamentals of acquiring, staging, and delivery of information and BI applications are done correctly. From a business perspective, a number of factors ultimately determine whether or not a BI application delivers an ROI. These readiness factors are types of business risk and can be managed accordingly. It is common for organizations to obtain a range of scores, from strong to weak, on individual BI readiness factors. Strong scores indicate a strength that can be leveraged for success. Weak scores indicate risks that need to be actively managed to mitigate risk.

3.3.1 Strategic Alignment

Much has been written about strategic alignment between business and IT. The discussion is generally about consistency among business strategy, business organization and processes, IT strategy, IT infrastructure, and IT organization and processes (Cooper et al., 2000). In the BI context, strategic alignment occurs when

- Business strategies and key management and business processes are consistent and reinforcing, whether this is achieved by strategy mapping or traditional strategic planning mechanisms.
- BI initiatives are focused on improving those key management and business processes that drive profits.
- BI initiatives are supported by appropriate IT strategies, infrastructure, and IT organization.

Absent any of these elements, there is the risk that a BI initiative will not deliver business value.

Tip
If strategic alignment *is* an organizational strength, then using a BI opportunity analysis framework (see Chapter 2) to develop a BI opportunity map will seem intuitive. If it is *not* a strength, then using a BI opportunity framework to develop a BI opportunity map may be initially uncomfortable. The result, however, will be the ability to make a "business case" for potential BI projects that are based on bottom-line considerations. This strategic alignment of BI opportunities will greatly improve the odds of BI success.

From an ROI perspective, BI initiatives should focus on business processes that make a difference, which was the focus of much of Chapter 2. We cannot expect much of an ROI on BI initiatives aimed at nonstrategic parts of the business. To have a profit impact, BI investments must be directed at management processes and/or business processes that have the greatest impact on profits. Accordingly, building ROI into BI initiatives requires that we ensure–up front– that a proposed BI portfolio or project is strategically aligned. The BI opportunity analysis framework and the BI opportunity map help ensure strategic alignment, as do having an appropriate BI infrastructure and a BI organization with the necessary BI/DW core competencies (see Section 3.3.6).

3.3.2 Continuous Process Improvement Culture

Using BI to improve management and/or business processes that make a difference in profits, productivity, and service requires some degree of process change. Experience at leading companies suggests that change management is often the most difficult aspect of successfully deploying a new BI application.

If process changes are needed to leverage BI and business users don't make them, then the company's investment in BI will be wasted. The money spent will have no impact on the economic well-being of the organization. However, organizations that have created successful process improvement cultures are adept at changing business processes, which prepares them to leverage BI effectively within processes that have an economic impact. Accordingly, you should assess whether an organization is ready to manage the process changes required to capture the business value of a BI initiative. If the organization is not ready, you need to know that up front so that you can formulate and execute appropriate plans for overcoming that liability (managing that risk). The differences in corporate cultures with respect to change and continuous improvement are evident in conversations we've had with several of the large companies with which we work. In one case in which we were developing a BI strategy for an industrial manufacturer, we asked about that company's orientation to change. Their response was, "All we do is change." In contrast, another company with which we've worked is very slow to change. A business adage popular at that company is that "there are 1,000 people who can say 'no' to a proposed change and only two who can say 'yes,' and nobody knows who those two people are." This is a major company whose consumer product brands are among the most well known in the world, so it is very successful. It's just that the company is very deliberate about change. From the perspective of capturing the business value of BI, these two companies present very different management and implementation challenges. An effective BI readiness assessment can help ferret out the specific change management and continuous improvement challenges that must be managed.

> **Tip**
>
> If continuous improvement *is* an organizational strength, then process changes that are needed to fully leverage BI capabilities can be incorporated into the existing organizational structures that are in place for this purpose. If it is *not* a strength, then you may consider identifying key business players that have resisted change, as well as those who may be open to change. "Sell" the need to change to key business players who can "market" to resisters in order to influence organizational change. Work with these change agents to develop a compelling business case for change. Use the BI opportunity analysis to discuss the "to be" organization and how using BI within changed business processes will support bottom-line performance improvement.

3.3.3 Culture Around the Use of Information and Analytical Applications

Organizations that embrace the use of information and analytical applications to improve profits are better able to leverage investments in BI than are organizations that do not embrace and reward such approaches to creating business value. We recently conducted a short survey of BI readiness via our Web site, and we found that major organizations differ markedly on this aspect of readiness. On a scale of 1 (low readiness) to 5 (high readiness), the survey respondents scored as high as 4.5 and as low as 2.5 on this factor. Although the number of respondents to the survey was small, the respondents are major organizations (most with revenues greater than $1 billion), which makes the survey responses valuable at least as anecdotal evidence.

Organizations vary in their readiness to use information and analytical applications to improve business performance. That fact is an element of corporate culture and is influenced by the environment in which the organization operates. For example, businesses that operate in high fixed-cost industries (such as airlines, hotels, trucking, and some manufacturing businesses) have long employed highly sophisticated revenue optimization models that they use every day in their business. These models dynamically manage pricing to optimize the tradeoff between price and capacity utilization. The goal of these models is to deliver the most profit possible under given constraints of supply and demand.

Such organizations are not daunted by the prospects of deploying new BI applications because their operating environment demands the use of BI applications and their culture supports it. In contrast, we have worked with leading companies where the predominant mode of operation was characterized by lack of information and analytics, decisions driven by force of personality, and the dominance of intuition at the expense of fact-based analysis. These different types of firms have different prospects when it comes to leveraging BI to capture business value. An effective BI readiness assessment will identify the relevant cultural obstacles to a successful BI application that delivers ROI.

> **Tip**
>
> If use of information and analytical applications *is* an organizational strength, then new BI applications that further enrich analysis will be welcomed by the business. If it is *not* a strength, then this capability will need to be developed in the organization. Finding business "power users" who can embrace new BI applications and demonstrate/model how these applications can be used to measure and manage business performance may be a good way to grow this organizational capability.

3.3.4 Business Intelligence Portfolio Management

A wide range of BI applications can improve the performance of the units within a given company, including some applications that help drive revenue growth and others that help reduce costs and optimize profits. Companies that have undertaken a comprehensive review of the major BI opportunities for sales, marketing, manufacturing, distribution, customer service, quality, and so forth are in a position to manage BI as a portfolio of investments, ranked by business impact and risk. This is important in an environment where capital budgets for IT are constrained, as they are almost always are.

The idea of managing BI initiatives as a portfolio is gaining increased attention in the context of discussions about the business value of BI. In many companies, a certain percentage of sales revenue is budgeted for IT, and then IT investments are managed as a portfolio (Broadbent and Weil, 1998). Within this IT capital budgeting context, BI fits as shown in Figure 3-3.

In any given company setting, a variety of IT capital expenditures for different purposes exists. Infrastructure expenditures—the foundation for the pyramid—can be thought of as basic plumbing in that they move data around, store it, and secure it. Infrastructure also provides the means for collaboration by providing such utilities as e-mail, workflow control, and intranets. The portfolio also includes transactional applications–the systems that the company uses to conduct transactions with or for the benefit of customers. Enterprise resources planning (ERP) systems are the most prominent example of a transactional application. Lastly, the portfolio includes informational applications and strategic applications, which is what BI has come to encompass. Informational applications provide key performance management

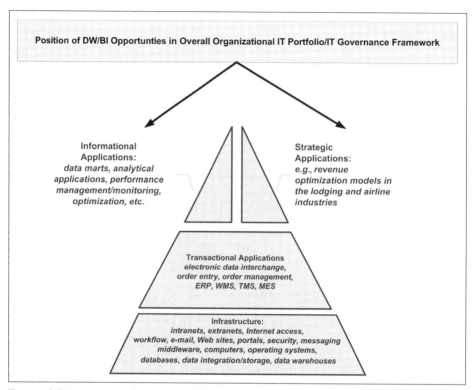

FIGURE 3-3 Business intelligence in the information technology portfolio.

information, and strategic applications are innovative IT applications that provide strategic advantages to the first mover.

Tip

If IT portfolio management *is* an organizational strength, then obtaining support for using a BI opportunity map approach to identify and evaluate potential BI projects for funding will likely be supported. If IT portfolio management is *not* an organizational strength, then the business may have to be sold on the concept. In organizations in which "pet projects" are funded based on influential business players rather than on the merits of the investment, this may be difficult. By selling key business players on the concept and enlisting their help to begin developing a BI opportunity map, you will be able to demonstrate to the business how this type of analysis can be beneficial to ensure that their BI/DW investments pay off.

Given its position in the IT portfolio, BI must compete for scarce capital funds, and the formal capital budgeting process frequently addresses the subject of ROI. If a given company has not examined the full spectrum of BI opportunities, it cannot know if the proposed BI projects are those that offer the highest risk-adjusted ROI to the company. Ideally, this analysis is conducted at an enterprise level, but this analysis can also be applied at a line of business, or functional level, based on the scope of the BI program. This may not make a difference if there is sufficient capital fund all BI projects that offer a positive ROI to fund all BI projects that offer a positive ROI. In a capital-constrained environment, however, not managing BI initiatives as a portfolio poses the risk of funding one BI project at the expense of another that may offer a higher ROI. In our view, companies who take a portfolio view of BI initiatives show a more strategic commitment to BI, and thus they are more ready to capture the maximum business value from BI investments. In our recent readiness survey, respondent scores ranged from 2.7 to 4.3 on this readiness factor, indicating that some organizations take a more strategic approach to managing BI for ROI.

3.3.5 Decision Process Engineering Culture

Decision process engineering is a term we have coined to convey the concept of using structured decision processes to increase the effectiveness of certain decisions that organizations face on a recurring or semi-recurring basis. These structured decision processes can incorporate the use of information, analytical applications, and/or quantitative methods as appropriate for the type of decision to be made. The decisions in which we are most interested are those that occur within the context of the core business processes that have an impact on profits.

For many companies in many industries, numerous routine and/or recurring management and operational decisions get made in the context of management and business processes. Such decision processes can be improved by using BI in ways that capitalize on the availability of information, analytical applications, and workflow technology to build structured, repeatable decision processes (Williams and Williams, 2003). Companies that understand this are well positioned to capitalize on BI applications to improve profits. In our recent "survey" of BI readiness, we found that survey respondents' scores ranged from 1.5 to 4.0 on this dimension of BI readiness.

Organizations that scored high on this readiness factor agreed with such statements as, "There is a standard decision-making routine for any well-structured problem situation we face." Having experience in engineering key decision processes means that an organization is accustomed to answering the kinds of questions associated with the example BI application, simple variance analysis, shown in Figure 3-4.

Tip
If your organization *has* a decision process engineering culture, then it will welcome better and richer information to use for organizational decision support. If your organization *does not have* a decision process engineering culture, then you can use new BI capabilities as an impetus to build one. This may be difficult and take time because in these cultures, individuals frequently have power based on their individual influence on decisions that are many times made in an ad hoc way. Again, the best way to address this is to demonstrate to the organization how moving from an ad hoc approach to a more structured approach regarding decision making will help bottom-line performance. IT is *not* the appropriate organization to make this case; the business organization is. Key business individuals should be enlisted to develop the business case and advance the argument. Finding very specific organizational "case studies" that everyone can relate to based on perceived business problems is a good place to start.

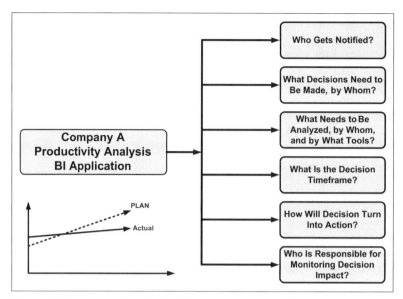

FIGURE 3-4 Key questions for decision process engineering.

Such experience translates into BI readiness because it prepares organizations to embed the use of BI applications into the core business processes that determine overall performance.

3.3.6 Business Intelligence and Data Warehousing Technical Readiness

A critical requirement for capturing the business value of BI is the technical ability to deliver the information and analytical applications that support BI. Fortunately, there is an extensive body of knowledge about how to do this. That said, some organizations are much more capable than are others at designing, developing, deploying, operating, and maintaining the appropriate technical environment to support DW and BI. Because you are interested in increasing the likelihood that BI investments will pay off, you must be concerned about reducing technical risk, which means that you need to assess technical readiness. By identifying technical risks up front, you can devise and execute appropriate plans to mitigate them. Accordingly, an effective BI readiness assessment should assess BI and DW technical readiness.

One proven tool that can be used to extend the technical readiness portion of the BI readiness assessment is the DW readiness assessment, a comprehensive instrument available from The Data Warehousing Institute (TDWI, at http://www.tdwi.org/Education/main.aspx?pageName=focus). Although the TDWI DW readiness assessment also includes organizational and business process readiness, it is strong on assessing technical and technical program management factors that affect a company's ability to do the technical work required to design, develop, and deploy a DW environment that will support the BI applications that will make a difference in profits. The TDWI instrument is designed to assess 12 specific capabilities, including the following:

1. **People readiness and business imperative.** The technical team's understanding and support for the business goals and objectives that the BI initiative is targeted to achieve, and their understanding and support for the role the data warehouse will play in meeting those goals and objectives.
2. **IT readiness and business imperative.** The IT organization's understanding of business goals and objectives that the BI initiative is targeted to achieve, and its preparedness and willingness to actively support the DW initiative.
3. **Business readiness and business imperative.** The business organization's understanding and support for the business goals and objectives that the BI initiative is targeted to achieve, and its preparedness and willingness to support the DW initiative.
4. **People readiness and executive sponsorship.** The executive sponsor's level of involvement and support, his or her understanding of what is required to achieve success, and the ability to set realistic business goals based on that understanding.
5. **IT readiness and executive sponsorship.** The executive sponsor's level of involvement and support for the IT organization, his or her understanding of what is required by IT, and the willingness to support or advocate necessary changes in the IT organization based on that understanding.
6. **Business readiness and executive sponsorship.** The executive sponsor is at an executive level in the business organization that will be directly affected by the BI initiative, he or she understands what is required of the business organization, and he or she is willing to make the necessary business resources available based on that understanding.
7. **People readiness and DW development method.** The technical team understands its role in a data warehouse development project and has experience in DW development.
8. **IT readiness and DW development method.** The IT organization has and follows IT standards that are compatible or that can be adapted to the DW development methodology; the IT organization can ensure a quality deliverable.
9. **Business readiness and DW development method.** The business organization is able and willing to participate in the data warehouse development and understands its roles and responsibilities under the DW development methodology.
10. **People readiness and business process orientation.** The technical team understands business processes and the value of information in the processes

> **Tip**
>
> If your organization *has* strong BI/DW technical capabilities, then it can support the technical skills needed to support BI/DW program. If your organization *does not have* these skills, they can be obtained, either through hiring new employees or by using consultants. Determining critical technical skill gaps is essential to ensure successful technical architecture and implementation.

11. **IT readiness and business process orientation.** The IT organization understands business processes and the value of information in those processes.
12. **Business readiness and business process orientation.** The business understands its business processes and how the targeted BI initiative(s) will affect or change those processes.

The TDWI DW readiness assessment is a very useful diagnostic tool for identifying technical execution risks, which is a key prerequisite for mitigating and managing them.

3.3.7 Effective Business/Information Technology Partnership for Business Intelligence

When we talk about an effective partnership between business and IT, we're not just talking about "playing well" with each other. The issue is business results that create business value, which concerns the business practices used to manage development and use of both IT generally and BI specifically. Organizations that have been effective in using IT to improve business results are more able to leverage BI to create value than are those whose practices do not create effective business/IT partnerships. Figure 3-5 shows key elements of effective partnerships.

> **Tip**
>
> If your organization *has* a strong business/IT partnership, then you are fortunate. Many BI/DW failures result from inadequate support from senior-level business management. That support, however, without a solid framework to guide your BI efforts is not enough. Executives will soon lose interest if you do not demonstrate how their investments in BI will deliver business value. If your organization *does not have* a strong business/IT partnership, it will need to develop one in order to succeed. Many organizations have used IT-driven prototypes to demonstrate BI opportunities. Although this "bottom-up"/IT driven approach is not optimal, it is often needed to get the business on board. The business/IT partnership will naturally be strengthened and continued funding will be provided when the business benefits that can result from this partnership are demonstrated.

The concepts in Figure 3-5 are not new: they are proven principles for effective use of IT to deliver business value (Dvorak et al., 1997). When these ideas are applied to management of a BI portfolio, the probability that individual BI initiatives will deliver business value is greatly increased. Accordingly, an effective BI readiness assessment will test for the presence of practices that implement these principles.

3.3.8 Summary: Business Intelligence Readiness Factors

The seven BI readiness factors we have described can be either stepping stones or barriers to deploying BI applications that create business value. Accordingly, you must know where the organization stands in relation to these factors, and you must take a holistic and realistic view of its starting position. No organization will achieve perfect scores across the board, and BI readiness is more easily improved in some areas than in others.

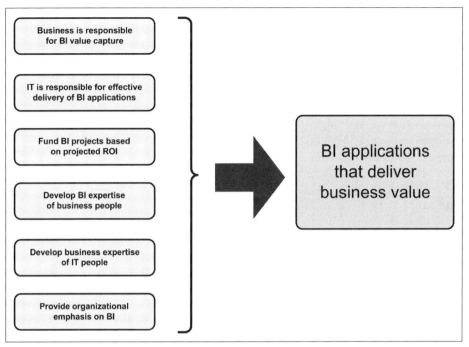

FIGURE 3-5 Elements of effective business/information technology partnerships for business intelligence.

For example, changing the culture around use of information and analytical applications will take longer than improving technical readiness, which in some instances can be addressed by strategic hiring, training, and/or use of consultants. The organization can use information from the BI readiness assessment as a guide to develop specific, customized BI strategies and implementation plans that effectively account for an organization's starting position. The result is that BI initiatives deliver *as much value* as possible *as quickly* as possible.

Performing an effective BI readiness assessment is a critical element of business-centric BI development methods because it helps the organization to assess how well it performs on factors that can be considered the preconditions for BI program success. A BI readiness assessment is a key tool for identifying the impediments to BI success and then systematically managing BI initiatives to overcome those impediments. Done correctly, it need not be an expensive or lengthy process, and the insight gained into the principal business risks associated with BI initiatives will pay dividends in the form of deployed BI applications that deliver real business value.

3.4 Case Study: BYTECO Business Intelligence Readiness Assessment

BYTECO is a multi-billion-dollar global manufacturer and marketer of semiconductor devices. Its products are key components used in a broad array of electronic applications, including personal computers, workstations, network servers, mobile phones, flash memory cards, USB storage devices, digital still cameras, MP3 players, and other consumer electronics products. Its customers are original equipment manufacturers located around the world.

BYTECO offers its products in a wide variety of package and configuration options, architectures, and performance characteristics tailored to meet application and customer needs. Individual devices take advantage of its advanced silicon processing technology and manufacturing expertise. BYTECO continually introduces new generations of products that offer lower costs per unit and improved performance characteristics.

BYTECO's manufacturing facilities are located around the world and generally operate 24 hours per day, seven days per week. Its process for manufacturing semiconductor products is complex, involving a number of precise steps, including wafer fabrication, assembly, burn-in, and final test. Efficient production of semiconductor products requires use of advanced semiconductor manufacturing techniques and effective deployment of these techniques across multiple facilities.

BYTECO sells its products into computing, consumer, networking, telecommunications, and imaging markets. Approximately 45% of its net sales for 2005 were to the computing market, including desktop personal computers, notebooks, servers, and workstations. The company markets its products primarily through its own direct sales force, and it maintains inventory at locations in close proximity to certain key customers to facilitate rapid delivery of product shipments.

3.4.1   The Business Intelligence Readiness Assessment

At the time of the case, BYTECO was in the early stages of *BI maturity*—a measure of organizational culture about which we will have more to say in Chapter 5. Given the nature of its business (and similar to many high technology companies), BYTECO exhibited a strong appetite for better information to use in such key business areas as

- **Manufacturing**, where yields and continuous process improvement are critical
- **Supply chain management**, where demand forecasting and inventory management have substantial impacts on supply in relation to demand, and thus pricing, and where collaboration with key customers has the ability to reduce costs and thus maintain or improve margins
- **Management accounting**, where better cost information can be used to improve pricing and product design-to-cost decisions

However, the company recognized that it needed to assess its ability to deliver the kinds of BI it could use to improve profits. It used the BI readiness assessment for that purpose. "BI readiness" is a state wherein an organization

- Recognizes and understands the key preconditions for leveraging information, analytical applications, and structured decision-making processes (collectively BI) to improve the management and business processes that drive profits/productivity
- Has achieved a broad consensus among its top managers to change its key management, decision-making, and business processes to leverage BI

- Has the financial, technical, governance, and change management ability/resources to execute programs to change its key management, decision-making, and business processes to leverage BI

A BI readiness assessment can be a good way to educate senior-level business management about the critical success factors needed for BI success and to obtain their support for the changes that are needed to improve the odds of success. In practice, BI readiness is the organization's starting point for a long-term evolution in how it uses information to improve profits and productivity. The BI readiness assessment survey that we use contains 100 questions grouped and scored across the seven BI readiness factors we described earlier in this chapter. Assessment participants are asked to respond to various statements on a scale from 1 to 5, where 5 means "strongly agree," 3 means "neutral," and 1 means "strongly disagree." The high-level results of the assessment at BYTECO are shown in Figure 3-6.

	Enterprise	Business Customers	Manufacturing Customers	IS Group	IS Business	IS Manufacturing	IS Data Services
Strategic Alignment	3.0	3.2	3.2	2.9	2.6	2.9	3.4
Continuous Improvement	2.8	3.0	3.0	2.7	2.2	2.9	3.2
Information Usage	2.6	3.0	2.9	2.4	2.0	2.6	2.9
Functional Use of BI	2.5	2.8	2.9	2.3	2.1	2.2	2.9
Decision Process Engineering	2.8	2.9	3.0	2.6	2.2	3.0	3.0
BI & DW Technical Readiness	2.5	2.6	2.7	2.4	2.3	2.2	2.8
Business: IT Partnership	2.5	2.6	2.3	2.6	2.3	2.6	3.0

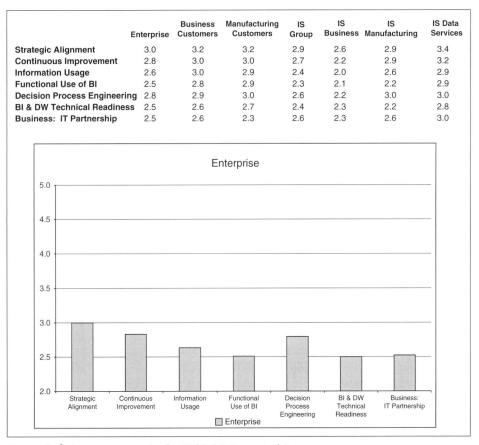

FIGURE 3-6 Assessment results for BYTECO (case study).

There are several key premises that underlie our use of the BI readiness assessment results to diagnose readiness and identify risk:

- Significant differences between groups in average scores for a given BI readiness factor may indicate a readiness challenge.
- Universally low average scores for a given BI readiness factor are indicative of a readiness challenge and risk factor that is a candidate for active mitigation and management.
- Low average scores and/or significant differences between groups indicate the need to examine responses to the specific questions for the given BI readiness factor in order to assess potential.

The results at BYTECO indicated that there were BI readiness challenges across the board. With a few slight exceptions, all groups were neutral to slightly negative in their assessments of BYTECO's BI readiness on the seven BI readiness factors. Although there did not appear to be any glaring weaknesses, all fronts indicated room for improvement. In general, respondents felt that BYTECO was the least ready in the areas of partnership between business and IT, BI and DW technical readiness, and managing BI as a portfolio. These indications were further explored and substantiated by using the TDWI DW readiness assessment instrument.

Based on the results of the BI readiness assessment and other supporting analyses, BYTECO developed a comprehensive program plan to move its BI initiatives forward and manage its risks. Specifically, BYTECO addressed strategic alignment by elevating the importance of BI within BYTECO and by changing from small, report-focused projects to looking at BI as a multi-year program, or BI portfolio. BYTECO addressed BI and DW technical readiness by investing in training and by adopting BI/DW design and development methods. The company now has a clear idea of how it intends to leverage BI to improve profits, and it is more technically capable of delivering BI applications. Under the leadership of a well-regarded vice president, and in conjunction with its enhanced BI management capabilities, BYTECO is successfully deploying BI as a key profit improvement tool.

3.5 Business Intelligence Readiness: Summary

BI readiness is ultimately about three things: the ability of the company to align and govern a BI program, the ability of IT to perform technically, and the ability of the company to change in order to leverage BI within core processes that have a profit impact. Absent these abilities, a company's investment in BI in a substantially higher risk proposition—and certainly more of a gamble than it needs to be. Any capital investment is made under conditions of risk, and thus the goal of management must be to identify and reduce those risks. The BI readiness assessment serves just that purpose, and when used proactively, it can identify specific risks to achieving BI-driven profit improvement. Armed with a clear idea of the risks, management can then mitigate those risks and increase the likelihood that its investment in BI will pay off.

3.6 Key Points to Remember

- A careful assessment of BI risks is essential to lay a realistic foundation for BI success. BI risks can be managed if they are known in advance.
- The BI readiness assessment identifies potential barriers to the success of your BI initiatives, and thus it is a key tool for ensuring your BI investments pay off.
- The BI readiness assessment can be used in the context of creating the BI opportunity map. It provides the BI risk assessment for the risk-reward tradeoffs that must be made to accurately place specific BI opportunities within the four quadrants of the BI opportunity map.
- BI risk is ultimately about the ability of the business units to leverage BI to improve profits.

3.7 Think Tank

3.7.1 Seven Questions to Ask About Your Company's Business Intelligence Readiness

1. Are we focusing our BI investments on business processes that really make a difference in our profits?
2. How good are we at managing a group of related IT investments that could cost several millions of dollars or more?
3. How good are we at using information and analytical tools?
4. Do we have the BI and DW competencies we need to minimize technical risk and optimize the BI/DW infrastructure?
5. Are there important business decisions we have to make on a recurring basis that require human judgment and that we can standardize in terms of the information needed, the way the information will be analyzed, and the manner in which the decision will be made?
6. How good are we at changing our core business processes to improve profits?
7. Are our business units held accountable for using IT to improve profits?

3.7.2 Quiz: How Prepared Is the Business to Leverage Business Intelligence?

1. Do our business units understand how the affected core processes must change in order to leverage our planned BI investments?
2. What plans have been made to provide BI tool training to business users so that they know how to access the business information and analytical tools that will be deployed via our planned BI investments?

3. What plans have been made to provide impetus from top management for the use of the business information and analytical tools that will be deployed via our planned BI investments?
4. Have we identified business unit stakeholders who stand to gain power or lose power as a result of the planned BI deployments?
5. Have we identified potential power users and key early adopters who can speed up acceptance of the new BI applications?

Chapter 4

Business-Centric Business Intelligence Development with the BI Pathway Method

"The key question is whether a firm's investment in information technology is in harmony with its strategic objectives . . . and thus building the capabilities necessary to deliver business value. This state of harmony is referred to as 'alignment.' It is complex, multi-faceted, and never completely achieved."
—Peter Weill and Marianne Broadbent, *Leveraging the New Infrastructure,* 1998

There's good news and bad news about the business value of business intelligence (BI). The good news is that management is paying more attention to it. The bad news is *why* they're paying attention: all too often, BI hasn't delivered the return on investment (ROI) that it promised. It has eaten up money and resources but, in the end, delivered little. However, the other good news is that things don't have to be that way. If we plan and manage BI as a business investment instead of a technological toy, it can outperform our most optimistic forecasts. What's been missing until recently is the evolution of BI methods to capture the full business value of BI. And that's what we'll tackle in this chapter.

All of the traditional BI methods encompass structures, components, activities, and deliverables that seek to put the right information into the hands of the right people at the right time. Some of those methods are stronger than others, but they are all address the need for BI to have a business impact. Where the traditional technically focused methods fall short is in ensuring that BI investments pay off. The principal limitations of the traditional methodologies, from the point of view of ROI delivery, are that they

- Do not take a BI portfolio perspective
- Do not systematically analyze how BI can be inserted into the core business and decision processes that affect profits

- Do not systematically address the business process change required to capture the business value of BI
- Do not adequately challenge the current organizational paradigms for information usage to determine how information can be best leveraged to deliver value

This is *not* to say that traditional approaches are deficient for designing, building, and deploying data warehouses. These approaches have proven excellent for those tasks. Rather, we simply mean that such approaches do not design ROI into the process, which sometimes results in BI investments that don't pay off as well as they should.

These shortcomings of traditional, technically focused methods are a consistent theme that we hear over and over, both as instructors and as consultants. We've observed that these shortcomings are owing to the following:

- Many BI project teams are heavy on technical savvy but light on business expertise. They rely too heavily on the limited access they can get to business subject matter experts (SMEs) as their source of BI requirements.
- Traditional methodologies are heavy on the data architecture and technical delivery aspects of data warehousing (DW) and light on the analysis and design activities required to ensure that the organization understands how it can use information to improve business performance. This focus reflects the information technology (IT) backgrounds of the creators of those methods.

This might sound heretical, but IT too often assumes that the SMEs understand BI and its potential—*when they don't*. Because SMEs come from the business and are considered to be experts in the business, IT assumes that they should be the natural source of BI requirements. IT too often assumes that SMEs have given sufficient thought to the subject so that they can articulate a cogent and comprehensive vision of how BI can be applied in their subject area—*when they haven't*. If you're lucky enough to work with visionary or enlightened SMEs, those assumptions can sometimes work—but just as often, they don't. In many cases, the SMEs don't understand BI and/or they don't have time really to think through BI opportunities and requirements. We've seen this time and again within major organizations in a wide range of industries.

To solve these problems, we have developed a business-centric BI method called the *BI Pathway method*. Many organizations are used to running the business based on inadequate access to information. Unfortunately, these legacy information delivery paradigms frequently go unchallenged as businesses invest in DW. The unfortunate result is expensive DW implementations that have minimal business impact. The BI Pathway method strives to identify new information delivery paradigms that identify how organizational performance can be optimized based on having adequate access to information to guide business decisions and take business actions.

DW has historically focused on the technical challenges, technical methods, and project management methods required to successfully deploy data warehouses and data marts. In contrast, the BI Pathway method extends the important contributions to DW that were popularized early in the industry by Inmon, Kimball, Imhoff, and others. The BI Pathway complements these contributions by adding business rigor into BI business analysis and design activities. ROI is designed into BI initiatives from the outset by systematically driving the use of BI into the core business processes and decisions that determine profits. The BI Pathway method goes beyond traditional approaches by defining the *business value capture mechanism* for each BI project (Williams and Williams, 2004). It recognizes that *the missing link in many DW efforts is the lack of clarity in the value proposition and/or the lack of business process change to capture the business value of BI.*

Up to this point in the book, we have focused on introducing BI to business executives. We have talked about what BI is, how it can be leveraged to improve profits, how to identify and prioritize BI-driven profit opportunities, and how to identify the business risks that must be mitigated and managed in order to ensure that BI investments pay off.

In this chapter, our focus is to provide information for chief information officers (CIOs), business executives, and managers with an interest in IT and process re-engineering methods, as well as for the BI project teams who are charged with delivering BI that makes a difference. We will describe the BI Pathway method, a full life-cycle, business-driven approach to designing, developing, and deploying BI applications that improve profits. This approach marries business-centric BI methods with proven traditional technical methods to reduce risk and ensure BI success.

This chapter focuses on BI methods that are essential to ensuring business value. These methods go beyond conventional DW industry approaches practiced by most organizations today. Incorporated into the BI Pathway approach are some of the "best practices" (e.g., the need for an "architectures phase") taught by The Data Warehousing Institute (TDWI) for many years. The BI Pathway's DW components, such as data acquisition design and data mart models, are not unique to the BI Pathway and are rather technical. Because other DW publications and books cover these topics very well, and each could warrant its own book, we have decided to cover these topics only as they relate to the BI Pathway.

Note: We've used as much plain English as possible, but parts of this chapter are unavoidably somewhat technical. Nontechnical readers can feel free to skip over these sections or refer to the glossary in the back of the book.

4.1 The BI Pathway Overview

In Chapter 3, we noted that a company's ability to leverage BI to increase profits depends on three things: the ability of the company to *align and govern* a BI program, the ability of IT to *perform technically*, and the ability of the business to *change in order to leverage BI within core processes* that have a profit impact. This concept is shown graphically in Figure 4-1.

We need business-centric BI methods that ensure business and IT managers are aware of these three success factors. These methods must provide an integrated, mutually reinforcing approach to addressing the success factors. The BI Pathway approach meets those needs, extending traditional methods while embracing the best of industry-proven technical approaches and tools.

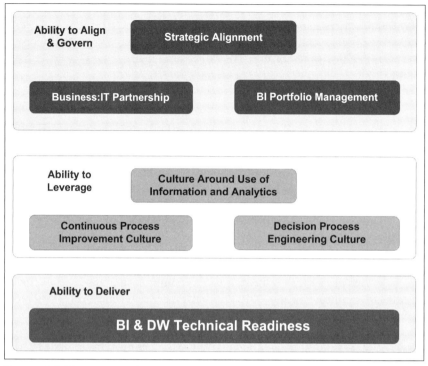

FIGURE 4-1 Three crucial business intelligence success factors: align, leverage, and deliver.

4.1.1 Unique Characteristics of the BI Pathway Method

The BI Pathway method ("the BI Pathway") is an iterative, full life-cycle method consisting of three phases, each with specific purposes and deliverables.

The architectures phase focuses on managing the alignment and governance of the BI program or initiative. Although other DW approaches include an architectures phase, the BI Pathway method incorporates a number of unique program-level activities, including the following:

- Development of a *BI opportunity portfolio* that identifies opportunities based on tradeoffs between potential business impact and technical risk.
- *Business process engineering* models that identify the "as-is" process and information and that compare and contrast the "as-is" state with a "to-be" process and information model.
- *BI readiness assessment* which identifies risk areas that need to be actively managed to in order to realize the full business benefit of a BI investment.

The implementation phase uses industry best practice approaches to iterative, incremental technical delivery. In addition, it applies analytical and design rigor to ensure a full understanding of requirements and the "value proposition" associated with a BI release, including the following:

- Explicitly documenting *detailed requirements* to make the "business case" so that expectations regarding the value of a BI release are communicated to and agreed to by business stakeholders. This documentation discusses the shortcomings of the "as-is" business process/information and discusses how BI can be inserted into a "to-be" business process to improve business performance. In line with industry best practices, it uses business questions as detailed requirements and prioritizes these questions to ensure that the most important questions are answered within a time-boxed BI release.
- Reviewing *logical models* of the data mart release with the business users, translating the contents of the model into standard business language. This ensures that as much analysis and design rigor goes into the release "on paper" before any development begins.
- *Prototyping* the data mart release with production data to "productize" the requirements and ensure that expectations are aligned before full development begins. This gives business users the ability to see their questions answered with production data and to validate the value of answering these questions before the investment is made to develop the release. It also provides insight into source data quality issues that might need to be addressed while development is in progress.
- Instituting *business process re-engineering* activities to implement the "to be" process/information and to ensure that the potential business value associated with a BI release is fully captured.

Pitfall

BI requirements are a common stumbling block for organizations because these requirement techniques are unlike operational system requirements techniques. They also go well beyond the techniques used to specify reports.

The operations and continuous improvement phase focuses on improving the cost-effectiveness of BI delivery to intended users and on discovering new ways to use BI to improve core business processes. The specific activities and deliverables within the three phases provide a structured, systematic way to design, develop, deploy, and continuously improve BI applications that increase company profits. This phase also provides the unique features of instituting *business performance metrics* that quantify improved business performance in line with ROI expectations for a BI application.

Although the basic flow of activities is shown in Figure 4-2 as a top-down flow, the architectures phase, via the BI opportunity map, effectively sets the stage for developing and deploying BI increments in a time-boxed, iterative fashion via repetition of relevant portions of the implementation phase.

4.1.2 Organizational Tailoring of the BI Pathway Method

The BI Pathway is designed to be used in practical, flexible ways based on the company context. For example, the approach to the architectures phase activities

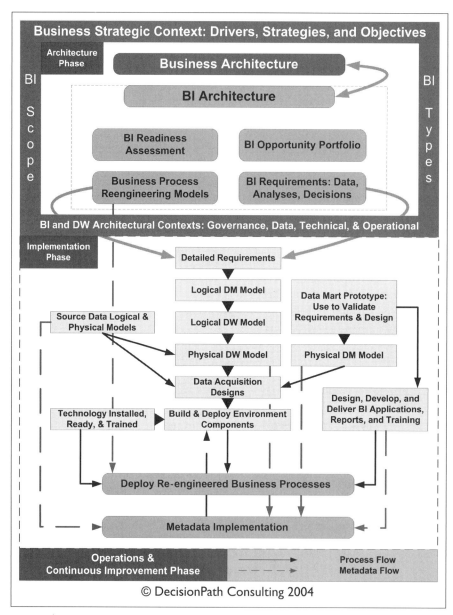

FIGURE 4-2 Overview of the BI Pathway method.

and deliverables can be and should be tailored according to such factors as the following:

- The scope of the BI initiative, that is, whether it is an enterprise-level initiative or a more narrowly scoped initiative, such as a functional or departmental BI application

- The maturity of the BI initiative, that is, whether the BI initiative is just getting started or whether the initiative is already well underway
- The degree of redirection needed, that is, whether the BI initiative has been successful thus far or has failed in some material way
- The relative emphasis of the BI initiative at a point in time, such as if the company is trying to integrate analytical silos and thus needs a unified BI opportunity map, which would dictate a certain emphasis
- The budget constraints on the BI initiative
- The preferences of the executive sponsor, such as a preference (or demand) that the BI initiative be delivered by a certain time, requiring the project team to do a higher level or abbreviated architectures phase

We have used the BI Pathway in a wide range of industries, such as lodging, financial services, government, consumer products, industrial products, and high-technology manufacturing. In these widely different contexts, our clients were at different stages of BI maturity. Some were essentially clean slates, and others had years of BI experience and had established large-scale BI environments. Based on these experiences, we find that business-centric BI methods in general, and the BI Pathway in particular, are appropriate in any organization, in any industry, and at any stage of BI maturity. The key is to effectively customize the application of the BI Pathway to the specific industry and company context.

The BI Pathway is a results-oriented framework for organizing a sequence of activities aimed at producing specific deliverables that fit together and guide effective design, development, deployment, and continuous improvement of BI applications that improve profit. It has been designed specifically to overcome the shortcomings of traditional technically oriented methodologies and to leverage the strengths of traditional methodologies, and the wide range of associated best practices, to execute the technical portions of the BI life cycle.

What this means is that the BI Pathway encompasses new, business-driven analytical, architectural, and business process re-engineering activities and deliverables that drive subsequent technical activities. The technical activities can be performed by using an appropriate, proven technical methodology that fits for the specific BI context. For the BI Pathway, the technical elements of the Implementation phase are based on proven approaches that have been taught by TDWI for more than a decade.

That said, the BI Pathway can be adapted to work with other organizational development approaches, as long as such methodologies are adapted to the need for business-driven analytical, architectural, and business process re-engineering activities that provide the distinct BI Pathway advantage.

The BI Pathway approach, although using standard implementation steps, deliverables, and guidelines as a starting point, can be implemented flexibly to work within any organizational context. For example, requirements activities are commonly tailored to an individual organization to ensure the optimal outcome. This may leave some development teams in an uncomfortable position if they are accustomed to highly formal, step-by-step, template-based methodologies from the transactional applications configuration or development worlds. For example, we worked with a team that had no BI or DW design or development experience. The team was led by an individual with years of experience configuring SAP R/3 ERP systems and was staffed by application developers accustomed to using the rational unified process to iteratively develop chunks of application code. This team was extremely uncomfortable operating without a highly prescribed, template-driven approach, and it had difficulty making the paradigm shift to the BI/DW way of designing and developing. We relate this story because we often encounter situations in which BI and DW methods are either new or not well ingrained in the IT organization. This can be overcome by training and by building the technical capabilities of the team around experienced senior BI and DW professionals. There is such a rich body of best practices for the technical side of BI and DW that it does not make sense *not* to leverage those best practices. That is what the BI Pathway does.

> **Tip**
>
> The BI Pathway, like any BI/DW approach, provides a guideline for your BI initiatives. It must be tailored to your organization to provide maximum value.

4.2 Part 1: The Architectures Phase of the BI Pathway Method

The architectures phase of the BI Pathway method encompasses all of the activities needed to institute and govern a BI program. It serves as an organizing framework for the business alignment, prioritization, planning, development, and support of individual, dependent BI projects. Organizations that begin DW and BI initiatives frequently overlook the need for an architectures phase. It is common that this need is identified once they have implemented several BI applications and experience some of the problems we will discuss in this section.

4.2.1 The Case for Investing in an Architectures Phase

According to *Webster's Dictionary*, a program is "a plan or system under which action may be taken toward a goal." When funding a BI initiative, the goal is to leverage information assets to support informed decisions that lead to actions that improve business performance. Architectures phase activities are critical to achieving this goal.

Common symptoms of organizations that do not adequately pay attention to and fund architectures phase activities are as follows:

- BI projects that are not explicitly aligned to supporting business goals
- Capital expenditures for BI projects that don't deliver an ROI
- Stove-piped BI applications that provide different answers to the same question
- Inconsistent business rules applied across BI applications
- An abundance of redundant BI tools and technology investments
- Technical performance problems across BI applications
- Inability to extend the data architecture to meet new business information needs
- Confused and frustrated business users

Although critical to the success of a BI initiative, there are frequently organizational impediments to instituting architectures phase activities. The first impediment is that the need for BI program is not always recognized by organizations because the concept of a program is frequently a paradigm shift for IT departments and business sponsors and stakeholders that are used to funding and managing individual application development projects. An additional impediment is a common organizational belief that the value of IT starts when the coding begins. Planning, analysis, and design activities are not assigned the same level of importance as technical activities. This, coupled with the imperative for IT to "deliver" an application, often gets in the way of critical program-level activities. Finally, even when there is a recognition that program-level efforts are important, many organizations lack ways to fund such initiatives.

> **Tip**
>
> Whether you use the BI Pathway or some other BI/DW approach, it is critical to include program level planning, analysis, and design activities to avoid business and technical problems later.

4.2.2 BI Pathway Architectures Phase Overview: Aligning the Business Intelligence Program to Deliver Return on Investment

Earlier, we mentioned the idea that to increase profits by leveraging BI, we need to be able to align and govern a BI initiative or program. This requires strategic alignment of BI with your company's competitive environment and critical success factors. It also requires creating an effective alignment between the business user community and the IT team charged with designing and delivering BI to support the business. Finally, it requires your ability to govern the business and IT processes required to deliver BI, whether as a single BI initiative or as a portfolio of BI projects. The *American Heritage Dictionary* defines architecture as "any design or orderly arrangement perceived by man." From a business and technology perspective in the BI context, we are concerned about designing, creating, and maintaining/adjusting an orderly relationship between the environment in which your company operates and your company's business strategy, business operations, IT strategy, and IT operations (Henderson and Venkatraman, 1990; Cooper et al., 2000). You create this relationship to ensure that your investment in BI is building capabilities that create incremental profit. The architectures phase of the BI Pathway (Figure 4-3) focuses on this crucial task.

The architectures phase of the BI Pathway focuses on creating an orderly alignment among the following:

- **The business strategic context,** which consists of environmental drivers such as demographic changes and competitor moves, as well as a company's business and IT strategies in response to environmental drivers.
- **The business architecture,** which is the arrangement of business processes, organizational structure, people, technologies, and systems used to serve a company's customers.

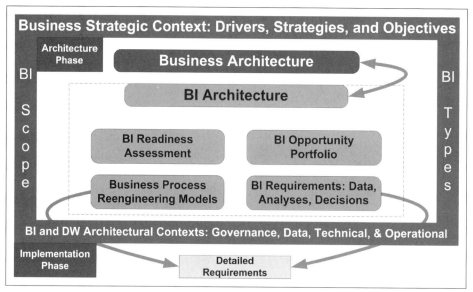

FIGURE 4-3 The architectures phase of the BI Pathway method.

- **The BI scope,** which determines whether you design and align the architecture at the enterprise level, at the strategic business unit (SBU) level, at the functional level, at the departmental level, or for a single BI initiative.
- **The BI capabilities/users,** which determine whether the architecture is being designed and aligned for a single type of business information, business analysis, and business decision or for a broader range of BI (for more information, see Chapter 7).
- **The BI architectural contexts,** which define the environment in which you must design and operate BI; in turn, those contexts are defined by the following:
  - Existing ways of funding and managing IT projects that may help or hinder BI program efforts
  - Existing organizational constructs for governance that can be used to support BI program-level efforts ranging from data stewardship, data architecture, meta-data management to technical standards
  - Existing arrangements of data stores, data flows, and data management approaches that will be considered when designing the BI data architecture
  - Existing IT tools, platforms, solutions, and products that can be leveraged to support the BI program
  - Existing IT operating policies that may support or compromise BI information delivery
- **The BI opportunity portfolio,** which is composed of the set of business-driven BI opportunities for profit improvement identified via the BI opportunity analysis.
- **BI requirements: data, analysis, decisions,** which include the specific business information, business analyses, and business decisions associated with each BI

opportunity in the BI opportunity portfolio. These requirements become the basis for designing a data and technical architecture that will support the range of known BI program analytical needs. They also are the basis for making decisions on tools and technologies that are best suited to supporting the business goals of the BI program.

- **The BI architecture,** which utilizes a BI program charter deliverable that documents the scope, direction, and priorities of the BI program and outlines the BI program organizational structure and responsibilities. It also contains program-level standards that will be used by all BI Implementation projects.
- **The state of BI readiness,** which identifies the business and technical risks that a company faces as a precursor to focusing management attention on mitigating and managing those risks.
- **Business process re-engineering models,** which depict current core management, revenue-generating, and/or operational processes at an appropriate level (such as IDEF 1 in the Integrated DEFinition methodology developed by the U.S. Air Force) and the "to-be" process or processes that will leverage BI to improve profit.

Practically speaking, alignment is "complex, multi-faceted, and never completely achieved" (Broadbent and Weil, 1998). Our experience with leading companies in different industries supports this assertion, and as with any conceptual framework, Figure 4-3 is an oversimplification of the business reality. That said, the relationships among the architectural components described above can be analyzed, characterized, aligned, and managed to improve profit if your company has the will to do so. It's vital that you convince business executives of the value of doing so, and that gets you deeply into tailoring the use of the BI Pathway.

Another key is to recognize that it is not practical or advisable to overanalyze these architectural components and their relationships. Massive project teams do not need to be used to accomplish the goal of understanding and aligning the factors that drive BI success. Compared with the tens or hundreds of millions of dollars that companies have spent on enterprise IT "solutions" to generate transactional data, the $100,000 to $1 million spent to align these architectural factors is a drop in the bucket that helps ensure returns in the tens of millions of dollars.

From an execution perspective, the architectures phase of the BI Pathway provides a framework for systematically analyzing and documenting the architectural components so that they can be adjusted, aligned, and managed to support BI success. The specific analyses, methods, and deliverables we use to do this are shown in Figure 4-4.

When done correctly, performing the analyses and developing the deliverables prescribed for the architectures phase of the BI Pathway provides empirical information that enables your company to

- Invest in BI with reasonable assurance of improving profits and performance
- Develop a comprehensive BI program plan (see Chapter 5) to focus, guide, align, and direct effective management of the preconditions for using BI to improve profits and performance

Analysis/Assessment Subject	Objectives	Methods	Deliverables	Business Value of the Analysis/Assessment	Supports	Relationship of Analysis to BI Readiness Factors	ROI Impacts
Business Strategic Context	Understand the external forces affecting the company and its strategic responses to those forces	Industry research and analysis; company research and analysis; Interviews with executives	Short written report describing drivers, strategies, and objectives	Provides a baseline for ensuring that BI investments support strategies and profit improvement	Ability to align and govern	Strategic Alignment	Helps ensure BI investment is aligned with strategies that will make a difference in company profits
Business Architecture	Understand arrangement of structure, business processes, systems, people, and technology used to serve customers	Company research and analysis; Interviews with executives	Strategy maps; Business design model or description; Description of management frameworks	Provides a baseline for ensuring that BI investments support strategies and profit improvement	Ability to align and govern; Ability to leverage; Ability to deliver	Strategic Alignment; Business: IT Partnership; Use of Information and Analytics; Continuous Process Improvement Culture	Helps ensure BI investment is aligned with strategies and processes that will make a difference in company profits
BI Scope	Understand whether the BI initiative in an enterprise, SBU, functional, departmental, or stand-alone initiative	Interviews with sponsoring executive(s)	Short written scope statement	Establishes clear understanding of boundaries for BI design, development, and implementation	Ability to align and govern; Ability to deliver	BI Portfolio Management; BI and DW Technical Readiness	Helps avoid costs by providing boundary for use in sizing IT investment to support BI
BI Types	Understand the kinds of business information, business analyses, and business decisions BI must support	Interviews with executives, managers, and knowledge workers; Formal utility theory models; BI taxonomy survey	List of prioritized business information, business analyses, and business decisions the BI Architecture must deliver	Establishes clear understanding of key factors for BI design, development, and implementation	Ability to align and govern; Ability to deliver	BI Portfolio Management; BI and DW Technical Readiness	Helps avoid costs by allowing team to design BI for specific anticipated uses
BI Architectural Context	Understand the information technology environment in which the BI initiatives is taking place	Surveys; Interviews with executives	Short written report describing BI context and the potential impacts and/or risks associated with the context	Anticipation and planning for known impacts on the BI initiative	Ability to align and govern; Ability to deliver	Business: IT Partnership; BI Portfolio Management; BI and DW Technical Readiness	Helps develop more realistic life-cycle cost estimates and manage to avoid overruns
BI Architecture	Understand the relationship between BI and the core business processes in which BI will be used to improve profit	BI opportunity analysis; BI requirements analysis; BI readiness assessment	Written report of suitable length to describe the business value capture mechanism for intended BI initiatives	Identification of core business processes that must change to realize improved profits, which enables change management	Ability to leverage	Culture Around Use of Information & Analytics; Continuous Process Improvement Culture; Decision Process Engineering Culture	Provides specific understanding of the business value capture mechanism so that profit realization can be managed
BI Readiness	Understand and manage risks	BI readiness assessment; DW readiness assessment	Readiness assessment reports	Remove barriers to improving profits; reduce BI investment by avoiding costly success	Ability to align and govern; Ability to leverage; ability to execute		Reduces risks and costs associated with BI and DW technical execution; Ensures BI is leveraged for improved profits
BI Opportunities	Understand how BI can be used to improve profits	BI opportunity analysis	BI opportunity map; Descriptions of opportunities and their value propositions; Business value driver mappings	Baseline for ensuring that BI investments support strategies and profit improvement; Identifies specific BI initiatives	Ability to align and govern	Strategic Alignment; BI Portfolio Management	Reduces risk of investing in BI initiatives that will have little or no positive profit impact
Core Business Processes	Understand the core business processes used to execute strategies and produce profits	BI opportunity analysis; business process modeling	Business process models of current and target core business processes	Baseline for ensuring that BI investments support profit improvement; Identifies specific process change initiatives	Ability to leverage	Culture Around Use of Information & Analytics; Continuous Process Improvement Culture; Decision Process Engineering Culture	Provides basis for ensuring that BI is leveraged for improved profits
BI Requirements	Understand the specific business information, business analyses, and business decisions the BI initiative must provide/support	BI requirements analysis	Information requirements matrix; Information needs glossary; Fact qualifier matrix; definition of terms	Combines with target core business processes as key deliverables for driving BI Implementation	Ability to align and govern; Ability to deliver	Strategic Alignment; BI and DW Technical Readiness (i.e. have good BI requirements to drive design)	Provides basis for delivering BI that can be used to improve profits

FIGURE 4-4 Analyses, methods, and deliverables in the BI Pathway.

- Develop the business case, cost-benefit analysis, and/or capital investment request documents required by your company's capital budgeting process
- Develop high-level architecture documents that may be required in your company's IT management environment
- Manage the risks and barriers to success so the investment pays off
- Optimize the magnitude of capital investment in relation to the potential profit improvement opportunities
- Engineer and manage the life-cycle costs (total costs of ownership) and avoid costly technical mistakes
- Use a comprehensive and strategically aligned set of BI requirements to drive design, development, deployment, and on-going operation of the BI asset as a core profit improvement paradigm

In effect, this empirical information increases the likelihood that your BI investment will pay off. That said, there are no silver bullets when it comes to BI and ROI. The analyses, assessments, and deliverables that compose the architectures phase of the BI Pathway are only as good as the quality of information, effort, rigor, and thinking that you bring to bear. For more information on the architectures phase of the BI Pathway, you might wish to take advantage of the full-day course on the BI Pathway method offered by TDWI (http://www.tdwi.org).

4.2.3 Setting the Architectural Foundation for Business Intelligence Project Success

The BI Pathway implementation phase consists of design, development, and implementation activities that create a BI project asset. Unlike operational systems that are designed independently to support a specific functional business area, BI projects are usually dependent projects, accessing the same source systems for data and overlapping in business subjects, and accessed by the same business users. Because of this dependency, it is critical that they use the same architectural foundation to avoid many of the problems outlined earlier in this chapter. The BI program architectural decisions that are made during this effort are documented in the BI program charter deliverable mentioned in the earlier BI architecture discussion. This architectural foundation is composed of four distinct but closely related architectures:

- **Governance architecture.** This identifies how program-level governance will be organized, detailing the items that will be governed at a program level and setting forth organizational responsibilities for these BI program needs. This includes organizational responsibilities for things ranging from data stewardship to metadata management, tools and technologies, and technical standards.
- **Data architecture.** This identifies the target data architecture standard that will be used to support the BI environment, whether hub and spoke, bus, or federated. It also identifies the roles of each part of the data architecture in supporting the business's information asset. In addition, it identifies the source systems that will be accessed to deliver the information, and the data marts that will be delivered over a series of BI implementation projects to support business information needs.

- **Technical architecture.** This identifies the platforms, standard tools, and technologies that will be used to support the BI environment. It strives to rationalize and optimize the technical architecture needed to support business information needs. It also serves to set forth technical standards that will be used across all BI implementation efforts.
- **Operational architecture.** This identifies the way in which the BI environment will be supported as releases move into production. For example, it discusses whether the production environment used for operational system support will be used or if a dedicated production environment for BI applications, separate from the operational system environment, will be used.

These architectures may exist in various stages of maturity in any given company, ranging from a blank slate for companies with no BI and DW experience to fully specified architectures for all aspects of BI and DW in companies with more mature BI and DW programs. In discussing the architectures phase of the BI Pathway, we noted that we need to understand the BI architectural context, but we did not elaborate. Before we describe the various implementation phase technical activities, let's take a look at the BI architectural context in which they occur. That context is largely determined by the governance structure, data architecture, and the technical architecture, as well as (to a lesser degree) the operational architecture.

> **Pitfall**
>
> Organizations often fail to appreciate that BI projects are unlike operational systems designed independently to support a specific functional business area. BI projects, in contrast, are usually dependent projects. They access the same source systems for data, overlap in business subjects, and are accessed by the same business users. Because of this dependency, it is critical that all BI projects use the same architectural foundation.

Governance Architecture

Because there is a wide range of issues in the BI arena that need to be managed across all individual BI project efforts, it is important to establish organizational authority, as well as roles and responsibilities, for these items. Typical areas of governance include the following:

- **Data ownership and stewardship.** Establishes authority for policy regarding access to information, naming conventions, definitions, business rules, standard business hierarchies, standard business metrics, and data quality issues.
- **Data and technical architecture.** Responsibility for data architecture and technical architecture standards and oversight is a role that exists at the BI program level. It is common that organizations have architectural review boards that oversee decisions regarding data and technical architecture policy. It may be necessary to present and defend BI data and technical architecture recommendations to this type of committee.
- **Technical standards.** To ensure consistency across teams and the ability to use standard technical approaches across all BI project efforts, you should establish

BI technical standards. These standards can range from conventions used by data modelers to testing standards and file-naming conventions. You should also establish standards for BI project development methodology, including a standard set of deliverables to be produced for all BI projects.

- **Meta-data management.** Meta-data, which is commonly defined as "data about the data" is used to ensure traceability throughout the environment and ensure there is a common understanding of the meaning of the information contained in the BI environment. It is also used to support and maintain the environment as changes occur. Because a variety of approaches are used in the industry to support meta-data management, it is important to establish meta-data standards that can be implemented and fully leveraged across all BI project efforts.

- **Operational support.** Roles and responsibilities for setting operational support standards to be used by all BI project efforts is another critical area of BI program governance. Are project teams responsible for supporting the data marts they develop, or is a centralized group used for this effort?

Data Architecture

As noted earlier, there are options for how you implement BI and DW, depending on your company's circumstances, BI maturity, and overall BI strategy. Generally speaking, data architecture is the means by which BI—in the form of business information, business analyses that use the business information, and flows of information to decision makers—is delivered for use in business processes that improve profits. This concept is illustrated in Figure 4-5.

The data architecture encompasses data structures, databases (source and target), data flows, and data integration. It also includes the data and meta-data requirements for the BI/DW environment. The data architecture is represented as a high-level model that illustrates the desired databases, the roles each will play, and the data flows between the databases. The typical roles that are discussed within the industry include the following:

- **Data intake.** The data architecture must account for systematic acquisition of relevant and detailed data from source systems (e.g., operational systems, enterprise requirements planning [ERP], spreadsheets) and the long-term staging and management of the data. The incoming source data is typically very detailed and is often referred to as "atomic-level data." In business terms, a good example is information from a customer order, such as the specific item that was ordered, what the price was, to whom it was shipped, the date of the order, the date the order was shipped, whether the order has been invoiced, and so forth. This detailed, atomic-level data is stored as the raw material from which BI is created. Because much of BI is about historical trends and analyses, it is typically necessary to store years of atomic-level data within the DW environment, creating specific technical data management challenges. Experience has shown that those challenges are often best met by creating a specific, flexible, and extensible data store that is dedicated to data intake and long-term storage.

- **Data integration.** The data architecture must also provide a means by which data from different sources, which can range from operational systems to enterprise

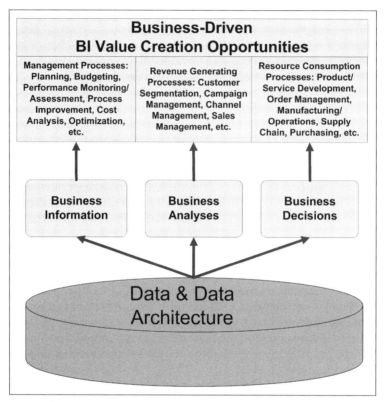

FIGURE 4-5 Architecture to deliver data for increased profits.

applications such as ERP to data from individual spreadsheets, can be brought together to create an integrated, consistent view of related parts of the company's business. This integrated view of the business, which is highly valued by the business, is referred to "the a single version of the truth." It is a common reason that organizations fund DW efforts. Integration is frequently a difficult endeavor because the underlying systems that we are attempting to integrate were not designed for integration. Problems include different names, definitions and business rules across systems, different levels of detail and history, and different key structures.

- **Data distribution.** One way to think of a BI and DW environment is as a supply chain in which data moves sequentially from sources to targets. Ultimately, data needs to be distributed out to the end users of the supply chain. Each of these users may be located in a different physical location and may have different information needs. Each end user may require a different view of the data based on considerations such as user roles and access control considerations. One job of the environment is to optimize for the job of distribution.
- **Data access.** The data architecture must provide a means by which various types of users can get to the data and use it for their BI purposes. Executives might want dashboards that provide status information on key performance variables

that the executives are expected to affect and by which their performance is measured. Power users might be more interested in time series information that they can use for sales forecasting or supply chain performance improvement. The range of possible business information and business analysis uses and users is quite broad. Thus, the data architecture must provide for the kinds of data access these different uses and users demand. A central data access concept is the user self-service, whereby users "pull" the data they need at a time of their choosing.

- **Data delivery.** The data architecture must also provide a means to "push" information to users who need information but are not inclined to go get it themselves. The typical example is the busy executive who doesn't have the time to learn a data access method and just wants standard reports and/or e-mail alerts when an important performance variable is out of line. This type of user is not going to personally perform a time series analysis, so data access methods aimed at power users are not appropriate. The data architecture must take account of the different BI needs of different BI users.

Within these broad parameters, a variety of technical means exist to provide for these roles, which means that there are a number of data architectures from which to select. The advantages and disadvantages of the various data architectures are beyond the scope of this section. The important point to consider here is that the choice of data architecture influences what tasks are undertaken and the methods for performing those tasks.

The implementation phase of the BI Pathway tasks are aimed at designing, developing, and deploying BI within a basic two-tier data architecture, as shown in Figure 4-6.

The data warehouse is responsible for intake, integration, and distribution needs. BI access and delivery is handled through data mart and other types of BI applications. Although the starting point for the BI Pathway data architecture is a two-tier hub-and-spoke data architecture, other configurations may be optimal depending on their specific organizational factors. The BI Pathway method can actually be used in conjunction with any of a number of traditional data architecture approaches, and thus from a technical perspective, it is "nondenominational." As long as the right business information is deployed within core business processes to support key analyses and decisions that affect profits, it doesn't matter which approach is taken. We'll have more to say on that in Chapter 5.

Technical and Operational Architectures

The implementation phase of the BI Pathway includes an activity labeled "technology installed, ready, and trained." This is a highly simplified, high-level shorthand for the idea that any BI initiative occurs in an existing or new technical architecture and technologies. Together, the technical architecture and the operating architecture can be thought of as the target technical environment. This is where "the rubber meets the road," where the business requirements for BI and the logical representations of the data must be converted into the physical IT processes and data stores that move and store the bits and bytes. Accordingly, we must either use the existing technical environment or design and implement a new technical environment. In the past

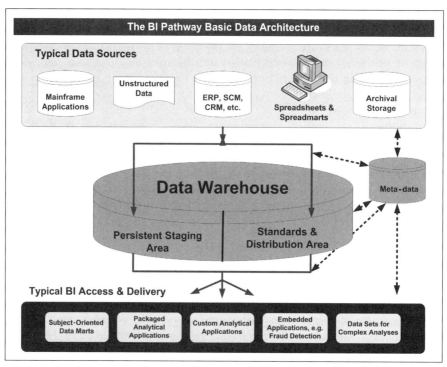

FIGURE 4-6 Basic data architecture in the BI Pathway.

few years, we have worked in a variety of companies with a range of technical environments. Two common situations are as follows:

- **A mixed-use BI technical environment.** One well-known financial services company needed to create a new BI environment to meet its BI needs. This required selecting and acquiring an extract, transformation, and loading (ETL) tool and a query and reporting tool. Although the environment was a blank slate from a BI perspective, its day-to-day operational applications run in a client-server environment that uses a specific relational database management system (RDBMS) and runs in a client-server environment. The company, like many others, wanted to leverage the existing technology, meaning its technical architecture consisted of new BI tools plus a shared hardware and RDBMS environment. This common approach presents challenges for BI. The BI initiative must accommodate development, testing, and operational policies that are optimized for operational applications. Such accommodation often slows down rapid effective deployment of BI applications. There are also issues around transfer costs from the shared hardware and RDBMS environment to the BI projects. Those costs often discourage companies from funding BI projects.
- **A dedicated BI technical environment.** Another well-known financial services company operates a dedicated technical environment for BI. The environment

contains servers, an RDBMS, an ETL tool, and a query and reporting tool. There are separate technical environments for development, test, and production, so each environment can be optimized for its role. Most importantly, having a dedicated environment means that the BI releases can be moved into and through the successive environments in accordance with BI best practices. As a result, a dedicated BI environment translates into more rapid and effective releases compared with mixed-use BI environments.

The maturity and characteristics of the target technical environment affect the cost, schedule, and technical risk for a given BI initiative, and thus they affect ROI. Understanding the technical environment allows you to make sound technical plans, ensure timely availability of technical expertise with the right skills for the environment, and anticipate technical risks. This understanding helps you avoid cost overruns and schedule delays that reduce—and in extreme cases, even eliminate—ROI.

4.2.4 BI Pathway Architectures Summary

Similar to building a house that contains many rooms that must work together, the job of the BI architectures is to provide the foundation for delivering business information that works together and provides a "single version of the truth" that guides actions that improve business performance. The required effort to achieve this is much larger than funding individual BI applications projects and requires a solid BI architectural foundation to guide and govern individual project efforts. There are numerous case studies within the industry of DW failures resulting from individual BI project efforts that delivered unarchitected information silos with little business value. In contrast, the architectures phase of the BI Pathway provides the solid BI program foundation needed to set a course for fully leveraging information assets to achieve business value.

4.3   Part 2: The Implementation Phase of the BI Pathway Method

During the architectures phase, we created the BI opportunities map, which is a tool to help prioritize BI projects. The implementation phase of the BI Pathway is an iterative approach that helps you complete BI projects (sometimes called "increments" or "releases") in as short a time as possible given the scope of the project and the constraints from the target technical environment, organization, and budget. By use of this approach, the BI opportunities identified during the architectures phase are incrementally developed and deployed during the implementation phase. This incremental, release-driven approach is shown in Figure 4-7, wherein BI projects sequentially flow from the BI opportunity map into the implementation phase for development and deployment.

The architectures phase and the implementation phase are connected by the BI requirements and the business process re-engineering models developed during the architectures phase, what we call the "information requirements." As we set about to build each increment, we further refine and complete the detailed requirements

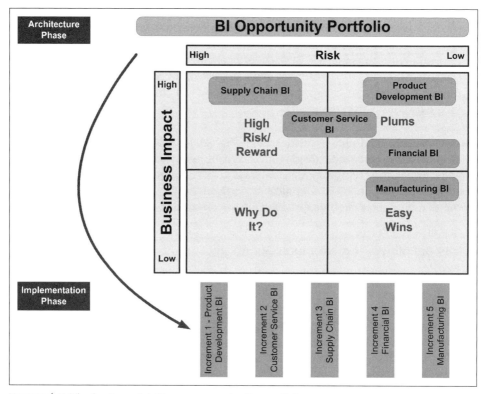

FIGURE 4-7 The business intelligence opportunity portfolio.

for that increment that support and reinforce the business justification for building the increment, and those requirements drive the implementation phase activities and deliverables. By use of such detailed requirements, we can apply proven BI and DW technical methods in a logical sequence aligned via an integrated set of technical deliverables. We can also execute the business process re-engineering required to ensure that the new BI delivered is fully leveraged to improve profits. The basic flow from requirements through the implementation phase activities is shown in Figure 4-8 below.

When all of the above activities and their associated deliverables have been completed for an individual increment, you have deployed a usable BI application within a new or modified business process that creates incremental profit for your company. You have created a BI asset, ready to be leveraged. As each project identified in the BI opportunity map is delivered, the BI asset increases in value and affords your company more ways to improve profits.

The implementation phase consists of an integrated series of activities that produce specific deliverables that feed or complement subsequent activities and deliverables. Because all activities are based on the requirements and business justification for investing in the BI application, there is full traceability throughout the process. In other words, there should not be information in the BI application that cannot be explained vis-à-vis the detailed requirements and the business value of

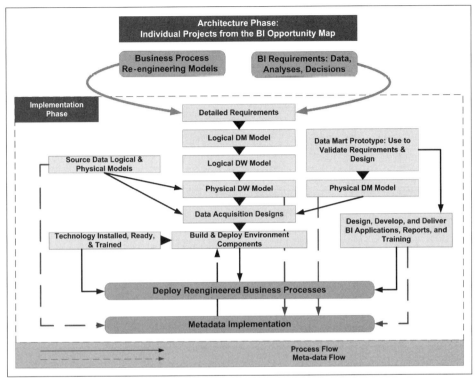

FIGURE 4-8 Business intelligence development process flow from requirements through implementation.

having that information. As noted earlier, the BI Pathway method leverages established technical best practices, about which there are many excellent reference books and courses. Accordingly, we will not get into the technical details here. Rather, we will share some high-level observations and case examples to highlight some of the key challenges and success factors that must beaddressed during the implementation phase.

Detailed Requirements and Re-engineered Business Processes

As shown in Figure 4-8, detailed requirements consist of the following:

- A business process re-engineering model for the given iteration or release.
- BI requirements, which in the BI Pathway method consist of a detailed description of the business information, business analysis, and business decisions that the specific BI increment must deliver and support. Detailed business requirements are usually stated as business questions that need to be answered to perform a business analysis that will support business decisions that lead to actions that improve business performance.

Notice that detailed requirements are much more than just a simple list of data elements. There is a very specific connection between a business process that has a profit impact, as determined via BI opportunity analysis, and the BI that would be deployed within the business process to improve profit. That connection is what we mean by the term *business value capture mechanism.* How must current business processes change to leverage BI to increase profit?

The detailed requirements, as described above, are absolutely critical in that they determine what physical IT processes and databases get built during the implementation phase. They also describe which business processes must change and how they must change and the intended *use* of the information once it becomes available to business users. It is unfortunately common that organizations do not have a common understanding of the intended use of information. Rather they simply expect the flexibility to perform ad hoc analysis as needed. This lack of clarity makes it impossible to determine the potential business value of a BI application, and this lack of a common understanding regarding how BI applications will be used once they are deployed also explains why may BI applications go unused once training is complete. Accordingly, it is imperative that the requirements be complete, well considered, and clearly defined. It is also critical that business users have a clear and common understanding regarding the intended use of the information, within the context of business processes, once it is made available. This understanding must be relevant to the business and must address a business problem that needs to be solved to improve business performance. In other words, we must explicitly "connect the dots" between the information, how it will be used, and how this will translate into improved business performance. We like to call it answering the "so what?" question associated with detailed information requirements. By building rigor into this analysis, BI applications are funded or not funded, as well as implemented or not implemented, based on the merits. Databases are designed for a purpose, rather than serving as a general "one size fits all" repository that serves no one very well.

The need for good requirements translates to the need for experienced business professionals to vigorously and rigorously examine the business value capture mechanism to assess its soundness. In effect, the business value capture mechanism is an up-front hypothesis that states: "If we change Process A by adding this specific business information and performing this specific business analysis to support this specific decision, we will be able to improve profit by $X\%$ or $\$X$ million." Before investing capital to build and deploy a given BI increment, companies would be well served to examine such hypotheses in detail. The results of the detailed requirements and re-engineered business process analysis get translated into the data and data relationships needed to satisfy the requirements. This is the input needed to create the logical data mart model.

4.3.1 Logical Data Mart Modeling

Once requirements are known, they need to be translated into a logical model that represents the type of analysis that will be made available through the BI application. This is an extra step of analysis and design that is done "on paper" to make sure that the type of the requirements for analysis are clearly understood by IT. These models use standard logical data modeling notation and are "translated" by the data modelers to the business audience to ensure that there is a common understanding of what will and won't be contained within the BI application. The value proposition of having this information is also confirmed during this review session. Frequently, questions about business definitions, business hierarchies, and data quality issues surface during these reviews. The results of the logical data mart model review becomes input into designing the data mart prototype.

The Importance of Data Mart Prototyping

One of the challenges of doing requirements well is that human language is often ambiguous. For example, we once spent the better part of four hours in a discussion with a small group in the marketing department of a major hotel company in order to arrive at a consensus on what the term "customer" meant to that company. Another key challenge of doing requirements well is maintaining sponsor enthusiasm for a BI project or program in the face of sponsor impatience with the development process. To overcome these challenges, we strongly recommend the use of a data mart design prototype, which is an inexpensive, time-boxed effort that uses a sample set of production data and the BI tool that will be used to deploy the BI application to help the business community refine what business information they want to see, how they want to see it on the screen, and how key terms are defined. By using "real" production data, it also serves to give business users a preview of the types of data quality problems that exist. This is an important first step in setting business user expectations regarding data quality issues and what is reasonable to expect based on the availability of source system data. The feedback from the prototype session is used to refine and finalize the user interface design for the BI application. The logical data mart model used to build the prototype becomes the starting point for building the production-ready data mart physical design.

An example of how this has worked on one of our projects is described below.

Financial Institution Cash Management Business Intelligence Prototype

A financial institution launched a BI program aimed at reducing cash collection costs, improving cash forecasting, and reducing cash balances. It contracted for a number of lockbox operations to serve different parts of the institution, and the people responsible for cash forecasting and for cash consolidation and management were in still other parts of the organization. By use of the BI Pathway method, we were able to identify and catalog a large number of business information needs. Although everyone agreed that gathering requirements was necessary, as often happens, there was a lot of impatience with the process. The business community also had a hard time envisioning how the BI would be presented and used.

To overcome wavering business support, we built a design prototype to present the kind of information the production BI release would provide. The prototype activity also included developing usage scenarios based on the business process re-engineering models. This allowed the BI team to present the BI in context, and this created tremendous enthusiasm for the entire BI program. It also allowed the BI team to clarify key terms, check on the reasonableness of cash collection amounts presented, and obtain feedback on how the information was delivered/displayed. Once the business users were able to visualize what they would be getting from the new BI application, they were willing to wait for the IT team to build it to production standards.

The Challenge of Data Sources

A quick scan through just about any book about DW and business intelligence will have a drawing that looks something like Figure 4-9, which shows an orderly flow of data from data sources to a data warehouse and on to specific BI applications.

The implicit assumption in these drawings is that there are mature, well-documented data sources from which we can readily extract the high-quality data we need to for our BI applications. Sometimes this is a valid assumption, and sometimes it is not. Because BI applications depend heavily on transactional data about a business and its customers, it is absolutely critical to develop a complete understanding of the potential data sources for the BI initiative in general and for a specific BI increment in particular.

During the BI opportunity analysis and the subsequent processes of developing detailed requirements, we identify the kind of business information and business analyses we believe will allow us to improve profits. We typically do not constrain these thought processes by considerations of whether data exists and/or can be obtained. Instead, we ask the fundamental kinds of questions posed by management theorist Peter Drucker, including the following:

- What information do I need to do my job?
- When do I need it?
- In what form do I need it?
- What information do I owe? To whom? When? In what form?

The central premise of this approach is that the business needs the information it needs, regardless of whether there is a currently available source for that information. Once that has been determined, however, analytical attention must be turned to understanding the data the business has at hand so that the degree to which

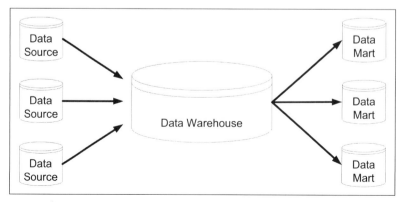

FIGURE 4-9 Data from sources through a data warehouse to business intelligence applications.

we can provide the business information needed can be determined, which in turn determines which business analyses can be performed. In other words, you must determine if there are gaps between the detailed requirements for business information and the potential sources of the data. This approach to source analyses has lead to some interesting and unconventional data sources that held valuable business information, including mainframe log files, a backend scanning equipment data base, and individual worker spreadsheets. It has also lead to organizations discussing the potential need to modify operational systems so that the systems would contain the information needed to better run the business. Although changing operational systems is never a popular or first choice, the possibility should not be dismissed outright. Instead, you need to weigh the potential benefit of making operational system changes against the cost of making them. We have worked with several clients who gave serious consideration to making operational system changes because of a strong business need to have certain information in order to improve business performance. The process of making the determination regarding the availability of source data is referred to variously as source analysis, source system analysis, source data analysis, or source-gap analysis. We will refer to it as *source-gap analysis*.

Practically speaking, there are a number of activities that make up source-gap analysis, including the following:

- Profiling source data and assessing its quality. Books have been written about the importance of data quality for BI/DW success. This is because the lack of data quality is frequently a BI program risk and often places serious constraints on an organization's ability to deliver useful business information. A full discussion of data quality issues and data cleansing techniques, however, is outside the scope of this book.
- Assessing whether data exists to satisfy the business's information requirements.
- Assessing the degree to which data from different sources can be brought together into a meaningful common framework (which is what is meant by the term "data integration").
- If the data doesn't exist, assessing whether existing systems can be modified to capture the data and, if so, assessing whether they *should* be modified.
- If the data doesn't exist internally, assessing whether it can be obtained from external data providers and, if so, determining how much that would cost.
- Identifying the technical and security requirements for connecting to selected data sources, and determining whether the project can expect cooperation from the system owners.
- Estimating how much data is potentially of interest, determining how often the data could be acquired, and determining whether the amount of data of interest can be acquired and moved from data sources to the data warehouse within batch windows.
- Determining the number of individual data sources from which data would need to be acquired.

The amount of time and resources needed to perform this kind of source-gap analysis depends on such factors as the size of the company, the number of source systems relevant to the analysis, who owns the source systems, the degree to which information about the source systems is well documented, and whether there are automated tools to use for data profiling and data quality analysis. That being said, BI initiatives absolutely depend on source data, so the source-gap analysis cannot be avoided.

The issue, in our view, is whether management has the patience to let the BI team do the job well, thereby reducing overall BI project risk. If management lacks this patience, the risk increases that the business information required for improving profit will either be lacking altogether, lacking in quality, lacking in meaning, or some combination of these. This, in turn, increases the risk of project failure. The old IT adage of "garbage in, garbage out" is absolutely true for BI initiatives. Nothing will kill the credibility of a BI application faster than the perception that the business information being delivered is no good. To overcome this risk, it is imperative to educate business sponsors about source data risk and to set realistic expectations about the time and resources that will be required for source-gap analysis.

> **Pitfall**
>
> BI applications, unlike other IT applications, rely upon source data for input. Data quality problems and the lack of data needed to meet information needs often present BI program risks.

4.3.2 Technical Development Work

There are a variety of technical steps needed to complete the design and development of the databases and ETL processes that make up much of the technical "plumbing" that support the BI application. Because there are industry books dedicated to fully discussing industry best practices related to these topics, they will not be discussed in this book.

Deploying Re-engineered Business Processes

The central premise of the BI Pathway method is that investments in BI cannot increase profits unless the BI is leveraged by business processes that affect profits. Whether these are new business processes or re-engineered business processes does not matter. What does matter is putting business information, business analyses, and business decisions into action. Toward that end, we set the stage during the architectures phase by creating detailed requirements. Once the BI is actually available, we have to ensure that it is leveraged as intended. This connection is shown in Figure 4-10.

We described the role and characteristics of detailed requirements earlier, and we noted that the requirements describe a business value capture mechanism. Where the rubber meets the road is when BI is put into action. Once the technical challenges of the implementation phase have been overcome, close the loop by ensuring the BI is used within the target business process to increase profit.

One substantial challenge to capturing the return on a BI investment lies in gaining user acceptance of the BI application. Assuming that you have solved any data quality issues, gaining user acceptance becomes a matter of how the business

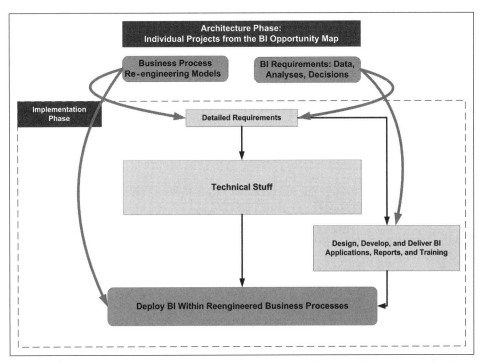

FIGURE 4-10 Connection between the architectures phase and leveraging business intelligence.

information and business analyses are delivered in support of business decisions and actions. All BI applications contain underlying data, and substantial effort is required to ensure that you have the right data and it is of high quality. That being said, many users sensibly care only about how the data is delivered, how easy it is to use, how it is displayed, and other usability issues. This points to the need to distinguish between

• The data processing aspects of BI, such as acquiring and staging the business information needed for business analyses and decision making
• The user-design aspects of BI, which are about segmenting user groups by their different BI needs and determining how they want to access the BI application

This activity is shown in the Figure 4-10 as "design, develop and deliver BI applications, reports, and training." The processes within this activity include user segmentation, development of usage scenarios for the various user segments, determination of which delivery and/or access methods are most appropriate for the user segments, development of the delivery and/or access methods, and training the various users in how to use the BI within the target business processes.

The other key challenge to capturing the return on a BI investment lies in making changes to the targeted business processes, which takes us into the province of business process re-engineering and change management. During the architectures phase, current-state and target-state business process models were developed, with the target state incorporating the use of the new BI application. During the implementation phase, the BI application was put into service within the target-state business process. This requires the business process owner(s), typically the business sponsor's organization, to accept responsibility for changing the business process and to make the changes happen as effectively as possible. If a BI readiness assessment was performed during the architectures phase, then the sponsoring organization will have identified strengths and weaknesses resulting from

- The organizational culture around continuous improvement and change management
- The organizational culture around the use of business information and structured business analyses to support decision making
- The readiness to define and standardize decision processes, including defining what business information will be used, what analysis will be performed, who will perform the analysis, who will be involved in making the decisions, what the decision timetables will be, and who will implement the decisions

Pitfall

Organizations often do not recognize that they need to change business processes in order to reap the potential BI value from their BI investments. Organizations that have been publicly recognized for BI "best practices" recognize and explicitly address business process change within their BI efforts.

Based on the assessment, the business unit can develop a change management approach and then execute the approach when the BI application is ready. Empirical evidence suggests that IT has the biggest impact on business performance when it is a business-driven line activity (Dvorak et al., 1997). The implementation phase is the point in the BI development life cycle when the business must drive process change if the BI investment is to pay off.

4.4 The Operations and Continuous Improvement Phase of the BI Pathway Method

There are two distinct components in the operations and continuous improvement phase. The first consists of improvements in the BI application and how it is used within the targeted business process. Metrics are developed during the operations and continuous improvement phase to objectively measure the ROI that was associated with the use of a new BI application. Most frequently the "current state" performance metrics serve as a baseline of performance. The "future state" process/information is then put into use to measure performance improvement based on the change process. This objective measurement helps to further refine additional improvements that can be implemented to further improve performance.

The second consists of improvements in the IT production processes used to acquire, move, and store the underlying data that supports the BI application. The improvements in the application and how it is used affect the level of incremental profits, and the improvements in IT operations affect the total cost of ownership. By working on both, we can improve the overall ROI of our BI initiatives.

As with any production environment, we can aspire to year-over-year cost improvements by achieving operating efficiencies and by leveraging the physical IT assets in the BI technical environment to support more BI applications. In the BI world, operating efficiencies stem from

- Improving the performance of the data extraction, transformation, movement, and loading processes
- Improving query performance in some cases
- Improving data storage strategies

By improving the operating efficiency of the BI technical environment, we are optimizing capacity, which gives us the ability to pump more work through the same technical resources. This translates to the ability to run as many BI applications as possible within the environment, which avoids the costs of unused capacity and/or the cost of adding capacity, which tends not to be linearly scalable.

The operations and continuous improvement phase also deals with improvements to the BI application and its usage within the target business process. Typical examples of improvements to the BI application include incorporating additional business information, refining the business analyses made possible by the BI application, refining the decision processes that leverage the business information and business analyses, expanding the number of users of the application, and refining the ways that the target user segments employ the application. Many BI projects have demanding timetables established by business executives who do not have the background to judge how long the project should take. In the BI world, this may mean that all the ways that the business information could be leveraged are not implemented at once, and/or all the potential users do not get trained at once, and/or that the delivery of business information may not be as sophisticated as it eventually can be. Over time, however, we can address these opportunities through continuous improvement efforts.

4.5 Chapter Summary

The BI Pathway method is essentially a business and technical strategy for improving profits by leveraging information and analytical tools. As such, it is aimed at establishing alignment across a wide swath of relevant organizational elements, including business strategy, IT strategy, business operations, and IT operations. As noted at the outset, this alignment is complex, multi-faceted, and never completely achieved. That being said, the BI Pathway method presents a logical way to achieve sufficient alignment to ensure a fighting chance that an investment in BI will pay off. As with any profit improvement strategy, there is the thinking and the doing, and we must do *both* to realize the full potential of BI to improve profits.

4.6   Key Points to Remember

- To profit from an investment in BI, your company must have the ability to align and govern BI, the ability to leverage BI, and the ability to deliver BI.
- The architectures phase of the BI Pathway provides empirical information that enables your company to invest in BI with reasonable assurance of improving profits and performance.
- The implementation phase of the BI Pathway is an iterative approach to completing BI projects in as short a time as possible given the scope of the project and the constraints imposed by the target technical environment, organization, and budget.
- The operations and continuous improvement phase of the BI Pathway method is aimed at reducing total cost of ownership of the BI asset and improving BI applications and the way they are used to improve profits.

4.7   Think Tank

4.7.1   Seven Questions to Ask About Your Company and Business Intelligence

1. Would our business leaders engage at a sufficient level for our company to gain the strategic advantages of the architectures phase activities?
2. If we were to undertake the architectures phase activities, how could we tailor it to our culture and other relevant circumstances?
3. Would our business leaders and key managers be willing to spend two or three days cumulatively over the next few months to help define our BI opportunities and requirements?
4. How easy would it be to gain a complete picture about the quality and availability of source data for our potential BI applications?
5. How many different user segments do we have and how might they be characterized from a BI usage perspective?
6. How ready is our BI technical environment?
7. Will our business leaders accept responsibility for leveraging BI within the targeted business processes? Will they demand it?

4.7.2   Quiz: How Prepared Is Your Company to Leverage Business Intelligence?

1. What is the risk that BI would not be effectively leveraged owing to your company's inability to effectively manage process improvement projects?
2. What is the risk that BI would not be effectively leveraged owing to a company culture that is averse to fact-based and analytically driven decision making?
3. What are the odds that your company could define a fact-based and analytically driven decision-making process within a key business process and make it stick?

4. How effective is the partnership between the business and IT communities in your company?
5. What are the odds that your company would establish a dedicated BI team consisting of hotshot business analysts and experienced BI and DW technical people?

Chapter 5

Leading and Managing a Business Intelligence-Driven Profit Improvement Program

"Strategic Planning, Benchmarking, Pay-for-Performance, Outsourcing, Customer Segmentation, Reengineering, Balanced Scorecard, and Total Quality Management are among the many management tools that companies have experimented with in recent years. Do companies using these tools do better than the ones who don't? There is no equivalent of the Consumer Reports for management to use in evaluating the tools available to them."

—Daryl Rigby, "Management Tools and Techniques: A Survey." *California Management Review*, Winter 2001

In previous chapters, we have described business intelligence (BI), shown how major companies are using it to improve profits, described how you can identify the relevant BI-driven profit improvement opportunities for your company, described how to identify and manage company-specific success factors, and described a practical, proven method for designing, building, and leveraging a BI asset that improves profits. This chapter presents top management-level information about how to manage BI for maximum business value.

As suggested by the quote at the beginning of this chapter, a wide variety of management tools are available, "sometimes costing firms tens of millions of dollars to implement" (Rigby, 2001). Although for some companies the investment may not be that high, BI-driven profit improvement sometimes does require that magnitude of investment. Thus, we would argue that it requires the same level of top management thinking and attention as any of the other tools that have proven successful.

Recent trends suggest that BI is making headway in this regard. For example, Harvard Business School recently held an executive symposium titled "Competing on Analytics: How Fact-Based Decisions and Business Intelligence Drive Performance." One of the key points of the symposium was that the ability to use BI for competitive advantage "starts with the CEO's commitment and involves building the necessary enterprise-wide infrastructure, analytical skills, and culture. When done successfully, competing on analytics creates value and strategic advantage" (Davenport, 2006).

Another recent example of how BI is drawing both top management attention and coverage in the mainstream business press is found in a *BusinessWeek* article titled "Giving the Boss the Big Picture" (Ante, 2006). Although the article does not delve into the substantial BI and data warehousing (DW) challenges associated with delivering accurate, relevant information, its discussion of dashboards, a visual way of presenting high-level BI, as "killer apps" for executives is on the mark in emphasizing that modern BI tools can present timely, relevant business information that improves business decisions that affect profits. The article points out that 40% of the 2,000 largest companies use dashboards. It quotes Ivan Seidenberg, chief executive officer (CEO) of telecommunications giant Verizon Communications, as saying that the "dashboard puts me and more and more of our executives in real-time touch with the business. The more eyes that see the results we're obtaining every day, the higher the quality of the decisions we can make."

These examples indicate that BI is moving into mainstream business thinking. In this chapter, we will discuss the leadership and general management challenges associated with leveraging BI to create value (improve profits) and strategic advantage. In doing so, we hope to elevate BI-driven profit improvement onto top management's agenda—if it's not already there. As you read this chapter, please keep in mind that we are now looking at BI from a top management perspective, where we are not concerned with how to manage specific projects or with narrowly scoped BI initiatives. Rather, the information presented is for the benefit of the top executives who have determined that BI is strategically important for their businesses and who need to know how to go about leading and managing a BI-driven profit improvement program.

5.1 A Leadership Perspective on Business Intelligence-Driven Profit Improvement

From a leadership perspective, BI-driven profit improvement is largely about vision and cultural change, whether at the enterprise level, the business unit level or the functional (departmental) level. Leaders must articulate a compelling and specific vision for how their organizations will use information to improve profits and business performance. Furthermore, these leaders must also guide the process of cultural change so that the use of business information, business analytics, and fact-based decision making becomes ingrained in the way the business operates.

5.1.1 Changing the Culture of Information Usage

The cultural changes that leaders must drive to realize the value of investments in BI include the following:

- **Redefining the role that information plays in the organization.** Historically, the right kind of business information had been hard to get. For that reason, information has often failed to contribute as much as it should contribute to profit improvement. The ability to obtain both detailed and summary, historical information in an integrated and timely fashion and to create new information using business rules (e.g., identifying "highly valued customers") affords companies an opportunity to rethink how they can leverage information to improve profits. BI has tremendous potential if leaders can redefine the role information and analytical tools play in the organization.

- **Changing the way that information requirements are defined.** Most organizations have had to make do with operational reporting and high-level summary reports produced by individual operational systems as core business information for years. A continuation and improvement on this "reporting" information paradigm is frequently the focus as organizations embark upon BI initiatives. The reporting paradigm is deeply ingrained in many companies and often gets in the way of defining business information, business analytics, and fact-based decision processes that can be used in core business processes that affect profits. BI can substantially improve core business processes if leaders can broaden and enrich the way their companies define information requirements.
- **Changing behaviors in using information.** In most companies, decision support processes arose in unstructured and ad hoc ways owing to managers' inability to obtain information easily. Because information delivery was inadequate and untimely, companies relied heavily on individuals who had institutional knowledge to make the best decisions possible with what little information they had. BI can inject business information and business analytics into fact-based decision processes if leaders can change behaviors that rely on inflexible and inadequate reports.

Companies that meet the leadership challenges presented by BI-driven profit improvement initiatives will reap the business and economic benefits that BI can provide. The process of BI-driven cultural change can be viewed as a journey along a predictable development path that we think of as a BI maturity model with three stages, as shown in Figure 5-1.

5.1.2 The Three Stages of Business Intelligence-Driven Cultural Change

As Figure 5-1 suggests, the process of changing an organization's culture to benefit from BI usually follows three distinct stages. To manage the change process effectively, you need to understand each stage of the process, as well as what you can—and *can't*—accomplish during the stage.

Stage 1

- **Information focus.** "What" do the users want (lists of data elements)
- **ROI potential.** Limited

This early stage of BI maturity looks a lot like information usage before BI. There has been no redefinition of the role of information. Information requirements are gathered much like report requirements and typically consist of lists of data elements provided by business users to the BI team. As such, the information requirement focus is on the "what" the users would like delivered. Users regard the day-to-day usage of information much in the same unstructured way that they did before. The perceived BI benefits center around improved and more timely end-user access to information.

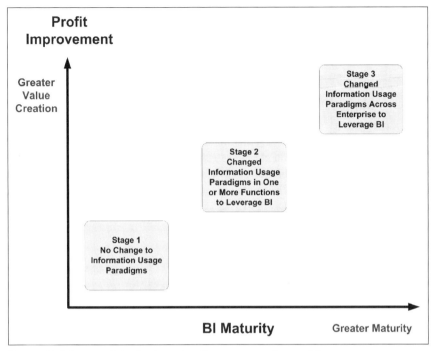

FIGURE 5-1 Stages of the business intelligence maturity model.

Stage 2

- **Information focus.** "Who"(some), "what," "when"(some), "where" (some), "why"
- **ROI potential.** High

The middle stage of BI maturity is a great improvement over the early stage. During this stage, the company recognizes that to reap the benefit of its investment, managers must rethink the role of information in the organization and go beyond the status quo. Information requirements go beyond devising a list of data elements and seek to closely tie information needs to business drivers, goals, and processes. They go well beyond the focus of "what" is needed and demand the answers to "why" the information is needed by business users. They also address some of the "who," "when," and "where," as information needs are directly tied to the business processes that support business goals.

Stage 3

- **Information focus.** "Who," "what," "when, "where," "why," "how"
- **ROI potential.** Optimal

The final stage of BI maturity improves further upon stage 2 by looking at overall organizational processes that are in place for using information. It does not stop at delivering the right information to the right people at the right place and time. Instead, it strives to fully understand the details of "how" the information can best be used once it is delivered to the business. It recognizes that the arbitrary and ad hoc decision processes that evolved when information was unavailable and untimely do not serve the business as well as they should. It strives to abolish decision processes that rely on individual business users and replace them with organizational decision processes that optimize the use of information throughout the organization. This is achieved in a number of ways. It can consist of standardizing responses associated with information. For example, an analysis of the effectiveness of campaigns can provide standard decision rules for future campaigns. The organization can redefine these standard rules as it gains more experience using them. This stage can also include automating certain decision rules. For example, an analysis of historical manufacturing capacity and demand patterns can be used to route orders to manufacturing facilities based on automated algorithms. Finally, once organizations approach this final stage of BI maturity, they are positioned to combine the power of information with institutional knowledge to fully optimize organizational decision making for competitive advantage.

Tip
To reap the benefits of BI, organizations need to rethink how information is being used in their organization and to envision opportunities to use new information in new ways. As organizations mature in their use of information, they begin to reap the bottom-line benefits that BI offers.

Based on our consulting experience and on what we hear from participants in classes we teach, we believe it is fair to assert that business use of information is in the early stages of maturity in many companies. To change that, business leaders must drive the evolution of their companies along the path to greater BI maturity.

5.1.3   Steps for Advancing Business Intelligence Maturity

The pace of evolution in BI maturity and the degree of success possible in your company depends partly on its ability to learn about, develop, and implement effective BI and DW competencies. We see this as a general management challenge, about which we will have more to say later in the chapter. The pace and degree of success also depends on your company's ability to change.

To accomplish the required changes depicted in Figure 5-1, leaders can apply a change model such as the one advocated by John Kotter, a highly regarded expert in the field of change management (Kotter, 1995). Adapted for BI, the cultural change approach consists of eight steps:

Step One: Establish a Sense of Urgency to Change the Company Culture to Leverage Business Intelligence

Kotter's research indicates that for change to be successful, as much as 70% of the relevant management cadre must believe that the status quo is untenable, that is, that the risks of change are lower than the risks of not changing. The state of adoption of BI as a management tool for profit improvement is at a point where there are BI success stories in just about every industry: those stories can be used to create a sense of urgency. External drivers can also contribute to increased urgency.

> **Tip**
>
> One way to establish a sense of urgency is to present managers with quantitative estimates of revenue lost owing to lack of BI information. Another is to identify competing organizations that are now or soon will be using BI to gain an advantage over your organization.

For one of our clients, the external drivers that have created the required sense of urgency include increased demand associated with an aging population, pending retirements within its aging workforce, economic pressure for efficiency, and ever-increasing customer expectations for near-instantaneous service in "Internet time." An organization's competitors can also provide a strong sense of urgency. For example, a perceived risk of "losing our best customers," if we aren't able to identify them and manage them more effectively, can be the catalyst needed to develop and leverage new BI capabilities.

Step Two: Create a Coalition to Drive Business Intelligence Use into the Company Culture

Driving BI use to the point that it is ingrained in the company culture takes consistent leadership over time. Change management experience suggests that cross-functional coalitions of powerful, respected executives are needed to provide such leadership. Absent such leadership coalitions, organizational inertia sets in and progress is slowed or stops all together.

> **Tip**
>
> Because higher levels of BI maturity require business change, organizations find that this is most successfully done by forming a coalition of well-respected senior business executives that can champion the business need to drive BI usage into the company culture.

For one of our clients, the prevailing culture around BI use had historically been report-focused (stage 1 of the information usage maturity model). To overcome that, the client developed a BI vision and formed a strong coalition of believers. This coalition is led by a well-respected executive who reports to the CEO, ensuring on-going executive attention to the BI initiative and the cultural change it requires.

Step Three: Develop a Clear Vision of How Business Intelligence Will Be Used for Profit Improvement

As you may recall from Chapter 2, we use the BI opportunity analysis to identify specific opportunities to inject business information, business analyses, and fact-based decisions into core business processes that make a difference in profit and performance. With that as input, we can create a clear vision of how BI will be used for profit improvement.

For example, we worked with one organization that determined through BI opportunity analysis that BI could be used to improve key treasury functions such as cash collection, cash concentration, cash forecasting, and cash balance optimization. This vision was communicated throughout the organization. A prototype BI application was used to generate enthusiasm and commitment to the changes that needed to occur for the client to reap the benefits of its BI investment.

Step Four: Share the Vision of How Business Intelligence Will Be Used for Profit Improvement

One mission of the BI coalition of business leaders is to share the BI vision, particularly with key thought leaders and potential early adopters within the management ranks. Companies are social organisms, and they evolve by achieving a shared vision about the direction the company must go to survive and thrive. Executive leadership is key to that process, as is gaining buy-in from the people in the company who are opinion leaders and exemplars of how the company operates.

> **Tip**
>
> Because BI is an expensive endeavor, it requires the formulation of a business case and active organizational marketing. Presenting a clear vision of how BI capabilities can be used to drive improved business performance is the best way to accomplish this.

At one organization with which we've worked, the operations function is driving change in how BI is used. Based on a vision of having more detailed, specific, and timely business information for improving business performance, an executive coalition keeps a focus on the BI vision and shares it via two thought leaders who have ties at the executive level. These thought leaders share the vision for how the new BI will be used to improve performance. In the process, they are driving cultural change.

Step Five: Empower People to Clear Obstacles to Business Intelligence Use

There are various obstacles that your company might encounter as it evolves in its ability to use BI to improve profit. Key cultural obstacles can be identified by conducting a BI readiness assessment, as described in Chapter 3. A few of the typical cultural obstacles we've seen include the following:

- Company cultures that downplay or denigrate the use of information and analysis for fact-based decision making
- Company cultures that are resistant to change
- Managers who are not comfortable with change
- Key individuals who have been the designated "go to" people for hard-to-get information feel threatened
- Decision-making cultures in which force of personality outweighs fact-based decision making
- Cultures that are locked into the reporting orientation that characterizes the stage 1 level of information usage maturity

> **Tip**
>
> Figure out how to turn adversaries into allies. If some people feel threatened by the changes that BI represents, show them how BI can make their jobs easier and give them higher status in the organization. If you "convert" one or two BI adversaries, they'll become your most vocal and enthusiastic supporters.

Overcoming these obstacles is really a business challenge: the impetus for changing how business information and business analyses are used for improving profits must come from the owners of the core business processes that must change to leverage BI.

Step Six: Secure Short-Term Business Intelligence Wins

Companies have been exposed to a number of management tools over the past few decades. Some of them have proven to be useful. Others have not borne fruit, whether because of data quality issues, because of failure to implement effectively, or because the tool itself was somehow flawed. As a result, some companies are cynical about new management tools, causing some observers to write about "fad surfing."

To overcome cynicism and resistance to change, a key tactic for any change initiative is to identify pieces of the larger initiative that can be successfully completed in the short-term, however that may be defined in a given company. For BI initiatives, this can be as simple as completing a design prototype that gets executive sponsors excited and that can be presented to key parts of the organization to sustain commitment.

When using the BI prototype for this purpose, we have found that it is essential to use real sample data of the type that would be provided by the BI application. For example, for supply chain BI one could use actual order history data to prototype of metrics and measures such as order-to-cash cycle time, demand by customer, demand by stock keeping unit (SKU), and so forth.

> **Tip**
>
> BI prototypes are an effective tool to demonstrate how BI can be used in your organization to improve business performance.

We have also found that it is very useful to present the prototype to business users by using a storyboard approach that approximates the actual business context in which the finished BI application would be used. In other words, show the business users how the BI would be used in an actual business situation in which a decision that affects profit is required.

Step Seven: Consolidate Business Intelligence Wins and Keep Moving

Achieving cultural changes in how information and analyses are used to support fact-based decision making ultimately means changing any and all aspects of existing operations that do not fit the vision for how BI will be used to increase profits. As the first production BI application is rolled out and successfully leveraged, the business must use the credibility that comes from success to force more change. In the BI world, this may mean such things as

- Rolling out the successful BI methodology to additional BI projects
- Communicating lessons learned about BI-driven process change to other units
- Publicly recognizing and rewarding the business unit and BI team
- Establishing a BI "center of excellence" (COE) to institutionalize BI use as a profit-improvement tool

Tip

Setting higher standards for performance based on BI can give users an incentive to jump on board. As they see other departments and coworkers enjoying BI's benefits, they will become more receptive and eager to take advantage of those benefits themselves. A BI COE can help.

At one of our client organizations, the success of an initial BI initiative has created a higher degree of consensus among top executives about the business value of BI. This, in turn, has increased the executives' willingness to change how BI is funded and how BI is handled within the broader information technology (IT) technical infrastructure. Seeing the business value of BI, the executives are consolidating the win and picking up the pace of BI adoption.

Step Eight: Institutionalize the Change in How Business Intelligence Is Used

The ultimate leadership goal for changing the culture around BI use is having the change become ingrained in company norms and shared values so that the change endures. The relevant norms when using BI for profit improvement are the decision-making norms within the context of business processes that affect profit. In Chapter 4, we talked about three general types of business processes: management processes, revenue-generating processes, and operational processes. To institutionalize the use of BI for fact-based decision making within these general processes, leaders have to model the behavior they are seeking.

In other words, they have provide what we call *adoption impetus*, which is a fancy way of saying that leaders must use and/or push the use of the new BI in a public way. If the CEO consistently asks the vice president of operations for business information and business analyses that can most easily be gotten from a BI application, the vice president of operations will make sure his or her people are using the same information the CEO is seeing.

We worked with a company that has institutionalized the use of BI for sales campaign management purposes. By using BI, the company can focus like a laser on the groups of potential customers who are most likely to accept direct marketing offers. Because this approach results in both higher revenues and lower costs, it has helped create company norms and shared values around the use of BI for profit improvement. People have seen the payoff, they take pride in leveraging BI, and there is little or no possibility of changing back to older ways.

5.1.4 Summary: A Leadership Perspective on Business Intelligence-Driven Profit Improvement

When we teach our BI Pathway course, class participants relate intuitively to the stages of our BI maturity model. Most identify their companies as being in stage 1, and they see the need for business leadership to get to the more advanced stages. Because many of these people are IT people, they do not feel they have the responsibility or the power to lead their companies along this developmental path. We agree. Only business leaders can change the behavior of people in the business units of the company, and to fully leverage BI, they must change the culture around information use and fact-based decision making.

The good news is that at well-known companies in many different industries, effective leaders have succeeded in doing just that.

5.2 A General Management Perspective on Business Intelligence-Driven Profit Improvement

From a general management perspective, BI-driven profit improvement is largely about strategic alignment, risk management, business process re-engineering, program and project management, IT infrastructure, and IT operations. In that sense, and except for the IT component, it is not different from any other strategic initiative launched in hopes of improving companies' business results. At the same time, the IT component is critical to success, and successful BI initiatives require different methods than traditional application development projects or enterprise-level packaged software implementations. Accordingly, the general management focus for BI-driven profit improvement must balance considerations of business strategy, BI strategy, business infrastructure and processes, and BI infrastructure and processes. This concept is shown in Figure 5-2, which is adapted from "Strategic Alignment:

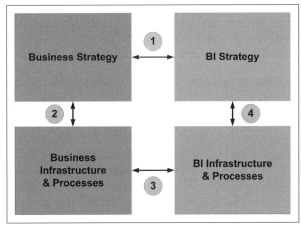

Figure 5-2 Balancing factors for business intelligence process improvement.

A Model for Organizational Transformation via Information Technology" (Henderson and Venkatraman, 2005).

The model, adapted for BI, shows that fully leveraging BI requires integration and/or alignment at four key points, which are numbered accordingly in Figure 5-2. These integration and/or alignment points are between

1. **Business strategy/BI strategy.** The BI opportunity analysis described in Chapter 2 is all about developing a BI strategy that supports and enables your company's business strategy. For example, if your company competes on cost, then your BI strategy should ensure that managers at the point at which costs can be controlled and reduced have the business information and analytical tools they need to make effective tradeoffs among costs, quality, and service.
2. **Business strategy/business infrastructure and processes.** The BI opportunity analysis explicitly uncovers the relationships between business strategy and business infrastructure and processes as a means of determining which business processes have the greatest impact on profits and performance and thereby are the most likely places for injection of BI to improve those processes. Generally speaking, we find that companies have good alignment and integration here.
3. **Business infrastructure and processes/BI infrastructure and processes.** The architectures phase of the BI Pathway method examines the integration and alignment among organizational structure, business processes, potential BI users, and BI readiness factors and the specific types of business information, analytical tools, and technical infrastructure and processes required to leverage BI to improve business performance.
4. **BI strategy/BI infrastructure and processes.** Any BI strategy has to be implemented in an IT environment, and in many cases, companies optimize total cost of ownership (TCO) at an enterprise level. This often means that BI must share IT infrastructure and must conform to IT operating policies and processes that are typically optimized for day-to-day transaction processing systems. This slows the pace at which BI applications can be deployed and profits can be improved. Ideally, IT policies and practices should be adjusted to accommodate the profit potential of rapid BI deployment.

By focusing general management attention on these integration and alignment points, we can explicitly assess and manage strategic alignment, risk, business process change, programs and projects, IT infrastructure changes, and IT operational changes. A vehicle for doing so is the architectures phase of the BI Pathway, the results of which can be used to create a roadmap, or program plan, for managing your company's BI-driven profit improvement program. From a general management perspective, company business and IT executives and managers can use the architectures phase analyses to focus their attention on general and company-specific business and technical challenges associated with leveraging BI to create improved profits.

5.2.1 The Program Plan for Business Intelligence-Driven Profit Improvement

In Chapter 4, we argued that the architectures phase analyses are critical because they provide crucial insights for addressing the multi-dimensional integration and alignment challenges that can be barriers to BI-driven profit improvement. These insights come together in a comprehensive BI program plan, which must address all of these challenges. At the applied level, the BI program plan must guide and coordinate systematic development of BI competencies that advance your company along the BI maturity path. The plan must also address risk management, business process reengineering, program and project management, IT infrastructure, and IT operations. To illustrate these ideas in action, we will use revisit Company B, the disability insurance company we introduced in Chapter 3.

> **Tip**
>
> Following a BI *program plan* instead of managing each BI effort as a separate, unrelated project enables you to see and implement the global changes your organization needs to get the maximum benefit from BI. It also ensures that BI efforts are not stove-piped, resulting in a suboptimal technical implementation and creating different and potentially conflicting information about your business.

Company B is an $8 billion company that faces substantial business challenges over the next decade. Those challenges come largely from increases in claims by the aging baby-boom generation, whose members are entering their disability-prone years. Other challenges come from heightened customer service expectations associated with the ever-growing number of business transactions that can be accomplished via the Internet. Accordingly, Company B needs to optimize claims processing productivity and improve service delivery. These challenges are complex owing to such factors as the following:

- The variable nature of disability claims—some are straightforward and some are very complex. Thus, they consume very different levels of resources and follow several different possible processing paths.
- The fragmentation of information across several legacy claims processing systems, which creates difficulty in gaining a total picture of the cost, processing time, productivity, quality, and service level of individual cases.
- The challenges of operating in a highly regulated industry, which drives claims processing and systems requirements that reduce operational flexibility.
- An IT environment that is optimized for highly secure, highly responsive claims processing in a shared services environment, which has slowed the pace at which BI can be developed and released.
- The fragmentation of BI responsibilities across several IT subunits, which has slowed the pace at which BI can be developed and released.
- The need to introduce new skills and tools into the technical environment.

Accordingly, the company has embarked on a BI program aimed at providing all levels of operations management with more timely and relevant business information, as well as with appropriate analytical tools so that managers can consistently improve productivity and service. The BI program plan at Company B has addressed a range of general management challenges specific to its situation. This particular program plan has seven elements.

Element One: Business Strategy for Leveraging Business Intelligence

Given its strategic position, Company B has articulated a vision for leveraging BI that encompasses providing all levels of management with integrated business information and analytical tools to support fact-based decision making within business processes that affect claims processing productivity and service delivery. Specifically, Company B has begun to deploy business information and business analysis tools that provide front-line managers with more detailed, timely, and specific information about productivity. In turn, this information allows for closer monitoring, more insight into performance trends, and more timely corrective actions. Before the development of this BI application, front-line managers were limited to highly aggregated information that was delivered long after the fact, thus providing very little actionable information in time to correct adverse trends. Company B is also beginning to develop BI that focuses on service improvement. The business information and analytical tools will provide a comprehensive view of the entire disability claims process, which will allow top managers, middle managers, and front-line supervisors to identify and correct service issues and thereby meet or exceed customer expectations.

> **Tip**
>
> Company B's experience is typical of the benefits an organization can derive from designing an overall BI program. By taking an organization-wide view, Company B can identify and prioritize *all* the information needed by managers in all departments to make good decisions.

Element Two: Program for Developing Business Intelligence Core Competencies

To achieve the business strategy for leveraging BI, the company is evolving toward a COE approach, which is a systematic way of developing and exploiting BI core competencies to improve profits and business performance. These core competencies are shown in Figure 5-3.

Developing these BI competencies has enabled Company B to increase the pace and effectiveness of its progress along the BI maturity improvement curve, resulting in a greater ability to leverage business information and analytical tools to improve performance. The specific BI competencies shown in Figure 5-3 each contribute to BI-driven improvements in profits and business performance:

- **Effective BI and business alignment capabilities.** The BI program at Company B has invested in BI methods to ensure that the BI projects undertaken support key business processes that make a difference in business performance. These methods have now been used on several projects and have become institutionalized.

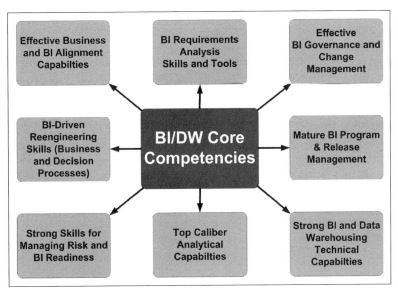

FIGURE 5-3 Business intelligence core competencies.

- **BI requirements analysis skills and tools.** BI requirements include identified needs for business information and analytical tools plus target business process models (or concepts) for leveraging those BI elements. Company B has invested in developing skills and tools that ensure that its BI requirements—which are crucial for driving what gets built and delivered to users—are effectively identified, validated, prioritized, and managed.

- **Effective BI governance and change management.** The BI program at Company B uses a steering committee composed of senior executives from the business (operations and finance) and from IT. This group is used to approve BI investment levels, approve and guide key projects, and ensure that the BI technical architecture supports rapid project execution and effective delivery of business information and analytical capabilities. The business representative is responsible for driving the business process changes necessary for realizing the business value of the BI investments.

- **Mature BI program and release management.** The BI program at Company B was initially a collection of individual projects. That approach worked up to a point, but it did not optimize the organizational learning achieved across individual BI project efforts. Different methods and standards were used, and the overall BI architecture was not well integrated. Recognizing these problems, Company B invested in establishing standard methods to be used under a uniform but flexible development approach. To ensure focus, a program manager was designated, and structured ways of defining and prioritizing releases were instituted.

- **Strong BI and DW technical capabilities.** Company B has made substantial investments in training and in recruiting skilled BI and DW professionals. The focus of training has been on BI and DW methods, technical skills, and tools.

Furthermore, Company B has invested in advanced technical tools to shorten development time and costs, thereby delivering more BI applications in a shorter period of time.

- **Top-caliber analytical capabilities.** Business information and analytical tools are of no use if the organization lacks the business analysis skills to use them to make better, fact-based decisions that improve profits. Company B's culture is operations oriented and has embraced the use of dedicated analyst groups in all of its regions. As new BI applications are delivered, power user groups are the early adopters. These power users then promote the BI applications to the wider audience of analysts.

- **Strong skills for managing risk and BI readiness.** As we see it, the primary categories of risk that the BI program must manage are business adoption risk and technical execution risk. At Company B, a BI readiness assessment was conducted as a means of identifying both types of risk. Situational constraints have sometimes limited the use of risk mitigation strategies. In other instances, however, the identified risks are being proactively managed and reduced or eliminated.

- **BI-driven re-engineering skills (business and decision processes).** As we've noted earlier, business information and business analysis tools will not have an economic impact unless they are used within business and decision processes that make a difference. Company B has an industrial engineering group and an automation support group, each of which is charged with improving productivity and service, with BI applications being one way to do so.

The COE approach at Company B has steadily and systematically improved its core BI capabilities. Because of Company B's size, progress has not always come as fast as executives wished, but the COE approach is a core element of the program plan and has provided constancy of purpose and direction. This is critical, because BI is as much about changing business behaviors and processes as it is about technology. Effective change in large-scale organizations requires persistence.

> **Tip**
>
> Developing a BI COE is a good way to set in motion a BI program aimed at maturing an organization's current BI capabilities. It signals an organizational commitment to developing world-class BI capabilities.

Element Three: Risk Management

As we discussed in Chapter 3, a BI readiness assessment is an excellent tool for identifying risks in advance. At Company B, the most salient risks that are being actively managed include (1) schedule risk induced by IT policies optimized for transactional systems at the expense of rapid BI development and deployment; (2) data integration risk due to having several different legacy transactional systems and culturally stovepiped and proprietary organizational units involved in the claims process; (3) technical risk (and potential reward) induced by the introduction of a new enterprise information integration platform; (4) schedule and technical risk induced by the need to migrate IT skills from older technologies to the newer platform; and (5) technical and schedule risk that result from cultural differences between BI development organizations and the shared services group that "owns" the IT assets.

The specific risks to be managed differ from company to company. The BI program plan is the place to identify them and describe the risk management techniques that you will use to mitigate them.

> **Tip**
>
> It is important to identify and actively manage the risks associated with introducing BI into your organization. A BI program plan is the best place to do this.

Element Four: Business Process Re-engineering

The business strategy for leveraging BI is to

- Deploy business information and business analysis tools that provide front-line managers with more detailed, timely, and specific information about productivity. This allows for closer monitoring, more insight into performance trends, and more timely corrective actions.
- Deploy business information and business analysis tools that provide a comprehensive view of the entire disability claims process. This allows top managers, middle managers and front-line supervisors to identify and correct service issues and thereby meet or exceed customer expectations.

To capture the business value of its investments in BI, Company B must leverage BI-driven reengineering skills, that is, the ability to use introduce and standardize the use of BI within business processes that affect profits and performance. Toward that end, the program plan addresses which specific business processes must change, how the change will be accomplished, by whom it will be directed, and how the benefits will be measured. As we noted earlier, front-line managers at Company B had been receiving only highly aggregated information that was delivered long after the fact, thus providing very little actionable information in time to correct adverse trends. Because they had never had timely, relevant, and detailed information before, the managers did not have established business processes for using such information, nor did they have analytical or decision support tools.

To address this, the BI program is using power users as early adopters, and the number of users has gone from six to 70 in six weeks and will soon be rolled out nationwide. Top management will also begin to use the information, which will further support changing management processes to include use of the new BI application.

Element Five: Program and Project Management

To succeed, a BI-driven profit improvement program must have effective program management and project management. In our experience, the most effective program managers blend general management skills, relationship-building skills, and IT strategy skills to set the program agenda and see that it gets carried out. At Company B, general management skills come into play in such areas as capital budgeting for BI investments, financial planning, facilities planning, and staffing. Relationship-building skills come into play at Company B

- In dealing with business executives and managers at the steering committee
- In working with the shared services group to influence the evolution of IT operating policies to better accommodate the specific needs of the BI design and development lifecycle

IT strategy skills come into play as the company adopts its standard IT system development lifecycle to fit the BI program, and as it evolves its IT platforms and tools to accommodate BI. At the project level, Company B is evolving its resource tracking system to provide better information for project managers.

Element Six: Information Technology Infrastructure

A BI-driven profit improvement program may require changes to the existing IT infrastructure, depending on the company and its starting position with respect to BI and DW. At Company B, the BI program has had to address two key IT infrastructure challenges. The first challenge is that the development, validation, and integration testing environments are heavily used shared environments that have been designed to support development and testing of transactional systems and modifications thereto. Accordingly, these environments are optimized for processing the typically small data sets associated with units or modules of transactional systems. As Company B moved into the larger scale data integration required for BI—in some cases processing 50 million records per day—the development, validation, and integration environments could not effectively accommodate such processing. That made it difficult to test data integration software routines and to predict performance in the target production environment. From a BI program perspective, the IT environment needed to adapt to accommodate the business imperative of rapidly developing and deploying BI releases.

The second IT infrastructure challenge stemmed from the fact that Company B invested in a new data integration platform that introduced an unknown into the tightly controlled, mainframe-centric IT environment. Although the data integration platform Company B selected was an established and widely adopted product, the process for obtaining architectural approval and getting the data integration platform installed in the environment had to be carefully planned and managed at the program management level. The managers of the shared services environment and the development environment had to be educated about how the new data integration

<table>
<tr><td>

Tip

Planning your IT infrastructure for BI involves both art and science. On one hand, your BI efforts should leverage your existing IT infrastructure as much as possible. On the other hand, your BI efforts must go beyond your existing IT infrastructure to deliver new value to the organization. You should consider the potential return on investment (ROI) for new BI technologies as well as (realistically) political factors such as the need to win support of groups that might have vested interests in parts of the existing infrastructure. All factors considered, what mix of old and new infrastructure will enable you to deliver the maximum BI value relative to your BI investment?

</td></tr>
</table>

technology would play in the existing environments before they would buy off on acquiring the technology. Furthermore, a range of technical issues and decisions needed to be managed as the technology was introduced into the environment, even down to topics such as selection of connection methods and designation of dedicated ports. Because of the mission-critical nature of Company B's transactional systems, it was important to proceed with caution. This generated the need for program-level planning.

Element Seven: Information Technology Operations

As business information and analytical tools become ingrained and fact-based decisions become the norm, it is critical that IT operations support both (1) the production operations of the data warehouse and (2) the BI applications it supports. In particular, the regular data integration processes must be run during batch windows, the relevant parts of the IT infrastructure must be administered, licenses must be managed, technology upgrades must be installed, and users must be supported. At Company B, these requirements are managed at the program level. In turn, that requires coordination with the shared services organization, with vendors, and with business user communities. To achieve this coordination, the BI program is establishing working groups for such topics as technical architecture, development environment, and user tools.

5.2.2 Summary: The Program Plan for Business Intelligence-Driven Profit Improvement

By using Company B as an example, we've illustrated some of the key topics in a program plan for BI-driven profit improvement. As you can see, there is a lot to manage. From a top management perspective, driving BI use into key management processes, revenue-generating processes, and operating processes that affect profits requires a multi-year perspective and an orchestrated alignment of business strategy, BI strategy, business infrastructure and processes, and BI infrastructure and processes. The analyses and activities of the architectures phase of the BI Pathway feed development of a comprehensive program plan for BI-driven profit improvement. As with planning in general, the planning document itself is useful and the format should be tailored to the situation. However, the most important aspect of the plan is the consensus, coordination, and communication it promotes. With the program plan as a navigation tool, top managers can ensure that the BI program is unfolding as planned, thereby leading to BI-driven profit improvement.

5.2.3   Business Intelligence-Driven Profit Improvement Is a General Management Responsibility

One of the most common challenges we have encountered—and one we hear about all the time when we teach BI courses–is the challenge of getting top management to engage on the subject of BI. We believe this is symptomatic of a broader problem faced by IT generally. For example, a McKinsey & Company study of IT use in manufacturing companies found that

OBSERVATION

Information management must receive the attention of top management. On average, the top managers at IT stars together spend about 45 hours per month on IT, compared with 20 hours for laggards. . . . Not surprisingly, top managers at low-performing companies, who spend an average of just 4.5 hours on IT per months, tend to have vague and unrealistic expectations. . . . At IT stars, by contrast, top managers devote time and energy to developing an IT strategy, and get actively involved in the introduction of new systems. *In particular, they play a critical role in defining projects and agreeing upon measurable goals in specific business processes and technologies* [emphasis added]. . . . Without the intimate involvement of top management in critical IT issues, information management rarely performs well. (Kempis and Ringbeck, 1998)

Although the survey population for this study was small manufacturers, the findings are very representative of what has come to be regarded as a universal truth in IT: that top managers don't get as involved as they should. This idea was echoed very succinctly in a conversation we had with the chief information officer (CIO) of a well-known consumer packaged goods manufacturer. When told about the findings from the McKinsey study cited above, he said, "I doubt that our CEO has spent 4.5 hours on IT in his life, let alone in a single month."

If we consider the business and technical challenges outlined above in our discussion of BI-driven profit improvement programs, it's clear that

- Many of the challenges are cross-functional between the business and IT.
- IT does not have the power to force the business to engage or to change business processes to leverage BI.

The implications for shareholders are unfortunate, because BI-driven profit improvement is a proven management tool that will become increasingly important over the next five to 10 years. Absent top management involvement, it is unlikely that BI will have as much profit impact as it could.

5.3 Business Intelligence-Driven Profit Improvement Is Crossing the Chasm

In his excellent book *Living on the Fault Line*, Gordon Moore (2000) describes a technology adoption life cycle and various classes of adopters. The order of adoption follows a predictable pattern: technology enthusiasts are first, followed by visionaries, pragmatists, conservatives, and skeptics. If they succeed, the highest incremental profit goes to the early adopters—enthusiasts and visionaries. The majority of the market consists of pragmatists and conservatives, who take less risk but consequently reap lower rewards. In fact, if they wait too long, they may have to invest simply "to stay in the game" if the technology is important enough.

For BI, the early adopters are well down the road and have achieved documented competitive advantages and incremental profits. For example, the *Wall Street Journal* recently published an article ("Gauging the Wal-Mart Effect," December 3-4, 2005) citing how Wal-Mart used information to predict that Hurricane Ivan would spur demand for toaster pastries, and was able to fill Florida stores to meet this anticipated increased demand. Based on the recent attention it is getting, we believe that BI is crossing the chasm between the early adopters and the mainstream market. We work with and talk with major companies in a wide range of industries who have invested millions in IT infrastructure and transactional systems such as enterprise requirements planning (ERP), supply chain management (SCM), and customer relationship management (CRM) and who still say, sometimes bitterly, that they don't have the information they need to run their businesses.

Given this state of affairs, BI is becoming more and more important as a profit improvement tool. We believe that the time is right for top management to embrace its potential and step up to the leadership and general management challenges of a BI-driven profit improvement initiative.

5.4 Key Points to Remember

- BI-driven profit improvement is an emerging management tool whose time has come.
- Using BI to improve profits poses specific leadership and change management challenges that can be met by using a structured approach adapted to BI.
- Using BI to improve profits poses specific general management challenges that can be met by establishing a sound architectural foundation and an effective program management office.
- Developing BI/DW core competencies reduces risk and ensures that the business reaps the rewards for its investment in BI.
- BI is a top management affair.

5.5 Think Tank

5.5.1 Seven Questions to Ask About Your Company and Business Intelligence-Driven Profit Improvement

1. What are the most difficult barriers to BI-driven profit improvement at our company?
2. Do the top managers at our company "get it" when it comes to IT in general and BI in particular?
3. Is our company inclined to try new management tools?
4. Where does our company stand with respect to BI maturity?
5. Do business units in our company take responsibility for the success of IT and/or BI projects?
6. Has our company had success in multi-year efforts to improve business performance?
7. Has our company had success in developing new core competencies?

5.5.2 Quiz: Where Does Your Company Stand in Relation to BI/DW Core Competencies?

1. Does our company have the patience for structured, thorough BI requirements analysis?
2. How does our company govern BI and is BI governance effective? If not, why not?
3. Does our company have an effective BI program management office with appropriate general management, relationship building, and IT strategy skills?
4. Does our company have strong BI and DW technical skills?
5. Do our business units have high caliber business analysts?
6. Is our company structured and effective in its approach to managing the business and technical risks associated with our BI program?
7. Is our company effective at managing business process change?

Chapter 6

Business Intelligence in the Broader Information Technology Context

"In the last 15 years, a litany of IT-enabled initiatives, from business process reengineering to enterprise resource planning, have elevated the importance of investing strategically in IT.... But while opportunities seem boundless, the resources required by these investments—capital, IT expertise, management focus, and capacity for change—are severely limited."

—Jeanne W. Ross and Cynthia M. Beath,"Beyond the Business Case: Strategic IT Investment"

Business intelligence (BI) initiatives take place in company-specific business contexts where they must compete with other information technology (IT) projects for resources. BI is downstream from day-to-day transactional systems and enterprise applications, and as a result, BI initiatives often must work within technical decisions that have already been made. Finally, BI is affected by a company's IT strategy and IT operating policies. These and related factors affect what BI can accomplish, how long it takes, how much risk it poses, how much reward it offers, and how much it costs.

6.1 Where Business Intelligence Fits in the Information Technology Portfolio

The mission of IT is to support the business. Although this is simple in concept, it is complicated in practice: supporting the business can mean many different things. Support can mean relatively straightforward activities, such as providing and managing Internet access for the company, and highly complex endeavors, such a migrating a global corporation to a common enterprise requirements planning (ERP) system. The latter often entails substantial changes to existing business processes or substantial customization of the packaged ERP software application—both of which have serious risks and life-cycle cost implications.

For the modern company of any size, managing IT amounts to making a series of investment decisions (bets) about technologies, productivity improvement, and, ultimately, profit and business performance. To complicate matters, many business

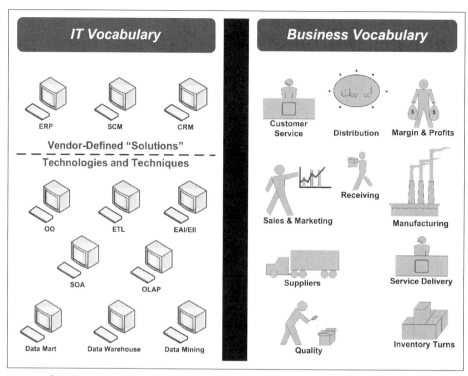

FIGURE 6-1 The modern Tower of Babel: information technology and business managers can't communicate.

executives in large companies are not well versed in IT. Although an effective chief information officer (CIO) can help, these business executives are called on to make multi-million dollar investment decisions that have substantial risks and substantial impacts on the business capabilities of the firm. Also, IT and business executives often speak different languages. IT concepts that have a very specific meaning to IT people often have little resonance for business people and vice versa. Figure 6-1 illustrates this language gap.

In the face of such complexity and risk, leading companies have adapted portfolio management techniques to the task of managing IT. The IT portfolio can be thought of as all the IT needed to support the business. It can range from basic infrastructure, such as networks and computers, to transactional systems, such as point-of-sales terminals and ERP systems, and finally to BI systems. A depiction of the IT portfolio is shown as Figure 6-2, which is adapted from an excellent book on IT strategy written by Peter Weill and Marianne Broadbent (1998) called *Leveraging the New Infrastructure: How Market Leaders Capitalize on Information Technology.*

The foundation of the IT portfolio is infrastructure, which can be thought of as a utility that promotes a company's ability to leverage IT. The utility provides many of its services as shared services, which is both a cost-optimization strategy for an agreed-upon level of service and a way to ensure that all the foundational elements of the infrastructure work together. A familiar example of this approach is

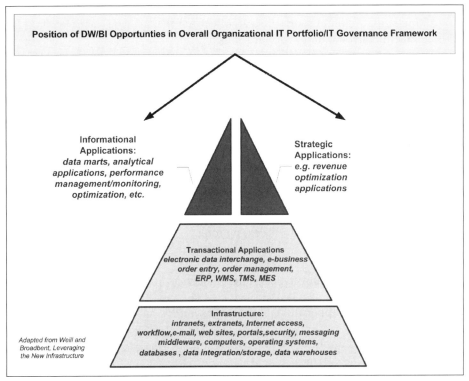

FIGURE 6-2 Structure of the corporate information technology portfolio (adapted from Weill and Broadbent, 1998).

the plumbing and wiring of a house, in which we want all the pipes to fit together and all the wires to support standard appliances.

The next layer of the IT portfolio is composed of transactional applications (transactional IT) that allow the company to conduct its day-to-day business. Transactional IT has evolved from "home-grown" custom-developed software to packaged, standardized applications that tackle various aspects of the business. These aspects include sales force management, customer interactions, order processing, inventory management, supply chain management, purchasing, warehouse management, manufacturing execution, and financial reporting. The general motivation for investments in transactional IT is operational efficiency and effectiveness, although in some cases having stronger transactional IT capabilities can confer a "first mover" advantage. Two companies that reaped this advantage are Dell and Cisco, whose transactional IT systems integrated their entire supply chains and allowed them to offer differentiated customer service combined with lower prices.

The top layer of the IT portfolio consists of strategic applications and informational applications. Strategic applications result in competitive advantage to first movers and early adopters. The classic example is revenue optimization applications developed in high fixed-asset businesses such as the commercial aviation and hotel industries. The combination of computing power and complex operations-research models allowed early movers to dynamically balance supply and demand by adjusting prices to fill airline seats and hotel rooms instead of leaving them vacant. Done well, BI has the potential to deliver strategic applications.

Informational applications, in contrast, aim to provide business leaders and managers with the information they need to effectively address strategic, tactical, and operational business challenges. In our view, this part of the IT portfolio is populated by a wide range of tools and techniques, including the following:

- Spreadsheets and spreadsheet-based databases, sometimes referred to as "spread-marts"
- Desktop databases for workgroups or departments
- Desktop query and reporting tools
- Desktop domain-specific packaged software, such as linear programming software
- Server-based query and reporting tools
- Server-based on-line analytical processing tools
- ERP-based reporting tools
- Portals
- Packaged management information systems, such as human resources information systems
- Packaged analytical applications for, for example, supply chain analysis and customer analysis
- Packaged analytical applications for business tasks such as budgeting or activity-based costing/management
- Data mining software
- Customized data marts and data warehouses

> **Tip**
>
> It bears repeating that better analytical tools *by themselves* won't make BI pay off for an organization. The organization must also be ready to restructure and adapt its processes to take advantage of new BI capabilities.

In practice, companies use IT in a lot of different ways to provide useful information. In fact, it's reasonable to say that information usage at many companies is ad hoc and idiosyncratic, which corresponds to level 1 in the BI maturity model discussed in Chapter 5. BI methods and tools exist to bring order, efficiency, and consistency to informational IT so that companies can manage their affairs with a single version of the facts. Further, BI can do more than just make information available. By providing better analytical tools and more structured, information-rich decision processes within core business processes, BI can improve profits.

In addition to its role in informational and strategic applications, BI methods and tools are also being used to enhance transactional applications. The classic example of this is the way that Amazon.com uses transactional history, data warehousing (DW), data mining, and BI to display individualized recommendations of additional items a shopper might wish to purchase. Other potentially fertile uses of BI methods and tools in operational contexts can be found in manufacturing, customer service, and order fulfillment contexts, in which highly profitable customers can be given preferential treatment based on business rules and access to transactional history and customer lifetime value calculations.

As just one of the types of potential IT investment within the IT portfolio, albeit an increasingly important type, BI investment opportunities are affected by each company's IT strategy and IT budget. IT strategy can be thought of as the set of choices a company has made around such key questions as:

- What is the scope of IT capabilities and services needed to support our business strategy?
- Which of those capabilities and services should we provide internally and which should we purchase or outsource?
- With which of our customers and suppliers must we collaborate and how will we use IT to do so?
- How do we create value for our customers and how can IT help us do that?
- Where do we want to be on the risk-reward spectrum when it comes to IT? Are we leaders, fast-followers, or late adopters?
- How can IT help us compete? Where do we want to stand in relation to IT use by our competitors?
- What strategic opportunities can IT enable for us?
- Are parts of the IT portfolio vital to our business? If so, which ones, and which can/should be outsourced?
- Do we see IT as a cost to be minimized or as a competitive weapon?

Based on the answers to these and related business questions, a company can then set about determining its IT budget, which includes capital and operating budgets.

Establishing Your IT Budget

Establishing an IT budget is like establishing any budget: it involves both art and science. One common approach is to compare your company to industry "norms," which are after-the-fact reports that present statistics about a survey population. For example, some data we've seen suggest that manufacturing firms spend an average of 1% of their revenues on IT. The problems with this approach are twofold. First, it assumes the companies in the survey know what they are doing—a tricky assumption. Second, it doesn't provide much insight into how the money was invested. On a more theoretical level, economists would argue that the firm should invest in every IT project that offers a return on investment (ROI) that exceeds the firm's cost of capital. The problem with that approach is that the ROI calculations for IT projects are sometimes difficult and intertwined with other projects. Because of the problems with these approaches, we think it's better to determine what IT capabilities your company needs to support its business strategies, develop bottom-up budgets, and then compare the results to available funding, however that gets determined in your company.

Coming to BI investment, we see that BI initiatives must compete with other IT investment opportunities for funding, and this often entails navigating the IT capital budgeting process. Whether the BI initiative is at the functional, business unit, or enterprise level, it must typically develop a business case, ROI analysis, cost-benefit analysis, or similar document. The specific requirements depend on company policies, and the mechanics are beyond the intent of this book. For an incisive analysis of the challenges of discounted cash flow analysis, you may wish to consult chapter 3 of *Dynamic Manufacturing* (Hayes et al., 1988). To understand some of the organizational dynamics associated with capital budget requests, you may wish to consult chapter 3 of *The Rise and Fall of Strategic Planning* (Mintzberg, 1994).

That said, the basic business case for any potential BI investment is profit improvement and (especially for government agencies and nonprofits) more cost-effective achievement of the organization's mission. The specifics for any organization can be developed via BI opportunity analysis (see Chapter 2) and the architectures phase analyses (see Chapter 4).

> **Tip**
>
> BI initiatives must compete with other IT initiatives for funding. To increase the odds of obtaining funding, it is important to understand your organization's IT strategy and IT budget. In this way you can tailor your positioning of BI initiatives to ensure funding.

By using the results of those analyses, we can develop a cogent description of how BI would be used to improve profits and what business process changes would be involved. We can discuss risks and rewards with some level of empirical rigor, and depending on how much cost analysis has been done, we may be able to define the level of investment required at a reasonable level of specificity. Whether we are developing the business case for BI-driven profit improvement as an enterprise initiative, for a BI portfolio for a business unit, or for an individual BI investment, a reasonable amount of structured analysis will leave us in a good position to discuss the business benefits (business value capture mechanism) and the order of magnitude of costs that must be incurred to achieve those benefits.

6.2   Information Technology Assets Required for Business Intelligence

The composition and scope of IT assets required for BI depends on your company's BI strategy. Informational applications can be—and are—implemented with desktop software such as Microsoft Excel and Access, often creating dozens if not hundreds of so-called "analytical silos." This approach has been shown to create different views of what should be the same business information, thus undermining confidence in the information delivered. The proliferation of analytical silos is often one reason that departmental, business unit, and/or enterprise BI initiatives are initially launched. For our purposes, we will assume that your company is planning an enterprise BI-driven profit improvement program.

From a business perspective, a typical BI environment consists of the elements shown in Figure 6-3.

When many executives, managers, and knowledge workers think of IT in general, they think in terms of what they can see and do with their computers and PDAs, and what they receive from others in the form of reports, memos, and e-mails. Although

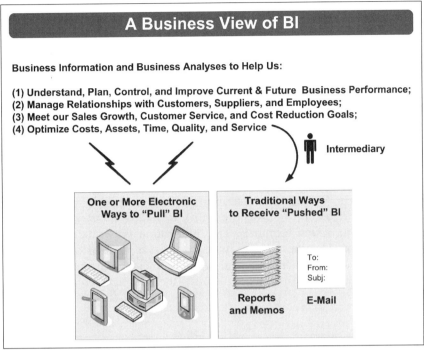

FIGURE 6-3 Elements of a typical business intelligence environment.

some power users can be quite deep in their understanding of data and databases, most users have a strictly utilitarian view of IT. Thus, to them, BI is just another name in the IT alphabet soup. What counts is what BI can help them see and do.

Because of this orientation and because of the magnitude and importance of the BI investment decisions that need to be made, it's important for business leaders and managers to expand their understanding of the scope and configuration of IT assets required to support a BI-driven profit improvement initiative. In saying this, we recognize that some business leaders and managers already have a good working understanding of this topic. In our experience, however, we have seen many cases in which it is tough sledding to get the IT assets that BI requires.

6.2.1 The Basic Scope and Configuration of Information Technology Assets for Business Intelligence

In Chapter 4, we discussed the fact that there are mixed-use BI environments and dedicated BI environments in use at major companies in a variety of industries. Although distinct operational impacts are associated with one approach or another, about which we will have more to say in Section 6.3, from a business perspective, the IT assets in play are the same. Accordingly, we will set aside that distinction for purposes of this section.

From a systems engineering perspective, creating a BI asset is a systems integration task wherein we add special-purpose BI tools into an existing IT technical infrastructure and we create specialized IT processes to move data along a value chain while preparing it for its intended business uses. For example, we might take raw transactional data from several of the thousands of data stores within an ERP system, combine it with raw data from a sales force management application, organize it by business unit and geographic region, summarize it at various levels of the organizational hierarchy, and push it into a special purpose data store used by business users for sales and operations planning. A generic (typical) IT technical infrastructure to support BI-driven profit improvement is shown in Figure 6-4.

Figure 6-4 highlights the BI assets and BI processes within the IT infrastructure, which is simplified for sake of discussion. In a typical company environment, transactional applications and other enterprise applications (in the "existing IT assets" box on the left) create databases. These databases and the associated applications are designed to present business information to business users via a variety of devices (in the "existing IT assets" box on the right), including PDAs, tablet computers, workstations, laptops, and terminals. The information presented can be seen on the devices and/or it can be printed out as standard reports. Most of the information presented is about the current state of the business for the current fiscal year, and that information is not organized to meet the complex requirements that BI addresses.

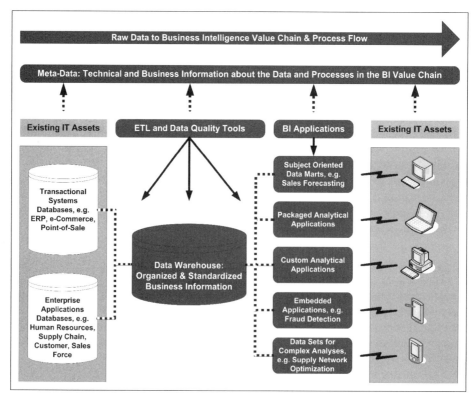

FIGURE 6-4 A typical technical infrastructure for business intelligence.

To meet the requirements for enterprise level BI-driven profit improvement programs, we introduce the BI assets and processes shown in the middle and at the top of the figure, with dotted lines to represent data flows and processes. Moving from left to right, we see that data contained in transactional and enterprise applications databases is moved into a data warehouse, which is a special-purpose database designed to meet BI requirements. Here, the raw information is organized and standardized to create the so-called "single version of the truth" for the various BI uses. This is also where we build subsets of business information that can be used by multiple BI applications. For example, the sales organization and the operations organization in many companies have a common need for business information about product or service sales—often by time period, by region, by product family or service type, by customer, and by other variables of interest. Given this common need, a single subset of business information can be prepared in the data warehouse for use by, for example, a packaged sales forecasting application for the sales organization and a customized sales and operations planning application for the operations organization.

Based on BI opportunity analysis and detailed BI requirements (see Chapters 2 and 4), data from the data warehouse is moved into BI applications (boxes in the middle-right of Figure 6-4), which we can think of as a combination of business information and one or more defined analytical approaches to gaining knowledge or insight from that information. Figure 6-4 shows some examples of BI applications, including the following:

- **Subject-oriented data marts,** which are subsets of business information selected and staged to address user-defined business information needs. Subject-oriented business information is analyzed by one or more structured approaches or tools. The typical BI application uses special-purpose applications to display, for example, sales by time period, by region, by product family or service type, by customer, and by other variables of interest.
- **Packaged analytical applications,** which combine vendor-defined subsets of business information with one or more structured approaches to analyzing the information. Typical packaged analytical applications include scorecards, dashboards, customer analytics, and supply chain analytics.
- **Custom analytical applications,** which are similar to packaged analytical applications in their use but are customized in their design. An important point to remember about customized analytical applications is that they are almost always designed, developed, and implemented with standard BI tools, so customization *does not* imply risk or materially longer development cycles.
- **Embedded applications,** which are BI applications that connect back to transactional systems and/or enterprise applications. Typical embedded applications include credit-card anti-fraud applications and e-commerce up-sell and cross-sell applications. Both of these examples examine past transactional data to identify patterns in real-time in order to *disapprove credit card transactions that differ from previous patterns or suggest other purchases based on prior purchases.*
- **Data sets for complex analyses,** wherein the data needed to feed complex analytical algorithms is staged in a form that can be used by, for example,

linear programming, network optimization, forecasting, scheduling, simulation, stochastic programming, mixed integer programming, and other operations research/management science techniques.

The above list of representative BI applications should not be viewed as exhaustive or as the only way to characterize various types of BI applications. Rather, it is intended to show that BI-driven profit improvement at the enterprise level is likely to require a variety of BI applications to improve the specific business processes that impact profit.

To enable the basic flow of business information within the BI asset, as discussed above, we need to enhance existing IT assets with special-purpose BI tools and processes. One key toolset consists of extract, transformation, and loading (ETL) tools and data quality tools, shown in a box in the upper-middle section of Figure 6-4.

Data quality tools can ensure that the quality of data feeding into the data warehouse and BI applications is appropriate for the intended BI application. It is not uncommon for transactional systems and enterprise applications to contain erroneous or incomplete data, which is fundamentally a business problem as business users are the people who enter the data into such systems in the first place. The key from a BI perspective is to understand the nature and frequency of data quality issues in order to determine whether the issues are material to the usability and credibility of the business information bound for the data warehouse and BI applications.

ETL tools are central to first-rate BI environments. They are mature tools that reduce development time, manage the flow of data along the BI value chain, and provide the means to manage changes to data over time as transactional systems and enterprise applications evolve. One key component of an ETL tool and other tools used to develop BI environments is a meta-data repository: a database that contains information about the business information in the data warehouse and BI applications and the IT processes that move the data along the BI value chain. Figure 6-4 shows the flow (in dotted arrows) from the various databases and processes in the environment into the meta-data repository environment (a box that extends across the top of the drawing).

To illustrate the role of meta-data, consider a simple example in which a transactional system such as ERP uses a month-day-year convention for dates and an enterprise application such as a human resources information system (HRIS) uses a year-month-day convention. For the BI asset to present date-related information in a consistent way, data from one or the other of these two sources must be changed to match the desired convention. The meta-data repository keeps track of data formats in the various feeder systems, keeps track of what changes are made to the data, maintains business rules for how business information is to be aggregated for higher-level presentation, keeps track of how often data must be updated, and performs a host of other tasks associated with being able to produce reliable, credible, and useful business information on a repeatable basis.

This subsection has concentrated on what IT assets are required for BI and the basic roles for those assets. In the following subsection, we will provide a high-level overview of the key IT products that are required for an effective BI environment. This is meant as a guide for business leaders and managers. A plethora of technical IT information is available about these products for IT professionals involved in selecting or tuning specific products, and it is not our intent to rehash that information here.

6.2.2 Key Information Technology Products for Business Intelligence

Although we acknowledge that many technology investments are made by companies to support BI initiatives, including data profiling tools, metadata repositories, and DW monitoring software, we have intentionally limited the discussion in this section to the products that we believe represent the core BI technology investments that organizations make.

Database Management Systems

Referring again to Figure 6-4, we see that databases are core to BI. Moving along the BI value chain (from left to right in the drawing), data is extracted from one or more databases. It's then placed in the data warehouse, which is a specialized database. Ultimately, it's moved into BI applications, which provide a way to store and analyze the data. Each database has a different job for which it is optimized.

The foundational IT product that allows us to create, manage, and optimize these databases is the modern relational database management system (RDBMS). From the early 1980s when RDBMSs first emerged as commercial software products, the field has narrowed from dozens of players to a handful of dominant products. We have no commercial relationships with any IT product vendors, and it is not an endorsement of any particular product for any particular situation when we state that IBM, Oracle, Sybase, and SQL Server dominate the RDBMS market. Teradata, a proprietary database management system, is also widely used in the industry. All of these products are very mature. Their vendors continue to add functionality that makes developing, deploying, and managing data warehouses, data marts, and BI applications more efficient.

Ironically, the very flexibility of RDBMSs, combined with the high cost for enterprise uses, creates a common business and IT challenge for BI. Specifically, companies wish to leverage their investment in RDBMSs across as many IT uses as possible, including BI uses. Therefore, this key technology product is often managed as a shared service to support transactional systems, enterprise applications, and BI applications. This can create business problems associated with cost allocation and chargeback among projects, as well as create suboptimization problems that can impact IT operations, BI development and operations, or both. We will discuss these issues in the section 6.4.4.

Extract, Transformation, and Loading Tools

As we noted earlier, ETL tools are central to a first-rate BI environment. They are key for developer productivity, for data movement efficiency and throughput, for configuration management, for job scheduling, and for managing change over time. Similar to RDBMS products, ETL products are mature and low risk. Without endorsing any particular product for any particular environment, our market research conducted on behalf of clients in a range of industries confirms that the most mature general purpose products are offered by Ab Initio Software, IBM, and Informatica.

Our research evaluated eight major areas for more than 20 vendors, including the following:

- Company background: technology, financial, market share, and strategy
- Product strategy
- Product architecture
- Functionality: data profiling, data cleansing, data auditing and validation, design and transformation, data movement, data extraction, data loading, system administration, and meta-data management
- Customer support
- Documentation and training
- Pricing

> **Tip**
>
> Because ETL tools are typically a large investment, you must understand the key features and functions that are needed to support your BI environment before making this investment. The BI program plan is a good place to get the "big picture" regarding the types of BI requirements that will need to be supported by the chosen BI technology.

Our research also confirmed that many excellent special-purpose products deliver one or more of the types of functionality listed above. Depending on your company's specific requirements, for example, a specialized data profiling or data movement tool might be needed to complement a more general-purpose ETL tool. As with many IT products, there is often a trade-off between products that do many things reasonably well and products that do one thing extremely well. As always, the trade-offs need to be made factors. Also, when choosing products from niche vendors, whether they are small generalists or specialists, it is important to evaluate product strategies and the financial stability of the company because these speak to product business viability during the useful life of your investment. That affects ongoing vendor support for the product or products you may be considering.

Business Intelligence Platforms and Analytical Applications

On the right side of Figure 6-4, we showed five generic examples of BI applications. Some of the examples represent customized BI applications, which tend to be designed, developed, and implemented using standard commercial products that can be thought of as BI "platforms." In the IT world, a platform provides a set of IT functional capabilities that in themselves do not solve a particular business challenge. Instead, the platform provides an integrated suite of IT tools that can be used to design, develop, and implement a customized IT capability that supports the business. BI platforms are specialized to address the specific tasks associated with delivering customized BI applications.

Market research conducted by a range of third parties suggests that the leading BI platform vendors include Business Objects, Cognos, Hyperion, MicroStrategy, and MicroSoft. Each of these BI platforms offers comparable functionality, although differences in product technical approaches make the different platforms more or

Table 6-1

Analytical application vendors and product types

Packaged Analytical Applications Vendors

Enterprise resource planning (ERP) vendors, e.g., Oracle, SAP, Great Plains
Enterprise applications vendors, e.g., Seibel, Deltek, i2, Lawson
Business intelligence (BI) platform vendors, e.g., Business Objects, Cognos, Hyperion, Microstrategy, MicroSoft
Niche specialists, e.g., CorVu, Geac, Pilot, Silvon

Packaged Analytical Application Product Types

Budgeting	Human resources/workforce analysis
Planning	IT systems performance analysis
Forecasting	Manufacturing and quality analysis
Accounts payable analysis	Supply chain performance analysis
Accounts receivable analysis	Balanced scorecards
Cost analysis	Dashboards
Activity-basedcosting/management	Customer relationship management analysis
General ledger analysis	Sales force management analysis

less suitable for specific BI environments, depending on the range and type of BI applications that must be delivered. For example, some of the platforms are better suited for large number-crunching BI applications than are competing products. Given these factors, it is important to have a clear BI strategy in mind when selecting a BI platform.

Figure 6-4 also shows a category of BI application called "packaged analytical applications." By "packaged," we mean commercially available software products, sometimes referred to as "shrink-wrapped" software. Many different types of packaged analytical applications are available, and they are sold by various types of software vendors (see Table 6-1).

At this point in the evolution of BI, products have been developed that analyze current and historical business information to assist with many recurring business management tasks and decisions. One challenge for such products is to be broad enough to meet the needs of many companies in many industries, which forces product design decisions that work well in the general case but may not be appropriate for any given company. To address a given company's sometimes unique or specific ways of looking at certain business situations, the products must be customized, which creates maintenance risks and adds costs. That said, many of the products offered are excellent products that can reduce the time it takes to deploy a BI application. If the application is targeted for an aspect of company operations that is not critical for competitive advantage, such as accounts receivable analysis, it may well make sense to invest.

Analytical Platforms

We noted earlier that a BI environment might also include data sets to feed analytical algorithms used by operations researchers and management scientists to perform computationally intensive analyses of large data sets and thereby gain insight into complex business situations. Analytical platforms are toolkits of precoded software routines that execute linear programming, network optimization, forecasting, scheduling, simulation, stochastic programming, mixed-integer programming, and other applied mathematical techniques.

A developer of a BI application of this type would work with an operations research analyst or management scientist to define what data inputs are needed and in what form. The analytical platforms have user interfaces that allow for selection of appropriate analytical techniques, and these platforms prompt for the input values, which can be obtained from the underlying data store. These platforms range in price from limited function desktop versions costing less than $100 to multi-function versions costing from several thousand to hundreds of thousands of dollars. For example, many of supply chain management software vendors have analytical platforms offering dozens of standard software routines and a sophisticated user interface for developers to use. Some well-known analytical platform vendors include SAS Institute, ILOG, and SPSS.

Data Warehouse Appliances

Data warehouse appliances are a new category of IT product that is beginning to be found in some BI environments. The value propositions for these products are that they simplify the systems integration required for a enterprise class BI environment and they are optimized for specific BI and DW tasks, thus they provide greater performance at a lower cost. In effect, the appliance would sit between the transactional system and enterprise applications database shown at the left of Figure 6-4 and the BI applications on the right of the drawing. Our research indicates that the leading vendors in this new product space are backed by venture capital and that the products are being touted by some industry analysts and observers, not all of whom can be said to be objective. As with any emerging, "disruptive" technology, substantial gains may be gotten, but probably not without risks. We believe that these products warrant assessment and consideration for inclusion in high-performance BI environments.

6.2.3 Summary: Information Technology Assets Required for Business Intelligence

The IT products required for BI, if installed and configured properly, are mature, low-risk products, and there are proven technical methods for building BI assets such as data warehouses and data marts. One key general management task, then, is to ensure that your company chooses products effectively in relation to (1) a specific BI strategy and (2) the specific requirements of the BI applications that constitute your company's BI portfolio.

Simply put—assuming that BI products are installed and configured properly—the risk is not in the product but in the selection process. Although it doesn't cost the tens of millions of dollars that ERP and other enterprise applications can cost, an effective complement of BI products can run to several million dollars at the enterprise level. Therefore, an effective and informed selection process is important to the long-term health of the BI-driven profit improvement program. This highlights again the importance of knowing what your company wants to do with BI so that intelligent, cost-effective choices can be made. The other key is using these assets well to meet BI requirements, and that is the focus of the next section.

6.3 Business Intelligence Environment in the Information Technology Environment

For our purposes here, we will define the IT environment as including a development environment, a testing and integration environment, and a production environment. The BI environment encompass all of the development, information processing, and support activities required to deliver reliable and highly relevant business information and business analytical capabilities to the business. The BI environment exists within the broader IT environment.

Tip

A dedicated BI environment is likely to deliver better performance with fewer problems, but those benefits must be balanced against the fact that it costs more up front than a mixed-use environment. If it's important to get top BI performance and your organization has ample funds, a dedicated environment might be the better choice.

From a business perspective, we must be concerned with how the IT assets required for BI are incorporated within the broader IT environment and how the business and IT policies governing that environment advance or detract from BI objectives. Because of business and technical differences between BI and transactional systems, an inherent tension exists within a mixed-use BI environment. Simply put, the policies that are appropriate for a large-scale transactional systems environment often impede aspects of BI development and operations. When a dedicated BI environment exists, the potential challenges are fewer, but in either case, the BI environment must be managed to achieve the following business and IT operational objectives:

1. Cost-effective and timely development of BI applications
2. Reliable production of high-quality business information for BI applications
3. Effective maintenance and administration of BI-related IT assets such as the RDBMS, ETL tools, BI platforms, and analytical platforms
4. Effective help-desk support for BI users

Essentially, the general management task is to ensure that the BI asset that has been created is managed in a way that supports the company's overall BI and business strategies. To accomplish this, we must recognize that BI capabilities should developed and managed in the same way that any other manufacturing or service delivery operations is managed: with a view toward supporting business strategy and delivering competitive advantage. Figure 6-5 and the associated thinking is adapted from manufacturing strategy ideas advanced by Robert Hayes, Steven Wheelwright, and others (Hayes et al., 1988) as Japanese companies were overtaking American companies in strategically important industries such as automobiles, steel, and electronics.

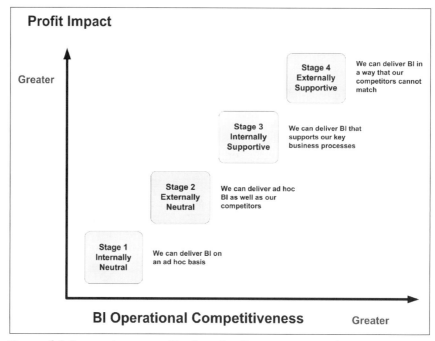

FIGURE 6-5 Progressive stages of business intelligence operational competitiveness.

Using the manufacturing example, a stage 1 company is capable of manufacturing the product or delivering the service in a way that does not detract from the overall operation of the company. The company's marketing and sales plans, for example, are not held back by lack of product or ineffective service. Similarly, a stage 1 BI capability would enable an organization to deliver BI on an ad hoc basis, not detracting from the overall internal operations of the company.

At stage 2, using the manufacturing example, the company has moved beyond that first level of achievement to the point at which its manufacturing processes or service-delivery processes are the equal of its competitors in relevant ways, for example, in terms of cost, quality, service, cycle time, and/or asset utilization. This ensures that the stage 2 company is not losing ground in the marketplace owing to the performance of the manufacturing or service delivery function. Similarly, a stage 2 BI capability strives to match the ad hoc BI capabilities of its competitors, resulting in BI capabilities that are equal to, but not better than, competitors.

At stage 3, using the manufacturing example, the company has advanced again, this time to the point at which its manufacturing or service-delivery capabilities actually enhance the performance of key business processes or functions, as opposed to not holding them back. Similarly, a stage 3 BI capability provides information that enhances performance of key business processes and functions internally.

Finally, at stage 4, using the manufacturing example, the company has advanced to the point at which its manufacturing or service-delivery capabilities cannot easily be matched by its competitors, delivering a competitive advantage. Dell and Cisco are excellent examples of stage 4 companies. Both aligned people, processes, and technology so that they could outperform their competitors on cost, quality, and service. A stage 4 BI capability also cannot be matched by competitors. It provides the information needed within key business processes that results in a distinct competitive advantage in the marketplace.

Applying this thinking to BI operations, the general management and IT management task is to evolve and optimize BI operations to a stage that is appropriate for the company's BI and business strategies. A number of major companies in a variety of industries have used BI to create competitive advantage, and thus they invested in people, processes, and technologies to become stage 4 companies, although they might not have thought of it in those exact terms. For other companies at a given point in time in their industries, it may be too late to achieve competitive advantage via BI, and thus becoming a stage 3 company may be the target.

Pitfall
Many companies fail to recognize that the technical environment and approaches needed to develop and support transaction systems are vastly different than those that are optimal for BI environments. Failing to adjust to the technical needs of a BI environment often results in technical failures.

Given the potential profit impact of BI, and given that more and more companies are seeing and exploiting the potential of BI, we believe that most companies should target becoming at least stage 2 companies, whereby their BI operational capabilities are equal to those of their strongest competitors. In effect, this means developing and optimizing two core BI technical environment processes: the development process, including testing and integration, and the production and support processes. We will discuss these in turn.

6.3.1   Business Intelligence Development Process

To support a BI-driven profit improvement program, the organization will need to invest in an effective BI and DW development environment. This environment should be used in conjunction with a suitable BI technical development methodology by IT people with suitable BI and DW technical skills. We talked earlier about the BI portfolio and the need to deploy BI applications as a series of releases, ideally every four to eight months once the appropriate BI infrastructure is in place. To accomplish this business objective, we need a suitable, repeatable, and cost-effective BI development process. Figure 6-6 shows the general development flow and the required tools.

Moving from left to right in the drawing, we see that the development process entails a flow between three environments, from the development environment through a testing and integration environment and into the production environment. The efficiency and effectiveness of those flows depends on having the appropriate tools, processes, and people. The specific processes may vary, but they will generally be akin to the processes described in Chapter 4 in the section about the implementation phase of the BI Pathway.

From a general management perspective, this all looks pretty simple, and it is indeed simpler in a dedicated BI Environment because the entire development

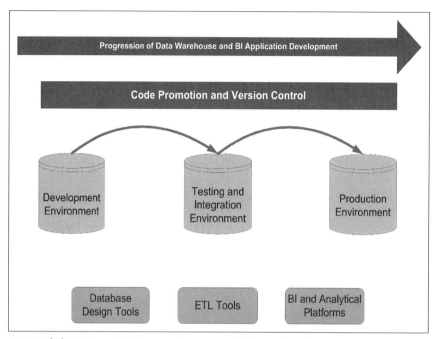

FIGURE 6-6 Business intelligence development flow and tools.

process can be optimized for BI. Where it becomes more complicated is in a mixed-use BI environment, in which the development environment, the testing and integration environment, and the production environment are shared among BI, transactional systems, and enterprise applications. This sharing sometimes makes sense from a total IT operating cost perspective. However, its drawback for BI development is that the respective environments are generally optimized around the needs of the transactional systems.

Transactional systems are essential to day-to-day revenue generation, and the cost of having down-time could be catastrophic. Imagine the impact on Home Depot if its point-of-sale system were to be down or dramatically slowed. Because of these stakes, IT shops value-controlled change or minimal change once they get the transactional and large enterprise systems tuned and running at suitable response times. As a result, they tend to favor lengthy, thorough testing processes before new applicationsare allowed in the production environment. Meanwhile, as a cost-containment measure, companies tend to deploy heavily shared development and testing/integration environments, which can add months to the development cycle for BI and other applications.

The net effect of all this is that IT investment, development, and operating policies that make sense for transactional systems trump the needs of a BI environment. As a result, BI applications take longer and cost more to deploy than would be possible in an environment optimized for BI. We certainly agree that the requirement for stable transactional systems is paramount.

Tip

In a mixed-use environment, transactional systems tend to have priority over BI development because they contribute *directly* to the organization's mission, whereas BI contributes only indirectly. That said, mixed-use environments can work well if you carefully manage the trade-offs between transactional systems and BI development.

That being said, it may be well for companies to evaluate the cost of a dedicated BI environment in relation to the opportunity cost of not fully realizing the incremental profits that could be captured if they had a more responsive BI development process that reduces "time to market" for new BI applications.

6.3.2 Business Intelligence Production and Support Processes

The BI production process is the means by which business information and business analytical capabilities are delivered for use in fact-based decision processes within core processes that impact profits. As such, the process must reliably produce high-quality business information, and the assets that support the process must be maintained and administered. The basic BI production process and key tasks are shown in Figure 6-7.

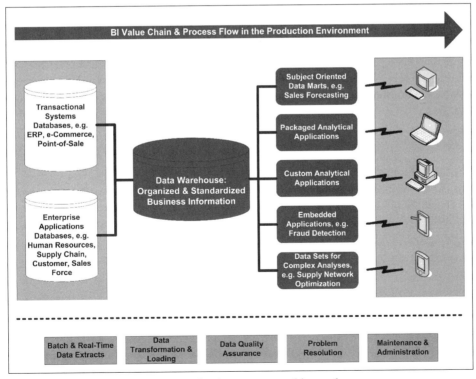

FIGURE 6-7 Business intelligence production process and key tasks.

Moving left to right, we see that data from the transactional systems databases and the enterprise applications databases flows into the data warehouse and then on to the BI applications, where it becomes available to users. As with the development environment, this all looks pretty simple, but the operational reality is more complex.

Whether operating in a dedicated BI environment or a mixed-use BI environment, the BI production process relies upon the production databases for the transactional systems and enterprise applications for data feeds, which means that the rules of engagement for BI are dictated by the needs of the transactional systems in the broader IT environment. The operational impact on BI is that, at a minimum, the regular batch data extract process must take place after the regular operating hours of the business so that the performance of transactional applications is not adversely impacted. Further, when operating in a mixed-use BI environment, other BI production processes, such as data transformation, data movement and loading into the data warehouse, data quality assurance, data movement, and loading into one or more BI applications, and resolution of any production problems must also take place after regular operating hours. In a global economy wired for electronic commerce via the Internet, the time available for such batch processes (the "batch window") is shrinking, and other system tasks must also run during this same time period using the same resources. Further, the volumes of transactional data being extracted and moved into data warehouses on a daily basis is huge, further taxing shared IT resources.

Aside from the resource contention issues, large-scale BI production processes are nontrivial. BI production processes require large-scale system integration among various computing assets. When one of the many IT jobs within the BI production process fails, something may have gone awry at many places. Although we have great diagnostic tools these days and BI processes themselves are mature, moving huge amounts of data every night during a short batch window is subject to process errors. Accordingly, the manufacturing paradigm we introduced earlier is certainly a propos. By continuously improving BI production processes, we can help ensure that BI fully supports the business strategy and achieving a competitive advantage.

In addition to the BI production process, the need exists for a robust support process that includes maintenance and administration of the BI tools and support to BI users who have encountered BI application errors or who need to know how to use the BI application. Both of these types of processes are mature and supported by cost-effective tools.

6.3.3 Business Intelligence Human Resources

In addition to configuring a BI environment that supports a successful BI program, attention also needs to be paid to the BI human resources that are needed to ensure success. Similar to the specialized IT assets that are needed to configure a successful environment, technical success also requires dedicated technical specialists who have general expertise in techniques that are needed to successfully design and implement the BI environment. In addition, specialized expertise in the selected tools and technologies is needed to ensure that the tools are installed, configured, and used as intended. Too often, BI is considered "another IT application" that can be handled by IT staff trained to design and build transaction systems. The need for specialized

Pitfall

Many companies fail to recognize the need for dedicated technical human resources that can focus on designing, building, and maintaining a large, and often highly complex, BI technical environment. Commonly, IT staff are asked to develop and support both transaction and BI environments. Inadequate technical human resources also adds a level of technical risk.

expertise, trained to design and build these frequently large and highly complex environments, is not appreciated. In addition, the need to train technical staff in the specific tools and technologies that will be used to support the BI environment is not appreciated. It is common that IT staff is spread too thin, assigned to build and support both transaction systems and BI systems. This often results in a different type of technical risk.

6.3.4 Summary: Business Intelligence Operations in the Information Technology Operational Environment

From a general management perspective, we must be concerned that the BI-driven profit improvement program is supported by an appropriate IT environment, IT operating policies, and specialized skills. This is harder than it seems because cultural differences exist within IT between the transactional systems and enterprise applications world and the BI world. Further, IT asset-optimization and cost-minimization policies, often driven by chief financial officers (CFOs), complicate the BI operation in ways that may not end up being supportive of the BI-driven profit improvement program.

Absent a strong CIO who "gets" BI and can drive for appropriate IT support for BI, the valid claims of both sides of the IT camp must be sorted out by general managers, many of whom are not IT savvy. What we've seen in these circumstances is that when the clamor for BI gets strong enough from senior leaders with profit center or cost-center responsibilities, the clout that the BI camp has increases and IT operating policies and asset decisions move toward greater enablement of world-class BI operations. Given the relatively low cost of a world-class BI environment and given the profit impact of BI, we believe companies would be well served to seriously evaluate establishing dedicated BI environments.

6.4 Summary: Business Intelligence in the Broader Information Technology Context

As we noted in Chapter 5, BI is but one management tool that can be used for profit improvement. Further, within IT, BI is one of many competing uses for scarce capital. Despite well-documented BI-driven profit improvement results by well-known companies in a variety of industries, we believe that BI continues to be underfunded within the IT portfolio. That is unfortunate because world-class BI capabilities with substantial profit impacts can be obtained for a fraction of what major companies have spent on ERP and other enterprise applications that have automated backroom activities but failed to impact the bottom line as promised. Looking ahead, the increased interest in BI that we see in the business community these days may be a harbinger of broader recognition of the profit potential of BI. With that recognition comes the general management task of ensuring that BI has its appropriate share of the management and IT resources required to turn BI into a competitive weapon.

6.5   Key Points to Remember

- BI-driven profit improvement requires an appropriate share of the IT budget.
- Using BI to improve profits poses specific leadership and general management challenges to ensure that BI has appropriate support within the broader IT operating environment.
- Using BI to improve profits requires investment in suitable BI people, processes, and technology.
- BI is underfunded in relation to its profit potential.

6.6   Think Tank

6.6.1   Seven Questions to Ask About How Business Intelligence Fits in Your Company's Information Technology Portfolio

1. Are IT investments managed as a portfolio at your company? If so, where does BI fit?
2. Are there well-known BI success stories from companies in your industry? If so, have your CIO, CFO, and chief executive office (CEO) heard about them?
3. Is your CIO a former data center manager? If so—or if not—do you think that affects how BI is viewed?
4. Does your CIO have the power and credibility to push BI operational requirements into the IT environment?
5. Do business leaders at your company understand the profit potential of BI?
6. On a scale of 1 to 10, how strong is demand for BI among your company's business leaders?
7. Do you see the possibility that effective BI use could lead to competitive advantage in your industry?

6.6.2   Quiz: Where Does Business Intelligence Stand in Your Company's Information Technology Environment?

1. Does your BI program operate with a dedicated BI environment or a mixed-use BI environment?
2. Assuming a mixed-use BI environment, is the BI development process suitable for rapid effective delivery of data warehouse increments and BI applications?
3. Assuming a mixed-use BI environment, are the BI production processes suitable for reliably delivering high-quality business information?
4. Assuming a mixed-use BI environment, can BI developers readily create tables in the development environment?

5. Assuming a mixed-use BI environment, do the lead time and processing time for validation and integration testing exceed three months?

6. Assuming a mixed-use BI environment, do the IT managers who control the IT environment understand what is needed for optimized BI operations?

7. Assuming a mixed-use BI environment, do the IT managers who control the IT environment have any interest in and/or incentives for advancing the proficiency of BI operations?

Chapter 7

Important Ways Business Intelligence Can Drive Profit Improvement

"The real competitive problem is laggards versus challengers, incumbents versus innovators, the inertial and imitative versus the imaginative. . . . At worst, laggards follow the path of greatest familiarity. Challengers, on the other hand, follow the path of greatest opportunity, wherever it leads."
—Gary Hamel and C.K. Prahalad, *Competing for the Future*

Before writing this book, we received feedback on the outline from respected peers in the business intelligence (BI) field. One reviewer offered an important challenge to us: Would it be possible for this book, or any book, to "generalize how to do BI when treatments for various industries may be so different"?

Another reviewer felt it would be useful if we could "treat some or a variety of specific industries in the book." We agree that these are important topics, and our short response is that we absolutely can generalize a systematic approach to analyzing and designing customized BI for a given company that operates in a given industry or in multiple industries. Furthermore, experience suggests that the *application* of BI by a given company is a potential source of competitive advantage and should be specific to the company, its industry or industries, and the manner in which it competes in the industry or industries. This ability to apply a standardized design approach to develop customized BI applications is exactly what we mean by "business-centric BI development methods," which our clients in a variety of industries have successfully applied. We will elaborate on this important subject in the first section of this chapter.

More broadly, and building on the quote above, we feel that companies need to decide whether they want to be innovative and imaginative in their use of BI or whether they can safely be content as followers, fast or otherwise. The innovator path requires greater investment, focus, and risk-taking, with the potential for greater profits. The follower path does not have the same upside profit potential, but it may be less risky. Furthermore, in more and more industries it will become necessary to deploy BI capabilities to neutralize the competitive advantages achieved by the innovators.

Evidence suggests that BI innovators are in most industries these days, and that they are well down the road in how they use BI to improve profits. Both in our role as judges for annual BI and DW best practices competitions sponsored by The Data Warehousing Institute and in our consulting practice, we see innovators in a range of service and manufacturing industries. For followers, then, the task is either to identify new ways to innovate with BI or to identify and implement BI capabilities that are strategically relevant for their organizations.

The good news is that a lot more is known about the business and technical aspects of BI than was known a decade ago. Thus, it is possible to proceed more cost-effectively and with less risk if companies are willing to learn from others' experience. Also, many published cases describe ways that BI has been successfully applied, and the later sections of this chapter will describe some of these BI applications. Our hope is that these examples will help you get a feel for where your company may stand in relation to competitors or other innovators.

7.1 The Impact of Industry, Competitors, and Company Business Design on Business Intelligence Opportunities

The North American Industry Classification System (NAICS) is an industry classification system that groups businesses into industries based on the economic activities in which they are primarily engaged (National Technical Information Service. NAICS, 1998). It is a comprehensive system covering the entire field of economic activities, producing and nonproducing. There are 20 sectors, 96 subsectors, and 1,170 industries in NAICS United States, and companies are grouped within these according to the similarity of the processes used to produce goods or services. For example, food manufacturing is a batch-oriented process manufacturing operation in which various ingredients are blended and converted into finished products. Food manufacturing is very different from other industries such as making fabricated metal products, which is a batch-oriented, discrete manufacturing operation with different parts requiring different operations performed by computer-controlled machine tools.

Because of the differences in production processes across industries and sectors, companies that operate in different industries tend to develop different vocabularies around the core operational processes of the business. For example, although food manufacturers talk of recipes and conversion processes, metal products manufacturers talk of bills of material and machining operations. Different production processes also cause industries to develop different performance measures, such as revenue or cost per ton-mile in the shipping industry or revenue per available room (revpar) in the hotel industry.

In addition to industry differences arising from fundamentally different production processes, industries also vary (Porter, 1980) with respect to the following:

- Economies of scale
- Degree of product differentiation
- Capital requirements
- Switching costs

- Access to distribution channels
- Potential cost advantages independent of scale
- Degree and intensity of competition
- Growth rates
- Threat of substitutes
- Bargaining power of buyers
- Bargaining power of suppliers
- Maturity
- Degree of concentration or fragmentation
- Degree of and potential for globalization
- Feasible strategies and competitive positions within industries

These differences between industries impact what BI information is relevant within a given industry and for a given competitor at a given time, thus raising the question posed earlier: Can we usefully generalize about "how to do BI when treatments for various industries may be so different"? These differences suggest a broader strategic line of inquiry that considers the impact of industry, competition within the industry, and a given company's business design on the BI opportunities for a given company within a given industry. In our view, looking at industry alone is too static because there are different ways of competing within the same industry. Those methods of competition can change over time as industries themselves evolve and mature and as their customers' needs evolve.

For example, Michael Porter (1980) advances the view that there are three generic competitive strategies: cost leadership, differentiation, and niche focus. Although written some time ago, his observation still holds true. He points out that "each of the generic strategies involves a fundamentally different route to competitive advantage" and that the "specific actions required to implement each generic strategy vary widely from industry to industry, as do the feasible generic strategies in a particular industry" (Porter, 1985). Porter further asserts that competitive advantage "stems from the many discrete activities a firm performs in designing, producing, marketing, delivering, and supporting its product" (Porter, 1985). By using the value chain construct, Porter then leads us to understand that there are many different combinations and permutations of ways that firms and entire value chains (now called supply chains) compete, pointing out that value chain activities such as logistics, operations, marketing, and procurement, among others, are "the building blocks by which a firm creates a product valuable to its buyers" and that "any activity in the value chain can potentially contribute to differentiation" (Porter, 1985).

Porter's seminal thinking about strategy and industrial economics has spawned elaborations, variations, and applications of his ideas that further suggest the need to customize BI for a given company competing in a given way within a given industry. Recognizing that industries are dynamic and their futures can be shaped, Gary Hamel and

Tip

What stays the same are the general principles of successful BI and management for results. What changes are the industry drivers of each organization, its BI readiness, its strategic needs, and thus the way in which you need to implement BI in that organization.

C.K. Prahalad (1994) argue that "companies not only compete within the boundaries of existing industries, they compete to *shape the structure* create differentiation and competitive advantage, as the company Owens & Minor has done in the medical products distribution industry. It uses a BI system called WISDOM (Web Intelligence Supporting Decisions from Owens & Minor) both to provide decision support information to its managers and employees and to help manage its supply chain.

As industries evolve, competitive positioning and the means of competing also evolve. Richard D'Aveni (1994) points out that "the most important aspect of competition is not current position, but the changes created by the dynamic interaction between rival firms" and that "cycles of change are growing progressively shorter. Although it may be difficult to generalize about how short change cycles are, because cycle duration varies by industry, there is little doubt that what customers value changes over time, and thus the ways companies compete must also change. Adrian Slywotsky (1996) talks in terms of "value migration" and the evolution of "business designs," where value migration occurs because customers' most important needs change. To meet those changing needs, companies' business designs must change. Customers give their business to the companies whose business designs best meets their needs, thus creating value migration from obsolete business designs to more effective business designs.

The concept of a business design is of particular importance for BI purposes. Slywotsky defines the business design as "the totality of how a company selects its customers, defines and differentiates its offerings, defines the tasks it will perform itself and which it will outsource, configures its resources, goes to market, creates utility for customers, and captures profit." To illustrate, let us consider Wal-Mart, whose business design is summarized in Table 7-1.

For many of the elements of business design, Wal-Mart could have made different choices. For example, it could have chosen to compete on service, as does Nordstrom, or it could have concentrated on consumer electronics, as does Best Buy. For any given company, the choice of business design dictates the performance objectives of core business processes and the elements of business performance that are important to plan, measure, control, and improve. To continue with the Wal-Mart example, its business design dictates that it be concerned with core business processes such as demand planning, forecasting, purchasing, supply chain management, category management, and cost management. That focus drives BI opportunities such as those shown in Figure 7-1.

In other words, the choice of business design suggests areas of analysis for determining the specific BI opportunities that are strategically and operationally relevant for a given company. Given that business designs vary by company and industry, we certainly cannot say a priori how a company in a specific industry should use BI. That being said, we can generalize that *for any given company in any given industry, we should systematically evaluate its industry, strategy, and business design as a means of identifying potential BI opportunities*. This is the essence of business-centric BI development methods such as the BI Pathway.

Table 7-1

Sample subjects and techniques for business analysis

Design Element	Value
Business focus	Retailing of a broad range of consumer products
Target customers	Cost-conscious shoppers
Competitive strategy	Cost leadership
Key points of differentiation	"Everyday low prices"; breadth of merchandise
Value disciplines	Supply chain logistics, information technology, merchandising, category management
Business scope	Some backward integration into logistics; no manufacturing
Value capture	Cost leadership allows gross margin maintenance despite low prices; low prices allow market share capture and incremental margin; expansion via new stores allows capture of incremental margin
Purchasing	Use market share clout to drive down manufacturers prices and push supply chain costs back upstream
Operating systems	Leverage information technology and strong socialization of work force to hold down costs, excel at category management, and excel at supply chain and logistics
Capital intensity	Build and own big-box stores on land purchased in suburban and urban areas; invest in internal information technology (IT) and IT capabilities (versus outsourcing); invest in logistics capabilities

Tip

The industry drivers faced by your organization partly determine its business design. In turn, your organization's business design, mission, and strategic goals determine its BI needs. If you can draw a clear logical connection backwards from your BI design to your business design and from there to your industry drivers, you've probably done a good analysis of your BI needs.

More broadly, we have tried to establish that industries are dynamic, that the ways that companies compete within industries and industry segments are variable and dynamic, and that business designs are variable and dynamic. All those facts point to the conclusion that the way a given company uses BI ought to be customized to its specific circumstances. That said, industrial economics is industrial economics, and all industries have customers and all companies use inputs and processes to deliver products or services to meet the needs of those customers. Further, the functions within businesses are common, for example, research and development (R&D) or service line development, operations, marketing, sales, finance, human resources, and administration. So although the permutations and combinations of value chain activities are many and although the bases of competition are different within different industries at different stages of industry maturity, it is fair to say that the building blocks with which a given business design is built are common piece

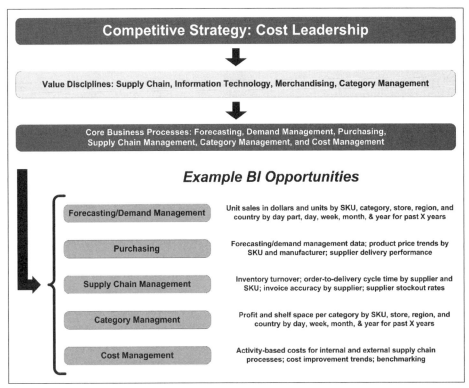

FIGURE 7-1 The connection of business design, business processes, and business intelligence opportunities.

parts. Accordingly, *what we look at in determining the appropriate BI investments for a given company is the same, even though the optimal BI portfolio for a given company in a given industry will certainly vary.* We described an approach for this BI opportunity analysis in Chapter 2, and we elaborated on the subject in Chapter 4.

We talked earlier about companies needing to decide whether they want to be innovative and imaginative in their use of BI or whether they can safely be content as followers, fast or otherwise. For either path, it helps to understand the state of the art, either as a means of stimulating thinking about how to innovate or as a means of understanding the path to follow. Toward that end, the remainder of this chapter will describe important ways that BI can be used to drive profit improvement, starting with a general overview.

7.2 A General Overview of Business Intelligence Opportunities

If we think of BI as business information and business analysis in support of fact-based decisions in the context of business processes that impact profits, it quickly becomes clear that BI is a broad concept. The nature of business information varies along a number of dimensions, including

- Whether the business information is about current business transactions and status or about transactions that occurred and were closed out in prior months or years
- Whether the business information is about the enterprise as a whole or about subunits of the organization such as strategic business units or functional departments
- Whether the information is about the company or about other entities in the value chain, such as customers and suppliers
- Whether the business information is generated by a company's internal information systems or whether it is obtained from external sources such as market research firms
- Whether the business information is used for management processes, revenue-generating processes, or operating processes
- Whether the business information is detailed transactional information or summarized information about many transactions
- Whether the business information is intended to be directly accessed by end users or whether it exists as input to simulations and models
- Whether the business information is intended for power users, general users, or executives
- Whether the business information is intended for broad distribution or for more limited role-based use
- Whether the business information must be retained for legal or regulatory compliance purposes

In addition to the wide range of types of business analyses, a broad range of business analysis techniques may be used alone or in combination with each other to support business analysis. The appropriateness of these techniques vary, based on the subject of analysis, for example, data mining techniques applied to risk analysis in contrast to trend analysis applied to sales performance analysis. Table 7-2 shows a sample list of analytical subjects and techniques.

As the above lists suggest, there are many different possible combinations of types of business information and business analyses. Selecting the relevant business information and analyses is a function of the kinds of business decisions that must be supported by BI, which in turn is a function of the type of business process within which the BI will be deployed. Business decisions are generally classified as strategic, tactical, and operational, although in practice the distinctions can be blurred. These classifications tend to imply differences in

- The importance of the decision, with strategic decisions accorded greater importance
- The frequency or useful life of the decision, with strategic decisions having a life of several years or more and operational decisions being more frequent and shorter lived (e.g., what products and amounts will we produce this month)
- The scope of the decision, with strategic decisions being associated with enterprise scope, tactical decisions being associated with departmental or functional scope, and operational decisions being associated with day-to-day business activities

Table 7-2

Sample subjects and techniques for business analysis

Analytical Subjects	Analytical Techniques	
Customer analysis	Aging	Modeling
Productivity analysis	Alerters	Optimization
Quality analysis	Benchmarking	Performance measures and metrics
Risk analysis (fraud detection, loss analysis, litigation)	Data mining	Probability analysis
Inventory analysis	Decision trees and expected monetary value	Simulation
Financial analysis (revenue, profit, cost, accounts receivable)	Decomposition	Statistical inference
Channel analysis	Descriptive statistics	Summarization
Supply chain analysis	Forecasting	Time series analysis
Sales analysis	Linear programming	Trend analysis
	Linear regression	Variance analysis
	Mixed integer programming	

Business decisions also take place in the context of business processes, such as management processes, revenue-generating processes, and operating processes. Depending on the process and whether the decisions to be made are strategic, tactical, or operational, different combinations of business information and business analyses will be appropriate. The general relationship between business decisions and business processes is shown in Figure 7-2.

At the core of Figure 7-2 is a highly simplified representation of value chain business processes, that is, supply chain processes, operating processes, customer relationship processes, management processes, intra-company processes, and support processes. In the context of these value chain processes, companies make a variety of decisions, shown in the arrows surrounding the core business processes. To illustrate, manufacturing companies make long-term strategic decisions about supply chain and operational processes, such as the number and location of plants and distribution centers and investments in information technology (IT) to enable planning and operational collaboration with suppliers. For a service company such as a bank, the long-term strategic decisions about supply chain and operational processes might address the question of whether to outsource check-clearing processes. In general, value chains differ by industry and product, and companies occupy different positions in those value chains. That said, the value chain construct is very useful for stimulating thinking about BI opportunities.

Faced with the many combinations and permutations of business information, business analyses, and fact-based decisions that BI can deliver or support, we need a general framework that delineates the major types of BI opportunities that can be

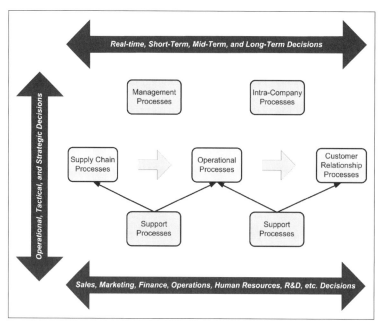

FIGURE 7-2 The relation between business decisions and business processes.

considered for inclusion in a given company's BI portfolio. With such a framework, we can further stimulate our thinking about potential BI opportunities as we conduct the BI opportunity analysis using the techniques described in Chapter 2. Table 7-3 presents some of the major types of BI opportunities on which companies in a variety of industries are capitalizing.

What we see in Table 7-3 is that BI opportunities can be segmented into three major business process categories: management processes, revenue generation processes, and operating processes. Within these major business process categories, proven BI opportunities are aligned with key business subprocesses, such as fore-casting, customer segmentation, and order processing. Although the exact way that a given company competing with a certain business design in a specific industry might design its BI applications will vary, the typical BI opportunities shown in Table 7-3 cut across industries. Furthermore, although the business vocabulary of industries might vary, the need for management processes, revenue-generating processes, and operating processes is a constant. Accordingly, we believe that the typical BI opportunities shown in Table 7-3 are a useful place to start when determining the specific BI opportunities your company should pursue.

7.3 Business Intelligence for Management Processes

Building on the information presented in Table 7-3, we see that BI is commonly used to improve basic management processes—be they strategic, tactical, or operational

Table 7-3

Major types of business intelligence (BI) opportunities and their relation to categories of business processes

Major Types of BI Opportunities	BI for Management Processes	BI for Revenue Generation Processes	BI for Operating Processes
Definition	Business processes aimed at managing the enterprise and/or its components	Business processes aimed at generating revenue for the enterprise	Business processes aimed at delivering the products and/or services of the enterprise to customers and day-to-day supporting business operations
Typical BI opportunities	Planning, forecasting, budgeting, performance management, controlling, process, improvement, quality management, cost analysis, optimization	Marketing analysis, customer segmentation, direct marketing, advertising, channel management, customer relationship management, category management, product or service development	Cycle time reduction, risk reduction, quality improvement, service level improvement, asset reduction, purchasing, order processing, benchmarking, process improvement
Scope	Enterprise and its functions/subunits, e.g., strategic business units, departments, cost centers, profit centers, revenue centers	Sales and marketing	Everything but sales and marketing
General objective(s)	Ensure long-term success and profitability of the enterprise; ensure alignment of enterprise functions/subunits with enterprise objectives	Generate profitable, appropriate revenue and revenue growth; develop products or services valued by target customers	Optimize costs, asset utilization, service levels, and quality in relation to the prices target customers are willing to pay for products and services
Typical decision scope BI supports	Strategic, tactical, and operational	Strategic, tactical, and operational	Strategic, tactical, and operational
Typical analytical subjects	Financial analysis, quality analysis	Channel analysis, customer analysis, sales analysis	Inventory analysis, productivity analysis, quality analysis, risk analysis, supply chain analysis

(Continued)

Table 7-3

Major types of business intelligence (BI) opportunities and their relation to categories of business processes—Cont'd

Major Types of BI Opportunities	BI for Management Processes	BI for Revenue Generation Processes	BI for Operating Processes
Typical analytical techniques	Aging, alerters (out of range detection), benchmarking, data mining, decision trees and expected monetary value, decomposition, descriptive statistics, forecasting, linear programming, linear regression, mixed integer programming, modeling, optimization, performance measures and metrics, probability analysis, simulation, statistical inference, summarization, time series analysis, trend analysis, and variance analysis		
Time focus of business information	Largely interested in business information about past transactions to plan and control future performance; also interested in information about current status, particularly as the BI application gets closer to daily operations	Interested in business information about current transactions and status for managing day-to-day revenue generation activities; interested in historical information for, e.g., forecasting sales, calculating customer lifetime value, or developing direct marketing offers	Interested in business information about current transactions and status for, e.g., managing order processing, supply chain execution, and customer service; interested in historical information for, e.g., business process improvement, optimization, and quality assurance

in orientation. The business information and business analyses used for fact-based decision making range from information about the current status of the enterprise or its subunits, to historical information about past business performance that can be used to predict future demand and guide process and quality improvement efforts. Overall, the goal of the entire set of management processes is to ensure the long-term success of the company, and BI has a proven track record of helping companies make better decisions toward that end. To illustrate this point, we will provide high-level descriptions and/or brief examples of some common ways that BI is used to improve management processes. We will describe two such uses in depth: balanced scorecards and management accounting.

7.3.1   Common Ways Business Intelligence Is Used to Improve Management Processes

Management processes are the core of any business. To the extent that BI improves those processes, it improves the efficiency of the business and the accuracy of the management decisions that drive it. BI typically can improve management processes in several areas, among others:

- **Planning and forecasting.** Generally speaking, planning is a future-oriented endeavor that often relies on business information about what has happened in the past. A common example comes from manufacturing companies, which have to make production plans and schedules to govern their supply chain and operations activities. Typically, those schedules are planned for a rolling 18-month period within which the first six months are planned in much more detail than are later months. A key input to such plans is business information about product sales in the past, typically for one to three years depending on the nature of the business. By knowing such historical information as unit sales and dollar sales by plant, by month, by product or product family, by customer, and by channel, a manufacturer can develop forecasts about future demand. Such forecasts are often augmented by collaboration with downstream supply chain partners. For example, the exemplar of this is the supply chain collaboration between Wal-Mart and Proctor and Gamble (P&G), whereby P&G stations people at Wal-Mart headquarters to ensure that it understands Wal-Mart's plans for opening new stores and for promotions. The combination of BI that delivers information about historical demand and detailed information about future events that will impact demand allows P&G to develop optimal production and supply chain plans, which in turn help optimize costs and gross margin.

- **Budgeting.** Similar to planning, budgeting is a future-oriented endeavor that often relies on business information about what has happened in the past. As with production planning, budgeting at the enterprise level generally starts with a forecast of the level of business activity, typically expressed in units and dollars. That forecast is often augmented to take account of revenue growth goals, known business events such as acquisitions and/or divestitures, known incremental business, and so forth. From a BI perspective, budgeting requires historical information about prior sales and prior expenses as a starting point for forecasting future sales and expenses. On the expense side, many companies are moving to activity-based costing/management (ABC/M) as a means of better matching demand with capacity and thereby optimizing expenses in relation to a forecast level of business activity. ABC/M requires an ability to relate expenses and outputs at the business activity level. Thus, historical information about, for example, departmental expense and output trends in relation to sales activity, is essential for calculating activity-based costs to use in budgeting. On a more traditional basis, historical expenses by chart of account code can be related to activity levels and used as inputs to project future expenses, subject to the need to distinguish between fixed costs and variable costs.

- **Performance management, process improvement, quality management, and performance optimization.** These and related management processes share the common requirements of (1) being able to measure performance along relevant dimensions, such as cost, quality, or relation to plan; (2) assessing the current state to understand whether performance is on target; and (3) being able to judge the efficacy of improvement activities and to assess progress toward a desired state.

Generally, these requirements drive a need for both current information and historical information, in which current information is used to understand the current-state performance and historical information is used to assess trends and provide inputs for establishing performance targets based on past performance. Further, in large companies there is generally a need to evaluate multiple dimensions of performance at multiple levels in the enterprise, as well as for the enterprise as a whole. From a BI perspective, many organizations have difficulty bringing together (integrating) all the business information they need for performance management, process improvement, quality management, and/or performance optimization. For that reason, they also have difficulty deploying appropriate analytical techniques because such techniques require appropriate business information. For example, statistical process control requires information on historical process performance in order to establish the upper and lower bounds of acceptable performance variation. As another example, companies often desire a comprehensive, multidimensional assessment of the performance of their organizational units, whereas the business information about all the relevant dimensions of performance is often found in multiple transactional IT systems. BI is designed to bring relevant business information together with appropriate analytical techniques to enable fact-based decisions that improve business performance, and ultimately profits.

> **Tip**
>
> Note that in each of the bullet list's examples, organizations adapted their BI implementations to their specific industry drivers and business design. Although there are good general-purpose BI tools, methods, and technologies, no rigid "one size fits all" approach is likely to succeed. If a particular tool, method, or technology is too difficult to adapt to your organization's situation, you should probably try something else.

7.3.2 Business Intelligence and Balanced Scorecards: Enabling Strategic Management

Over the past decade, business performance management (BPM) frameworks such as the Balanced Scorecard (see http://www.bscol.com) have been adopted by a growing number of major organizations. A 1999 Bain & Company survey of adoption of management tools revealed that almost 44% of firms in the survey used the Balanced Scorecard, and that the mean satisfaction rating among users was 3.85, with 5 being the highest rating (Rigby, 2001). Although a number of other management tools had higher adoption rates and higher satisfaction rates, the data suggest that BPM frameworks such as the Balanced Scorecard may become a staple within large organizations.

The business requirement for BPM frameworks stems from the fundamental limitation of "managing by the numbers." Executives have long known that managing by the numbers, instead of managing the business processes that drive the numbers, ignores the root causes of business performance and often leads to gaming. To overcome this, performance management frameworks have been expanded to incorporate *nonfinancial performance measurements.* Examples include capacity utilization percentages, customer satisfaction ratings, cycle times, units of output, and cases handled, to name but a few of the thousands of different nonfinancial performance measures.

The need for BPM frameworks manifests itself at all levels and across all functions of an organization. Many executives now recognize the need to manage business performance strategically, to understand the key linkages between strategy and the business processes undertaken to execute strategy, and to measure the performance of those business processes. This need for strategic performance management tools has been the impetus for the Balanced Scorecard and other BPM tools. At the same time, functional managers and middle managers need performance management tools appropriate to the business processes they manage, which hopefully are aligned with the business strategy. This need has given rise to different strategies for using Balanced Scorecards. These range from the traditional top-down approach with supporting scorecards "cascaded" down from corporate, to bottom-up approaches in which business units devise scorecards that are meaningful for their purposes and there is no aggregated view of the whole company owing to local differences in measures.

Recognizing these broad needs for scorecard frameworks and tools, BI software vendors have developed packaged performance management offerings that are certified by the Balanced Scorecard Collaborative to meet Balanced Scorecard functional standards. Those standards are defined in the Balanced Scorecard Functional Release Standards Release 1.0a published in May 2000 by The Balanced Scorecard Collaborative. As of June 2004, there were 19 vendors with certified products, including all of the leading BI and ERP vendors. Balanced Scorecards are essentially analytical applications that map/model, accumulate, display, and report multidimensional performance information, including financial and nonfinancial performance targets, actual performance measures, variance and trend analyses, and associated meta-data. Given these functions, traditional BI tools are ideally suited to the task of automating the data collection, aggregation, and presentation tasks associated with using the Balanced Scorecard as a performance management framework.

To develop a Balanced Scorecard, one typically does a top-down mapping between business drivers, business strategies, and value-driving business processes. One then selects financial and nonfinancial performance measures for those value-driving processes, with the measures drawn from four perspectives: financial performance, performance for the customer, internal operating performance, and learning. So, for example, if a business competes on price, its Balanced Scorecard might include the following performance measures:

- Financial perspective: operating margin dollars and percentages
- Internal perspective: unit cost, capacity utilization
- Customer perspective: order-to-delivery cycle time, percentage perfect orders
- Learning perspective: certified customer service reps numbers and percentages

These financial and nonfinancial measures may be specific to the Balanced Scorecard initiative. More likely, some or all of these measures may be used within other BI applications, such as customer analytics, where measures such order-to-delivery cycle time are standard fare. In order to avoid stovepiping and to achieve the so-called "single view of the truth," we must ensure that the data used by the Balanced Score-card is consistent with the data used by other BI applications that use the same measures. This means that the Balanced Scorecard and other BPM approaches should be managed as part of the overall BI Portfolio.

One of the key assumptions in almost all of the books, articles, and other literature about the Balanced Scorecard is that the performance measurement data required for using the performance management framework is readily available. Based on our experience with major private sector and public sector organizations, and based on BI and data warehousing experience generally, we believe this is really a huge leap of faith. In fact, in a 2001 survey by International Data Corp. (IDC) and the Balanced Scorecard Collaborative, survey respondents from a broad range of industries stated that complex data sourcing remains the single biggest challenge to automating Balanced Scorecards, followed by the unavailability of needed source data (Morris, 2002). Fortunately, a well-architected business-centric BI environment can overcome the complex data sourcing issues. Within this approach, a Balanced Scorecard initiative is just one application in the portfolio, albeit a strategically important one.

> **Tip**
>
> The strength of using a Balanced Scorecard approach with BI tools is that it lets you connect strategic business drivers, goals, and performance with your specific informational needs. One challenge of using a Balanced Scorecard approach is that required performance measurement data is often not readily available; although if you plan and implement your BI program creatively, you can usually get the data you need.

7.3.3 Business Intelligence and Management Accounting: Improving Operational and Financial Performance

As Johnson and Kaplan (1987) elegantly describe in *Relevance Lost*, managerial accounting evolved in the early days of the industrial revolution as a tool for measuring and managing resource consumption, outputs, and productivity at the operational level of the firm. Early management accounting systems were devised by industrial engineers, and the business information these systems provided was essential for managing operational and financial performance.

The principal type of information provided by early management accounting systems was *standard cost* information, which was used for planning and controlling the productivity and efficiency of internal processes. Other key attributes of early managerial accounting systems were that (1) they were devised to provide the kind of information required to manage operations in the specific industry in which the firm operated; and (2) they combined financial and nonfinancial information.

An example used by Johnson and Kaplan to illustrate this was drawn from the railroad freight shipping industry, where a basic productivity measure was *cost per ton-mile*. Cost per ton-mile could be compared with revenue per ton-mile to calculate contribution margin, from which period costs and other indirect costs could be subtracted to determine how the business was doing overall. Furthermore, this information could be used by operations managers to plan, control, and improve efficiency. The combination of financial information and nonfinancial information that was specific to the industry, and type of operation was directly relevant to the operations management task of optimizing cost, time, asset utilization, and service.

Today, most observers agree that management accounting information derived largely from modern financial accounting systems is obsolete. A review of the management accounting literature finds this theme time and again: see, for example, Cokins (2001), Kaplan (1988), and Cooper and Kaplan (1991). Our discussions with operating managers in a variety of industries reinforce this finding. For example, during the course of our work with a $7 billion service organization to modernize and increase the relevance of its management accounting system, we conducted dozens of interviews at all levels of the organization, and we identified the need for the following:

- Information about the direct costs of delivering each of the different types of services offered to customers
- Cost information that is specific to each of the 1,500 field offices, as opposed to average cost information derived from aggregated financial accounting data
- Cost-to-serve information that allowed for cost comparisons by service delivery channel, that is, teleservice center channel, Internet channel, and field office channel
- Activity-based costs for assigning the costs of indirect activities based on the true resource consumption characteristics of the service lines that benefit from the indirect activities
- Cost-to-serve information that allowed for comparison by type of customer
- Full cost information for budgeting and pricing purposes
- Relevant cost information for process improvement and capital budgeting uses

As with many organizations, the current system of allocating expenses found in the general ledger (G/L) system down to service lines, channels, customers, and so forth generates cost accounting information in which the organization's managers have no confidence. And yet the managers use that information because they have nothing better.

In addition to lacking cost information, the organization also lacks the information to systematically, consistently, and routinely perform fundamental operations management tradeoffs between asset levels, costs, process times, quality, service, outputs, and backlogs. In other words, the organization, similar to many organizations, does not have an integrated set of facts about organizational performance from which it can model, project, and analyze resource consumption under various customer-driven operating scenarios.

The commonly found deficiencies in cost information and the lack of integrated information about the other key operating variables of interest point to the need for expanded functionality for managerial accounting systems and for an expanded role for BI. To illustrate the differences between where we are and where BI can take us, we first examine traditional managerial accounting systems and the management tasks they support, as shown in Figure 7-3.

Figure 7-3 shows a representative managerial accounting framework, which we would note is concerned only with costs and not with the broader set of financial and

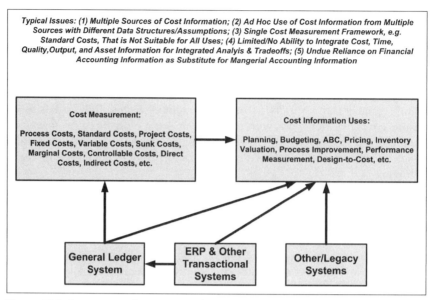

Typical Issues: (1) Multiple Sources of Cost Information; (2) Ad Hoc Use of Cost Information from Multiple Sources with Different Data Structures/Assumptions; (3) Single Cost Measurement Framework, e.g. Standard Costs, That is Not Suitable for All Uses; (4) Limited/No Ability to Integrate Cost, Time, Quality,Output, and Asset Information for Integrated Analyis & Tradeoffs; (5) Undue Reliance on Financial Accounting Information as Substitute for Mangerial Accounting Information

FIGURE 7-3 A representative managerial accounting framework.

nonfinancial information found in early managerial accounting systems and much needed today. The graphic shows the commonly used distinction between cost measurement and cost information uses. For cost measurement, the typical approach is to draw information from the G/L system and allocate it into a cost accounting model, which might be a standard cost model, a project cost model, or a process cost model, depending on the nature of the business. The costs thus allocated are then reported out on a period-by-period basis during the accounting year, with the reported information being aggregated or disaggregated according to a selected taxonomy of cost objects, such as organizational units, product lines, customers, geographic regions, sales territories, or other objects of management responsibility and attention. The reported costs can then serve as raw materials for various cost information uses, such as planning, budgeting, and performance measurement, as shown in the right-hand box near the top of the graphic. Figure 7-3 also shows some of the commonly encountered issues associated with traditional cost accounting systems, as reported in the literature and as we have encountered in practice. To move beyond these limitations, we need to provide a modern conceptual framework for managerial accounting information, such as the one shown in Figure 7-4.

The modern managerial accounting information framework (MAIF) encompasses a broader set of information than a traditional cost accounting framework, including information about costs but also information about assets, quality/service, time (e.g., cycle time or process time), and outputs. Further, the MAIF is built on a single integrated source of managerial accounting information, which for sake of discussion we have simplified and shown functionally as a BI environment. Properly designed and built from proven BI products, the MAIF can serve as a relatively inexpensive but robust source of managerial accounting information that can be used to

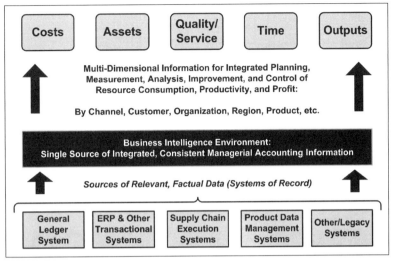

FIGURE 7-4 The modern managerial accounting information framework (MAIF).

1. Improve management processes, such as planning, budgeting, control, and performance improvement
2. Improve specific key business processes that impact revenues and/or costs, such as the "customer order to cash" processing cycle

The BI products from which the MAIF can be constructed are proven and widely adopted. So are the management and technical methods for doing so.

With a customized MAIF in place, an organization is then positioned to truly leverage managerial accounting information to improve revenues, reduce costs, or both. This can be accomplished by deploying BI applications and incorporating their use into the key management and business processes that drive revenues and/or costs. An example of the range of such applications is shown in Figure 7-5.

Here are some examples of how a MAIF based on BI technologies and methods can be used:

- Western Digital is a global manufacturer of computer hard disk drives with annual sales of more than $3 billion. Western Digital uses BI technologies to better manage its inventory, supply chains, product life cycles, and customer relationships. BI enabled Western Digital to reduce its operating costs by 50% from their previous levels, thereby enabling increased profit.
- Capital One, a global financial services firm with more than 50 million customer accounts, uses BI to analyze and improve the profitability of its product lines, as well as the effectiveness of its business processes and marketing programs.
- BankCo is one of the largest banks in the world. It has more than $500 billion in assets, more than 10 million individual customers, and more than 1 million business customers. BankCo uses BI technology to better understand the major drivers of the profitability of its loan business, for example, default risk, and to

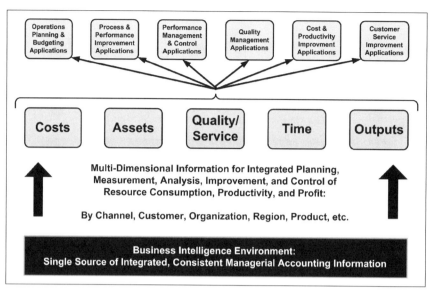

FIGURE 7-5 How the modern managerial accounting information framework (MAIF) can support resource management applications.

better segment its customers on the basis of lifetime value so that it can offer targeted, differentiated service levels and pricing.

- TransCo is a leading manufacturer. Its parts supply operation provides more than 4,000 authorized dealers with service parts. It has more than 2,000 suppliers, hundreds of thousands of parts, and more than 1 million stock keeping units (SKUs) in its North American distribution facilities. It uses BI technology to improve order fill rates (improve customer service) while reducing safety stock levels (improve asset utilization).

> **Tip**
>
> Modern managerial cost accounting is another area where BI can make a surprising contribution to an organization's effectiveness. One way to gain top management support is to show how BI can provide a far higher quantity *and quality* of managerial accounting information than can be obtained from current methods.

There are many other examples of how leading companies in a variety of industries are using enhanced managerial accounting information—delivered by BI tools—to drive improved profitability.

7.3.4 Summary: Business Intelligence for Management Processes

In this section, we have illustrated some of the typical ways that BI is used to improve key management processes. In addition to needing business information about the current status of the enterprise and/or its components, which typically comes from transactional IT systems, managers today need to understand the past so they can better influence performance in the future. This is particularly true of larger enterprises in which customers number in the millions, employees number in the tens or hundreds of thousands, multiple business units compete in different industries, and operations are multifaceted and multinational. Without BI, it is extremely difficult for managers to cope with the complexity of modern business. With BI, innovators in a variety of industries are shaping the future, establishing competitive advantage, and delivering strong profit growth.

7.4 Business Intelligence for Revenue-Generating Processes

Some of the earliest uses of BI were driven by the desire to improve revenue-generating processes. Simply put, companies wanted to understand their customers better, retain their best customers, and sell them more products or services. Achieving those goals can be relatively straightforward in some business-to-business contexts, for example, if a company has a couple dozen key customers that drive a large percentage of revenue. However, companies that have millions of customers and that annually process tens or hundreds of millions of business transactions with these customers often can't see the forest for the trees. Many such companies can't identify their most profitable customers, they don't know when profitable customers are about to defect, and they can only guess at what direct marketing offers will be most attractive to which customers.

To address these gaps in understanding customers, companies in such retail-oriented industries as consumer product retailing, telecommunications, and financial services were early adapters in using BI to sift through the data about the millions of customer transactions to better understand what drives revenue. By building on the information presented in Figure 7-3, we see that BI is commonly used to improve revenue-generating processes such as market analysis, customer segmentation, campaign management, advertising, channel management, customer relationship management (CRM), sales force management, and pipeline management. To illustrate this point, we will provide high-level descriptions and/or brief examples of some common ways BI is used to improve revenue-generating processes. Some of those ways are

- **Marketing analysis.** By marketing analysis, we mean the analytical activities in which companies engage in order to understand such revenue generation fundamentals as who buys their products or services, when they buy the products, where they buy the products, how often do they buy the products, what price do they pay, how do they respond to promotional offers, which products or services generate what percentages of revenues, what are the sales trends for each product or service, which products or services tend to be purchased together, and so forth.

For companies with millions of customers, perhaps thousands of points of sale, and perhaps multiple channels, such analyses clearly depend on access to relevant business information and appropriate analytical tools, that is, on access to BI. With a well-architected BI environment, marketing analysis can be done in near real-time to see current and long-term revenue trends and to understand the underlying drivers of revenue growth. With appropriate tools, data about hundreds of millions of individual transactions can be mined to answer the fundamental marketing questions posed above. Armed with better information, companies can be more effective in attracting new customers, retaining profitable customers, and achieving a sustainable revenue portfolio. Furthermore, they can understand the relationship between channels and profitability and introduce incentives for customers to use the more profitable channels. In general, experience in a range of industries has shown that one of the most profitable uses of BI is in better understanding the relationship among customers, products or services, and revenue generation.

- **Customer segmentation.** With the ability to sift through millions of detailed records about business transactions with customers, companies have gained the ability to substantially extend the practice of customer segmentation. In the past, most bases for customer (market) segmentation were so-called a priori bases; that is, they were based on information one could know about customers as a group and in many cases without having any insight into individual customer purchasing behavior. So, for example, *demographic segmentation* grouped customers by common characteristics such as age, income, occupation, and so forth, and *geographic segmentation* grouped customers by where they lived. In the business-to-business world, demographic segmentation grouped customers by such common characteristics as industry, role in the value chain, and revenues. Volvo Cars of North America uses these techniques to analyze and predict the behavior of its customers and sales prospects. Among other things, BI enables Volvo to prequalify prospects by predicting their probability of buying a Volvo even if they've never contacted the company or walked into a Volvo showroom.

Beginning in the late 1970s, *psychographic segmentation* sought to group customers by such potentially common characteristics as personality, leisure activities, and values. It became common to associate zip codes with psychographic profiles, with groups often labeled with catchy phrases as "pools and patios" or "shotguns and pickups." With all of these a priori bases of segmentation, the connection between association with the group and actual purchasing behavior was not clear. To overcome this gap, marketers began to investigate differences in customer behavior as the basis for segmentation, initially with focus groups and market pilots and, in the past decade, by using BI tools and techniques. Specifically, by mining data about millions of individual customer transactions and marrying such information with traditional demographic, geographic, and psychographic information, companies have been able to group customers by purchasing behavior and to understand the relationships, if any, between purchasing behavior and, for example, demographic variables and product characteristics. These BI tools do not replace traditional segmentation and market research tools: they simply provide powerful new tools that work well with existing tools to help companies define narrower customer segments, understand the needs and values of those segments, create products and services that better respond to those needs and values, and develop more selective and effective ways to reach and acquire new customers and/or expand business with current profitable customers.

- **Advertising, direct marketing, and public relations (PR).** BI-driven market analysis and customer segmentation provides a much richer understanding of customers and what they value as input for advertising, direct marketing, and PR campaigns, whether they are focused on product or service awareness, product education and positioning, brand building, countering rival campaigns, public image, or a call to purchase. Aside from effective presentation, advertising, direct marketing, and PR campaigns are about message, and BI provides an effective means of understanding the intended recipients of a given message. Further, BI can provide the ability to measure the effectiveness of advertising and direct marketing that is directed toward increased revenues. In some cases, this is done by observing changes to a product or product family's sales trend line after an advertising campaign has run. In other cases, the specific purchasing behavior of targeted individual consumers in response to a direct marketing campaign can be identified. For example, a hotel chain that sends a time-limited promotional offer to a specific known individual can determine from its reservation system or property management system if the individual accepted the offer. The power of such BI is substantial because it promotes both revenue increases, by targeting those who are most likely to accept an offer, and reduced costs, by narrowcasting the offer, which reduces campaign execution costs. Firms as different as Harrah's Entertainment, which runs casinos, and Capital One, which provides financial services, use BI to measure and improve the cost-effectiveness of their marketing and PR efforts.
- **Channel management.** The nature of channels varies by industry and position within the value chain. For product retailing and retail services, channels used to mean stores or branches and sometimes mail-order and/or telephone channels. Today, the Internet, ATMs, kiosks, and other point-of-sale mechanisms are also in the mix. For consumer product manufacturers, channels include both distribution channels (how the product gets to the store) and the different types of retail stores. For industrial product manufacturers, channels include direct sales and a variety of often industry specific distributors and wholesalers.

  Except for enterprises that are completely vertically integrated, a rarity in most industries these days, companies face strategic decisions about what channels to use and which partners to use within a given channel. They also face the task of evaluating channel and/or channel partner effectiveness over time. All of these channel management tasks can be made more effective through adoption of BI. For example, we talked earlier about using BI for marketing analysis, from which we gain insight into how much revenue comes from which channels; through which channels volume is increasing, decreasing, or holding steady; and how different products fare in different channels. If we can integrate that information with appropriate channel cost information, we can determine which channels are most cost-effective for us as a means to margin optimization. By use of BI, we can also assess channel partner performance. For example, suppose a company uses different distributors in different parts of the country. With appropriate BI tools and techniques, we can assess their relative performance in terms of revenue growth and customer service. All of these BI opportunities, and others not detailed here, can enable more effective channel selection and management, which supports more effective revenue generation and growth.

- **CRM.** CRM means different things to different people. To the vendors who coined the term, CRM is the packaged enterprise software they sell, which has both transactional and BI functionality relating to customers and to sales activities. For BI vendors, CRM means (among other things) prepackaged software applications for analyzing customer behavior and sales force performance. To companies that want to improve their revenue generation processes, CRM may have both a BI appeal and a transactional system appeal, and there is an associated idea of a centralized repository (database) of customer information that can be used for cross-selling and/or up-selling customers. Setting aside the potential of CRM to automate such transactional functions as campaign management, the BI appeal of CRM is basically that it helps companies better understand their customers (as discussed earlier under "Marketing Analysis" and under "Customer Segmentation"). In that sense, the technologies enable more effective marketing analysis and customer segmentation. If coupled with appropriate changes to marketing and sales business processes, those can lead to more effective revenue generation and revenue growth. Harrah's Entertainment and Continental Airlines are two outstanding examples of using BI to tune up customer service and relationships to a high pitch of excellence and profitability.

- **Category management.** With the consolidation in consumer product retailing that's been driven by Wal-Mart's successful competitive strategy, more and more retailers and consumer product manufacturers are using category management techniques to optimize revenue and margins. The fundamental principle of category management is that retailers want to optimize contribution margin per cubic foot of retail shelf space. Accomplishing this goal is a function of pushing inventory and shelf stocking costs onto suppliers, avoiding stockouts, and optimizing the allocation of shelf space to product categories based on understanding customers' purchasing habits and on knowing the revenue and gross margin characteristics of each product and product category. IT in general and BI in particular have dramatically advanced the state of the art in category management. By bringing point-of-sale data into a BI environment, retailers can understand product-level demand trends and how they vary by relevant dimensions such as geography and service area demographics. Further, they can track the revenue increase ("lift") associated with promotions, which can be more effectively targeted by using BI to analyze

> **Tip**
>
> A key strength of using a business-centric BI approach is that it explicitly connects the information BI delivers with the revenue-generating processes that pay back your BI investment. Because of that explicit connection, you get a clear picture of what kind of ROI your BI efforts generate.

customers' past purchasing behavior in response to promotions. The combination of multidimensional demand trend data and the ability to track the effectiveness of promotions allows retailers to have the right product mix on the shelves, to optimize shelf space allocation to product categories, and to optimize revenues and gross margin at the store level. Category management BI also can be used to optimize supply chain performance, which of course improves both margins and profits.

7.4.1 Summary: Business Intelligence for Revenue-Generating Processes

In this section, we have illustrated some of the typical ways that BI is used to improve key revenue generation processes. Fundamentally, these BI opportunities are about using detailed and specific business information about customers' past purchasing behavior to better understand their needs and preferences and, thereby, to become more effective at growing revenue and retaining profitable customers. Having such information is especially valuable for companies with millions of customers. It enables application of marketing concepts such as customer lifetime value analysis, needs-based segmentation, and collaborative filtering. Using BI to improve revenue generation processes is also important in business-to-business contexts because it allows companies to evaluate product sales trends in the aggregate, customer purchasing patterns in particular, product mix with specific customers, product sales by relevant dimensions such as geography and customer demographics, and customer profitability. In some distribution industries, having BI about product sales to end customers has enabled the distributors to offer BI to upstream and downstream supply chain partners as a value-added service that has resulted in competitive advantage and increased revenues. All in all, using BI to improve revenue-generating processes is one of the most effective ways BI can be employed to drive profits.

7.5   Business Intelligence for Operating Processes

If we look at today's operations management challenges, we see that the fundamental economic relationships among costs, time, service, quality, asset levels, outputs, and backlogs are still at the heart of what operations and supply chain managers must be concerned with if they are to optimize profits. The need for relevant business information about operating performance is even greater when one considers the trend toward extended enterprises and competition based on the performance of constellations of organizations up and down the entire value chain. We observed this need when we were engaged by a $2 billion food ingredients manufacturer for a supply chain collaboration and optimization project with an international fast food chain. In that engagement, the goal was to quantify and model the relationships among demand, inventory levels, service levels, costs, cycle time, warehouse locations, and operating policies so that the supply chain links from the manufacturer to the retail level could be optimized and periodically rebalanced as conditions changed. We found that we could get some of the information needed through ad hoc studies. In other cases, however, the information simply wasn't available, either from the manufacturer's systems or from the third-party systems distributors who were the link to the retail level of the supply chain. Yet this is exactly the type of information today's managers need to optimize operations and operating profits among the companies in the extended enterprise.

7.5.1 Common Ways Business Intelligence Is Used to Improve Operating Processes

In our earlier discussion in Section 7.3.3, we illustrated how BI tools and techniques can deliver business information and analytical capabilities to help companies optimize operating performance in support of their business designs. By bringing together multidimensional information about all aspects of operations, BI provides the tools needed to improve asset utilization, reduce cycle times, improve quality, improve service, and reduce costs, all of which contribute to improved profits. To illustrate this point, we will provide high-level descriptions and/or brief examples of some common ways BI is used to improve operating processes.

To frame the discussion, we are concerned here with the highlighted operating processes (darker boxes) shown in the simple value chain representation shown as Figure 7-6. The fundamental operations management challenge is to optimize the highlighted processes to support the business design and thereby optimize operating margins, a key determinant of profit. Here are some common ways you can use BI to improve operating processes:

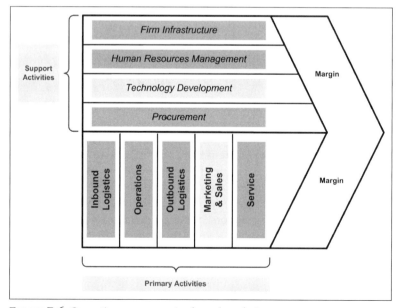

FIGURE 7-6 Operating processes in the value chain.

- **Cycle time reduction.** From a customer perspective, the time it takes to fulfill an order is often a key determinant of customer satisfaction, whether in a retail context or a business-to-business context. From a cost perspective, cycle time impacts capacity and asset utilization and can drive fixed costs up or down. With more and more companies today operating in lean environments and/or competing on time, cycle time reduction is increasingly important. Further, cycle time affects cash flow and working capital requirements, and thus it impacts profits. Accordingly, using BI to reduce cycle time is often a key business opportunity. Cycle time reduction is effectively a dimension of business process improvement, and thus having accurate and specific information about the end-to-end process is a prerequisite for knowing where improvement opportunities may lie.

  For example, many companies pay a lot of attention to the so-called order-to-cash cycle time: the total elapsed time between when a customer's order was received and when payment was received for the order. That entire elapsed time is a function of the elapsed time for all the steps in the end-to-end process. By using the kind of detailed transaction data that is often available from ERP and other operational systems, we can determine where most of the time is taken. By using analytical techniques from the operations research field, we can then identify improvement strategies and make operating changes. Furthermore, we can use the BI environment to gauge the effectiveness of the changes by examining post-change transactional information to see if cycle time has been reduced.

- **Risk reduction.** In operations, risk can convert to costs, which affect profits. The risk may be in potentially obsolete inventory, in warranty repairs, in fraudulent transactions, in bad debt, in employee turnover, in supplier performance, or in any number of other places. Because of the cost impact, being able to identify and quantify the likely economic impact of risk is an essential precondition for risk mitigation. As with many other BI opportunities, the business information needed to support informed risk analysis techniques can often be found in detailed transactional information.

  For example, a very popular BI application in the credit card business is fraud detection, whereby a customer's previous card transactions are examined by using data mining techniques to detect his or her purchasing patterns. This information is used to create a profile so that future transactions that appear to be out of the norm for an individual can be flagged and disapproved, thus reducing fraudulent transactions under circumstances as credit card theft. As another example, a major automobile manufacturer tracks warranty repairs by make, model, part, mileage, and so forth as a means of identifying the costs of quality problems. Armed with such information, the manufacturer can initiate value engineering changes to parts that show a higher propensity to cause warranty repairs. In general, by sifting through detailed transactional history, companies in a variety of industries have identified and quantified risks and then systematically reduced them, thereby reducing costs and increasing profits.

- **Quality improvement.** As with cycle time, quality improvement is effectively a dimension of business process improvement, and thus having specific business information about process quality, product quality, and/or service quality is a precondition for being able to improve quality. If we refer to Figure 7-6 and the value chain processes it depicts, we can say that the quality of every shaded process area can be the subject of quality improvement efforts. For example, in the firm infrastructure box, we might look at the invoicing process and track the percentage of correct invoices as a measure of quality. In the inbound logistics box, we might track supplier performance on a measure such as percentage of perfect orders, which we might define as all orders shipped on time, complete (no backorders) and billed correctly. By storing and analyzing detailed transactional information, BI can deliver essential information for identifying, measuring, and quantifying the economic impact of quality issues. This is a key step to improving quality and thus avoiding the cost of sub-par quality, thus improving profits. Brother International, for example, uses a data warehouse and BI techniques to glean information about product quality problems from its technical support calls. It then uses this information to improve both its products and its technical support.

- **Service level improvement.** Service level is defined differently under various circumstances: it may be simply a function of cycle time, which we discussed above; it may reflect more than one dimension of operational performance, such cycle time and quality; or it may be expressed as product availability to meet demand. In all these cases, we are concerned with being able to measure and manage service levels, and once again, we can use BI tools and techniques to analyze detailed transaction records to discern service level performance and identify improvement opportunities.

- **Asset reduction.** One of the principal ways that BI can be used is to reduce assets, particularly inventories of finished goods in product industries, inventories of operating supplies in various industries, and property, plant, and equipment in various industries. All of these opportunities are related to using BI to better understand demand and demand variability, or to improving process efficiency and thereby reducing capacity requirements in relation to level demand or enabling capacity to stay level in relation to increasing demand.

- **Purchasing.** In many industries, the percentage of the final product cost contributed by purchased raw materials, subassemblies, or finished goods is increasing for a variety of economic reasons. With purchased goods being a larger determinant of costs, many large enterprises need to maximize their purchasing power on a global basis. That said, many such companies have lacked a central repository of purchasing history, and thus they often do not know how much of a given product was purchased by their various operating units. Accordingly, strategic purchasing programs, which are generally organized by commodity, have lacked essential information to optimize their purchasing power. By using BI, this barrier to reducing costs can be overcome, as has recently been accomplished by a global automobile manufacturing company.

- **Order processing.** One view of order processing is from the cycle time perspective. In that vein, we can use BI to analyze and improve the process and reduce the cycle time, as we discussed above under the topic of cycle time reduction. Another view of order processing is from a customer service perspective, wherein we want to order better service to our most important and profitable customers. From that perspective, BI about customer profitability and/or customer lifetime value can be incorporated into business rules that prioritize order fulfillment to favor our best customers.

For example, in one business-to-business context in which we have worked, manufacturing scheduling was done on a first-in, first-out basis until it was determined that numerous small orders from infrequent customers would sometimes result in large orders for key customers being delayed. By using BI to identify its most profitable customers, this company was able to define business rules that could automatically be implemented by its manufacturing scheduling system, thus avoiding the costs of expediting large orders.

- **Benchmarking and process improvement.** Effectively, BI is a generalized process improvement tool, as the discussions above have indicated. An added wrinkle in the operations realm is benchmarking, whereby a company uses BI to analyze its processes along such key dimensions as time, cost, and quality and then compares its results to benchmark data. Benchmarking is a popular approach in operations, and some leading BI tools include reference databases of benchmark data.

7.5.2 Summary: Business Intelligence for Operating Processes

Although early adopters of BI tended to live in the marketing and sales arena, more and more BI success stories are coming from the operations arena. As more companies seek further cost reductions in response to profit pressures, the power of BI for pinpointing costs, cycle times, asset utilization, service levels, risks, and quality levels at specific and detailed operating process levels has become apparent. Armed with better business information and analytical tools for improving operating processes, companies have succeeded in improving profits.

7.6 Summary: Important Ways Business Intelligence Can Drive Profit Improvement

We have seen in this chapter that the way specific companies compete in their industries drives how BI can be used to improve their profits. We have also seen that there are many different possibilities for using BI, which creates some opportunity for innovation and competitive advantage. That said, we can use BI opportunity analysis to identify the best BI opportunities for a given company.

To stimulate your thinking about opportunities that may be relevant to your company, we have provided a wide range of examples of how BI is being used today in companies around the world. Whether your company wishes to innovate with its use of BI or simply keep pace, the BI opportunities described in this chapter are a good place to start. The bar has been set high in many cases, but not so high that BI cannot deliver competitive advantage and/or increased profits to companies that leverage what has been learned to date by successful BI innovators and apply appropriate methods for BI design and development.

7.7   Key Points to Remember

- The specific BI information that a company needs is determined by the company's industry, business design, value proposition, and competitive strategy.
- You should identify and then prioritize your company's BI opportunities by the amount of additional profit they will generate relative to their costs in money and process change.
- Most companies can find BI opportunities to improve their management processes, revenue generation processes, and operating processes.
- BI doesn't (and shouldn't) measure only financial factors, but unless you connect your BI efforts quantitatively and specifically to your business goals, you won't know if you're making a profit or a loss on your BI investment.

7.8   Think Tank

7.8.1   Seven Questions to Ask About How Business Intelligence Can Improve Profit in Your Company

1. What role do you see your company adopting in its BI efforts? Will you be a leader, taking greater risks to achieve greater competitive advantages? Or will you be a follower, taking less risk but using BI to stay even with your competitors? There's no one "correct" answer: it depends on your company, culture, industry, and ultimately on your business judgment.
2. What factors in your industry make specific BI information relevant for your company?
3. How does your company's business design determine what BI information is most important to you?
4. How does your company's competitive strategy determine what BI information is most important to you?
5. How can you apply BI to improve your management processes?
6. How can you apply BI to improve your revenue-generating processes?
7. How can you apply BI to improve your operating processes?

7.8.2   Quiz: How Does Business Intelligence Improve Profits?

1. How can BI information help a company improve its supply chain management?
2. Is BI likely to affect a company's core business processes? If so, how should the company plan to deal with that impact?
3. How can business decisions be classified? For which type(s) of decisions is BI likely to have the greatest positive impact on a company's profits? Why?
4. How can BI help a company improve its planning and forecasting?

5. What are Balanced Scorecards and how can BI help a company use them to improve profits?
6. How does a modern MAIF differ from its traditional counterpart? How does BI enable companies to use the modern framework?
7. What are some examples of how BI can improve marketing, channel management, and CRM?

Chapter 8

Common Mistakes Companies Make on Business Intelligence Initiatives

"The structure that a mature enterprise takes on at any point in time essentially represents the accumulation of a long series of prior resource allocation decisions. . . . If these decisions are made without a coherent guiding philosophy or strategy, the organization that results will be like a stalagmite: shapeless, inefficient, and of little usefulness."
—Robert Hayes, Steven Wheelwright, and Kim Clark, *Dynamic Manufacturing*

It can be argued that the emergence of the term "business intelligence" (BI) within the data warehousing (DW) industry was spawned largely as a result of the many mistakes that organizations unwittingly made as they pursued DW initiatives. Those mistakes were often costly, resulting in the implementation of large unused data warehouses that represented significant wasted investments.

With the arrival of the new BI buzz, the discussion turned away from how to build large data warehouses toward the acknowledgement that the data warehouse was only a means to an end. What was really needed was BI: the ability to identify and deliver actionable information that could be used within the organization to improve bottom-line business performance. Data warehouses would be repositioned as the technical means to achieve BI.

Once management's eyes turned toward BI, their interest in identifying return on investment (ROI) associated with BI/ DW investments also resurfaced. Unfortunately, much of the BI discussion is still relegated to buzz and has not been truly embraced and adopted by organizations. With new BI vendor offerings in the areas of analytical applications, scorecards, and dashboards, many organizations are faced with even more choices, which heightens the potential for chaos.

This problem is illustrated by a recent discussion we had with a student of ours. As an exercise, the student had been assigned to determine which key process indicators (KPIs) from the plethora of choices offered within his company's new BI vendor tool should be used by their organization to measure business performance. The tool had clearly been purchased to address information requirements that had not yet been defined, Without a sound framework to sift through all the possibilities that are offered in the BI/DW arena, there is a very real risk that organizations will repeat history and make more costly mistakes. Instead of improving the informational capabilities of an organization, BI initiatives, just like DW initiatives, can have the *opposite* effect. Several years ago one of our clients, a vice president of marketing, said it well: the problem used to be that there was too little information; now the problem is that there is too *much* information. It's like being a child in the F.A.O. Schwarz toy store in Manhattan: you don't know which way to turn.

Back to what we are trying to achieve. The BI ideal would be to make optimal use of information within the organization to achieve measurable improvement in business performance. It would be to have exactly the right information at the right time to make the business decision and take the actions needed to achieve optimal business performance. Although this is the ideal, very few organizations have come close to achieving it. Advances in technology offer the promise of BI, but achieving incremental improvements in information usage within organizations has proven to be difficult. The following section outlines the most common and damaging mistakes that managers make within the context of critical BI success factors. The BI Pathway approach was developed to address these critical success factors and to avoid those mistakes. Although much of this information is covered obliquely in other sections of this book, this section is meant to distill the most common mistakes we've seen that have thwarted BI success.

8.1 Critical Success Factor: Establishing the Value Proposition

The first step to BI success is to establish a clear understanding of how business performance can be improved by investing in a BI program and to define the scope of the BI initiative. You can define scope as enterprise-wide, limited to a single line of business, limited to a single function, or limited to a group of users. Define scope any way that makes sense, but *define it you must*. Until you know what you're *not* going to do, it's very hard to speak with confidence about what you *are* going to do. Establishing the scope of the BI initiative is a vital first step and prerequisite for defining the value proposition. These activities set the foundation for everything to follow.

Once you've set the scope, focusing on how a BI program can improve business performance explicitly addresses the ROI issue: Why should we embark upon a BI initiative? What business problems exist and how will a BI program address these problems? What will a BI investment give us that we can't already get? Is the investment worth the potential business value? How will having this information translate into bottom-line results? Why should we fund the BI initiative instead of another potential IT capital investment? Why should organizational stakeholders support the BI initiative?

8.1.1 Mistake #1: No Explicit Alignment Between Business Intelligence Strategy and Business Strategy

In their quoted statement at the beginning of this chapter, Hayes et al. (1988) were concerned about manufacturing strategy and competitiveness. It is clear that aligning resource allocation decisions with business strategy is just as important for BI competitiveness. In our experience, one of the most common and critical mistakes is the lack of explicit alignment between BI strategy and business strategy (Figure 8.1). Accordingly, BI investments are made without a coherent guiding philosophy, and the organizational result is an inability to fully leverage BI as a profit-improvement tool.

Clearly, organizations would never develop business processes such as order processing and inventory management without knowing the purpose of the processes and how they contribute to achieving business results. It is common, however, that organizations invest in BI/DW initiatives without having a clear understanding of what informational capabilities they are building, why they need those capabilities, and how they will contribute to achieving business goals and objectives.

This problem is illustrated by a conversation we had recently with a company in the midst of a major undertaking to integrate customer information across all lines of business. When asked why the company needed this capability and how this information would be used to support business goals and improve business performance, managers had no answer. Clearly, this linkage had not been explicitly discussed and communicated within the organization. If BI capabilities are to be optimized, the business needs a clear understanding of the opportunities that exist to deliver and use information in support of the business strategy. It provides the critical foundation for all that is to follow. Companies that think about how they use information to improve strategic results will be ahead of companies that don't.

8.1.2 Mistake #2: Not Knowing How to Define Information Requirements

Once you have a well-reasoned understanding of the relationship between BI strategy and business strategy, it is critical to understand the details of the information

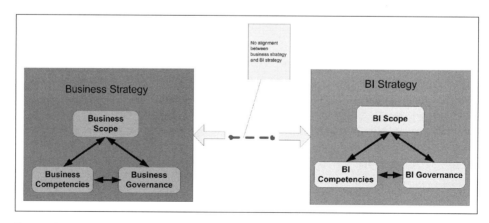

FIGURE 8-1 Connecting business strategy to BI strategy.

requirements and how they relate back to supporting the business. Because business users have been trained over the years by information technology (IT) departments to provide reporting specifications for operational system reporting, these business users reasonably think that information requirements should be defined as reporting requirements. IT departments also tend to resort to this seemingly logical approach. As a result, it's common for all concerned to specify requirements as data elements rather than as true information needs associated with a clear business purpose. Accustomed to not having information, business users often request the ability to have lots of data so that they can do ad hoc reporting. This approach has typically lead to expensive, monster-sized databases that are not designed for a specific purpose and do not perform well. Because they tend to be large, unwieldy, and confusing, containing "everything and the kitchen sink," they often end up not being used by the business.

Because of this approach to defining requirements, it is very common for information requirements to exist with little if any business context. Why particular information is needed, how it will be used, and how the intended use would contribute to improved business performance are not clearly understood or articulated. Based on conversations with many people from many organizations over the past years, we've concluded that this problem has been a major contributor to many failed DW efforts. A recurring theme that we have heard from IT staff is that "we built what they asked for and they aren't using it." Companies that both align BI strategy with business strategy and explicitly link how information can be used for competitive advantage by enabling and/or supporting business strategies will be ahead of companies that don't. By putting analytical rigor into "connecting the dots" to clearly understand *what* information is needed by the business, *why* it is needed, and *how* it will be used to improve performance, they are providing a solid foundation for achieving both business and technical BI program success.

8.1.3 Mistake #3: Not Marketing the Vision to Obtain Organizational Support

Many organizations are surprised to discover that it's not good enough merely to develop a BI/DW application and train business users—not if they want to ensure that the application will be used. This approach, which is common for operational systems, does not always work. One reason for its failure is that many organizations consider BI/DW applications to be optional. Unlike most other IT operational applications that replace existing applications and have to be used by the business, BI/DW applications often exist in parallel with old reporting capabilities. As a result, business users who are uncomfortable with the new BI/DW capabilities can frequently fall back on using their old reports to get their jobs done. This makes it harder to ensure that business users will use the new BI/DW capability and that the benefit of this investment will be realized.

By definition, embarking on a BI initiative changes how the organization accesses and uses information. For that reason, it is important that the organizational stakeholders are "on board" with the vision. This should not be a daunting task if

- Key business stakeholders have been actively involved in defining and linking the BI strategy and the business strategy
- Information requirements have been developed so that they clearly outline what new information will be available, why it is needed, and how it will be used to improve performance

Providing a clear articulation of the "current state" of information availability and usage, as well as the vision for the "future state" and how it is better, sets the stage for organizational buy-in and support. Organizations that explicitly embark on a marketing program to obtain organizational buy-in for their BI initiative actively communicate the value proposition to key organizational stakeholders, thereby setting the stage for BI success.

> **Tip**
>
> Establishing the BI value proposition is critical to BI success. It includes using a sound BI requirements framework that explicitly links BI requirements to business need. It also includes promoting the BI value proposition within the organization.

8.2 Critical Success Factor: Establishing and Managing a Business Intelligence Program

Many organizations get started with a single BI project. If it's successful, they realize that there is business demand for more BI capability. Unlike operational IT projects that develop stand-alone systems, such as order entry systems, procurement systems, and human resources (HR) systems, BI applications are *interdependent* and need to be managed within a program context. This interdependency includes BI projects sharing such things as tools and technologies, data architecture, standards, methodologies, and ETL (extract, transformation, and loading) processes. Many BI mistakes result from not fully appreciating the need to manage a BI initiative as a series of projects managed within a unified program.

All BI project opportunities within the stated scope of a BI initiative are *not* created equal: the relative cost/benefit of each potential BI investment varies. Organizations must consider what opportunities exist and how each opportunity sizes up relative to other opportunities. For example, within the scope of an enterprise DW program, there are numerous opportunities for getting started:

- Should we embark upon a project to identify the most important KPIs that will be used by senior management to run the entire business?
- Should we develop a BI capability to improve sales forecasting so that we can improve operational efficiency?
- Should we embark on a project to integrate information across business lines so we can track and provide high service levels to our most profitable customers?

To ensure that BI capital investments are made wisely, organizations must ensure that there is a way to sift through all of the possibilities and evaluate them and fund them based on relative cost/benefit considerations.

8.2.1 Mistake #4: Using Ad Hoc Practices to Select and Fund Business Intelligence Projects

It is always interesting to talk with organizations about their BI projects and the considerations that led the organizations to choose these projects instead of others.

Unfortunately, it's common to hear about (1) a key business individual who unilaterally decided to fund a project, (2) an IT manager who decided to build a BI proof of concept in hopes that it would be funded, or (3) a key individual in management who saw a demonstration of a vendor scorecard and decided to purchase it. It is rare that organizations use a framework for analyzing the merits of the potential BI projects to determine which ones are more worthy of funding based on their potential business value. Organizations that use a structured approach to evaluate and determine the relative cost/benefit of competing BI project efforts are more likely to make optimal use of their BI investments.

8.2.2 Mistake #5: Providing Inadequate Governance for the Business Intelligence Program Management

In most organizations, the job of IT is to run projects that build individual, stand-alone IT applications. By use of this IT paradigm, many organizations mistakenly conclude that BI simply requires an IT project that will result in a BI application. As a result, organizational expectations, business resources, technical resources, and funding often focus on individual project efforts and are insufficient to support the needs of a successful BI program. Although an initial BI project may be needed to spark the interest of the business organization in the possibilities of using information to support business goals, it is important for organizations to understand that a BI initiative ideally goes well beyond any single project. If positioned correctly, it is a long-term program undertaking to leverage information assets to support business success. As such, it requires a long-term commitment, a program perspective, and a governance structure.

To get the most out of a BI initiative, organizations must strategically position them as programs made up of individual BI project efforts, each of which furthers the organization's ability to use information for competitive advantage. If there are organizational impediments to achieving BI program success—such as insufficient funding, resources, and management of BI program activities that cut across individual project activities—then these impediments need to be resolved. Companies set a course for success when they understand the goals and opportunities of a BI initiative and provide adequate resources for both a BI program governance structure and BI project level activities. It's more costly up front to fund BI program governance activities, but this investment is needed to ensure that the right projects get funded; that supporting tools and technologies, data architecture, and ETL processes are rationalized across project efforts; and that sound standards are put in place for use by all projects.

Many of the "problems" we hear about are symptoms of the same mistake: the lack of coherent BI program governance. These problems include the following:

- "Stovepiped" data marts with different answers to the same question
- A new business need to integrate individual BI applications that were developed separately and can not be integrated without redesign

- Redundant ETL processes developed for the same purpose by individual projects that consume resources and don't perform well
- Expensive tools and technologies that were purchased for one project but now don't work for others

Organizations that invest in formal BI program governance in support of all BI projects make a wise investment and avoid expensive future problems associated with a project-centric approach to BI.

8.2.3   Mistake #6: Establishing De Facto Program Governance Based on the Initial Business Intelligence Project

We often have conversations with individuals who are responsible for their organization's "first BI project." Typically, these individuals are overwhelmed by all of the activities they must do to get started. The problem is that in addition to performing all of the activities needed for their individual BI project, they have also become the de facto program managers. Decisions related to tools and technologies, data architecture, technical standards, meta-data management, methodology, and other program-level activities are made by them. They are optimizing their decisions for their current project. As a result, it is common that these decisions sometimes fail to work for future project efforts. Organizations that use the initial BI project to make long-ranging decisions that will affect future projects are risking expensive mistakes.

8.2.4   Mistake #7: Not Strategically Positioning the Business Intelligence in the Business Organization

BI initiatives are often positioned organizationally as an improvement on "reporting" and are viewed as something done by IT. This frequently explains why there is little, if any, advancement of information usage in many organizations. Organizations are on the right track when they appreciate that BI is far more than reporting and can serve as an important tool to advance their competitive position in the marketplace. These organizations tend to view BI as a new strategic tool that has great potential if applied properly. They clearly understand that to make the most of this potential, senior-level business resources need to be actively involved to exploit it. If companies position BI as an important business initiative to be led by senior members of the business organization and supported by IT resources, then they're ahead of companies that don't.

8.2.5   Mistake #8: Not Providing Adequate Resources and Funding for Supporting Efforts Needed for a Successful Business Intelligence Initiative

As part of a BI program effort, it is necessary to provide resources and funding for new supporting functions such as data management and meta-data management. Data management requirements can range from defining enterprise-level naming conventions, definitions, and business rules to ensuring standards of data quality. Meta-data management efforts provide for the management and traceability of all components of the BI environment. Meta-data needs range from ensuring that definitions and business rules associated with BI applications are made available to business users to providing source data mapping information to manage the environment or answer questions regarding the sources of information in a BI application. These efforts can often be significant, but they are needed to ensure the success of the BI initiative. Organizations that recognize the need for and provide the resources and funding for supporting efforts needed to support a BI program will be laying the groundwork for success.

> **Tip**
>
> Establishing and funding a BI program are critical to ensuring a solid foundation for BI initiatives. The BI program provides a business, technical, and organizational framework to guide BI projects.

8.3   Critical Success Factor: Optimizing Information Technology Infrastructure for Business Intelligence

In many organizations, management information and reporting systems are relegated to the status of second-class citizens. Operational systems that take orders, replenish inventory, pay bills, and process paychecks have always been considered the lifeblood of the organization and have always been given priority over systems that deliver information.

In combination with the fact that the technical underpinnings and requirements of these different classes of systems differ greatly, this results in BI technical environments that are optimized for operational systems and don't serve the needs of BI technical environments well. Most business users believe that IT is just IT; they don't understand that there can be distinctly different needs for different classes of systems. If BI is truly being positioned in the company as a strategic tool to improve bottom-line performance, then it needs to be considered by itself and given equal consideration to be successful.

8.3.1   Mistake #9: Using a Technical Infrastructure That Does Not Adequately Support Business Intelligence

Operational systems are designed and optimized to capture individual business transactions (usually current year) as they occur. Those systems also update these business events, as needed, to run the business. Reporting needs are considered secondary when designing these types of systems.

In contrast, a DW environment, typically used to support a BI program, receives high volumes of data, including historical data, from many different systems. The DW environment must be optimized both to load this data efficiently and to provide high-performance information access. Because the underlying purpose and focus of these classes of systems are vastly different, considerations regarding storage, processing, network needs, and tool/technology requirements are vastly different. Unfortunately, it is common to hear about DW environments that don't perform. A major contributing factor to this problem is often an inadequate technical infrastructure. Organizations that recognize the need to invest in a technical infrastructure optimized to support BI requirements will avoid technical risks that lead to performance problems.

8.3.2 Mistake #10: Using Operational System Information Technology Design and Development Approaches

Many organizations do not recognize the inherently different nature of DW. They try to use operational system design and development approaches to get the job done. Although some of these approaches might be useful to address "real-time" DW approaches, many of these approaches do not support other DW needs and result in design, performance, and time-to-delivery problems.

For example, analysis techniques used to identify and document requirements that work well for operational systems do not do a very good job of capturing BI application requirements. Approaches used to specify report design are also not adequate at all. Design techniques used for operational systems, such as data modeling approaches, also are inadequate to support DW needs.

New types of testing to ensure adequate load and query performance are not needed for operational systems, but they are critical for DW environments. Organizations frequently do not appreciate these differences. Without knowing it, they use the wrong approaches to design and develop their DW environments, which results in mistakes that compromise quality and performance. Organizations that recognize that different design and development approaches are needed to support BI requirements will avoid quality and performance problems.

8.3.3 Mistake #11: Using Information Technology Standards and Policies Designed for Operational Systems

In most organizations, IT standards and policies have evolved over time and have been adjusted when problems have occurred. Many of these standards and policies have their roots in the days of mainframe system design, when time was measured in years rather than months. As a result, many of these standards and policies are not conducive to rapid application development: a stated goal for BI applications.

Several years ago, we were working with a client who had a very cumbersome project planning policy. It had been developed in response to sloppy project management practices that had caused problems in the past. This process included developing a very detailed project plan and incorporated several review cycles. If followed properly, it would take more than two months to complete before any project activities began.

The problem was that the BI project on which we were assisting was slated to be completed in four months. Doing the math, we pointed out that 50% of the time slated for the project would be consumed in planning the project. Although this process might be appropriate for a large-scale, multi-year system, it was not appropriate for this organization's BI project.

> **Tip**
>
> BI has its own development and infrastructure needs that often differ from the needs of operational systems. You can save money and time at the beginning by using operational resources and methods for BI, but you end up in the long run with less effective BI systems that deliver less value to the organization. It's wiser to recognize and address the unique requirements and potential of BI at the outset.

Another client had a charge-back system that was in place for business users who requested ad hoc reports. The purpose was to provide a disincentive for users to make ad hoc report requests that affected the performance of their operational systems. This policy, when it was applied to BI applications, made using the DW environment cost-prohibitive. Organizations that review and revise existing IT standards and policies to ensure that the policies adequately support BI program needs will be more successful in developing and deploying BI applications.

8.4 Critical Success Factor: Managing Organizational Change Needed to Capture Value

It is one thing to build a BI asset. It is another thing to ensure that the potential value of that asset is realized. Managing organizational change is critical to ensuring that the BI asset, once built, is put to good use to deliver bottom-line results. Typically, organizations grossly underestimate the effort required to institutionalize and optimize the use of the BI asset. Because business users can often avoid using BI applications, they often do. Training alone is not usually adequate to ensure that business users will get on board with the BI program. Organizational incentives may need to be put in place to ensure that business users will make the changes needed to leverage the new BI asset.

Organizations also are often unwilling to make changes needed to operational systems to ensure that the information they need to run the business is available and of high quality. Because of the organizational challenges associated with change, it is also common that the potential for the use of BI to improve business performance is not optimized.

8.4.1 Mistake #12: Not Utilizing Business Process Reengineering Approaches to Optimize the Use of New Business Intelligence Capabilities

Old IT paradigms usually persist when BI deployment activities are developed. Because acceptance testing and user training have usually signaled the end of a project, most BI efforts stop at this point. The problem with this approach is that business users are often confused about how to do their jobs "the new way" now that they have a new BI application. In some cases, the effect of the new BI capability is minor; in others, the effect is dramatic, completely changing the way that a job has been done in the past.

For example, we worked with a client several years ago who was used to generating a campaign mailing list from valid names in a database. To improve the response rate and reduce the marketing costs associated with obtaining a response, a BI application was developed to support customer segmentation analysis and to generate a targeted list of high-probability prospects. This new capability fundamentally changed the way that the identification of campaign targets was to be performed.

Training alone would have been inadequate to ensure that this new "to be" business process was put in place and used as intended. If business users are not helped along with understanding and adjusting to changes in underlying business processes needed to optimize the use of a new BI application, odds are that the application will not be used as intended. As a result, the potential business value will be compromised.

In addition, the IT department is not the organizational unit that should be charged with this activity. The business organization must work in conjunction with IT staff during the requirements phase to fully articulate both the "as is" business process and information capability and the desired "to be" business process and information capability. As the BI application is implemented, the business organization is responsible for ensuring that business process changes needed to realize the potential value of the new BI application are put in place. Organizations that manage organizational and business process changes needed to capture the value of the BI asset are more likely to achieve a good return on their investment.

8.4.2 Mistake #13: Unwillingness to Make the Organizational Changes Needed to Obtain Data Needed to Deliver Business Intelligence

By definition, BI is about change. In addition to business users needing to adjust to new informational capabilities, changes are also often required so that the organization can capture new types of data needed to provide a BI capability and to ensure the quality of that data. This change usually affects owners of the operational systems who are charged with designing the systems needed to capture business data and set standards for data quality. It also affects business-side people who are charged with inputting the data into the systems. A BI program can be limited by the organizational will to make these changes. Often, the need for more and better data collides with the organizational desire to speed up and reduce the cost of operational processing.

One client several years ago had a need for richer demographic data in order to better profile and understand customer behavior. Rather than putting in place efforts to add to the data currently available about customers, an effort was underway to reduce the amount of available customer data to shorten the length of time and cost required to take customer orders. Because the client's BI strategy was not explicitly aligned with its business strategy, the impact of this change was not visible to key business decision makers. As a result, they had no vote and the operational needs to reduce the time and cost of taking customer orders won out.

8.4.3 Mistake #14: Not Creating Organizational Incentives

Most people in organizations do not like change, even if they understand logically why change may be beneficial to the business. Even when given a BI application that can help them do their job better, and provided with the necessary training and support, resistance is often met. It is common that people may want to resort to what they know and have done for years. To ensure that the people who are needed to capture the value of the BI asset are using it in the way that is intended, it is important to create organizational incentives for "doing the right thing."

One organization built in management objectives affecting bonuses for actively using the BI application. Other organizations send strong signals that senior management will be using new BI application capabilities to manage the business and expects that the rest of the business will use them as well. Organizations that recognize the need to institutionalize the use of BI assets through creating organizational incentives are more likely to capture the potential ROI of their BI asset.

8.4.4 Mistake #15: Not Exploiting the Full Potential of Information

Many organizations have a hard time moving away from the status quo. Accustomed to having little to work with, they have a hard time thinking about the full range of possibilities of how they could use information for competitive advantage. Some organizations, by nature, resist change and will only embrace it when forced to. Other organizations are so focused on the present that they don't seem to have the organizational bandwidth to fully exploit the possibilities.

> **Tip**
>
> To get the most value from BI, you must change your processes from those based on *not* having information to those based on *having* information. Identifying the need for change, and proactively managing it, will increase the odds of success.

There are organizations, however, that are capturing the potential of BI for competitive advantage. These organizations will be the leaders in defining new ways of competing, and will reap the rewards of exploiting this new capability.

8.5 Key Points to Remember

- The first step in getting maximum value from BI is to identify how BI can improve business performance and to define the scope of your BI efforts.
- You should define your BI information requirements so that they are explicitly connected to your organization's business strategy.
- You should manage your BI efforts as a coherent program with long-term goals and global standards, not merely as a series of one-off projects.
- You should actively market the value of BI both to top management and to your business users. This helps ensure adequate support for *developing* BI and profitable *use* of BI after it's developed.
- You should make sure that the organization provides adequate technical infrastructure for BI.
- You should make sure that both top management and IT understand that BI is not "just another IT project."
- You should provide incentives for people to use the new BI capabilities that you've developed.

8.6 Think Tank

8.6.1 Seven Questions to Ask About Business Intelligence Mistakes

1. Has our organization analyzed the value proposition of its BI efforts? If not, when is that going to happen?
2. Have we aligned our BI strategy with our business strategy?

3. Have we actively marketed the value of BI to get management support and user buy-in?

4. Have we understood the difference between a stand-alone BI project and a BI program?

5. Have we defined our BI program in close cooperation with IT and top management? Does everyone understand and is everyone "on board"?

6. Have we defined our BI standards and practices based on a careful review of our BI program as a whole, or have we simply adopted the standards and practices that worked for our first BI project?

7. Have we really understood and communicated to the organization how BI differs from traditional reports?

8.6.2   Quiz: Do You Know How to Avoid the Worst Business Intelligence Mistakes?

1. Why is it important to define the scope of your BI efforts?

2. When should you analyze your organization's BI value proposition and relate it to your business goals?

3. How can you connect your organization's BI strategy with its business strategy?

4. When is the right time to begin marketing the value of BI within your organization?

5. How do the resources for a BI program differ from those required by traditional IT projects?

6. Can BI realize its full value in your organization if people continue to operate in the same way as they always have? If not, how can you identify and make the needed changes?

7. What kind of incentives do your people need to embrace BI?

Chapter 9

A View over the Horizon

"The most important . . . contribution of management in the 20th century was the fifty-fold increase in the productivity of the manual worker in manufacturing. The most important contribution management needs to make in the 21st century is similarly to increase the productivity of knowledge work and the knowledge worker. The most valuable assets of the 20th-century company were its production equipment. The most valuable asset of a 21st-century institution . . . will be its knowledge workers and their productivity.

"Knowledge-worker productivity is the biggest of the 21st-century management challenges. In the developed countries, it is their first survival requirement. In no other way can the developed countries hope to maintain themselves, let alone to maintain their leadership and their standards of living."

—Peter Drucker, *Management Challenges for the 21st Century*

Being in the business of helping companies leverage business intelligence (BI) to improve profit, we find it encouraging that such an esteemed management philosopher as Peter Drucker has devoted a third of *Management Challenges for the 21st Century* to the topics of the information managers needs and knowledge worker productivity. Drucker clearly understood that information and its effective use by managers and other knowledge workers is crucial for business success—"the creation of value and wealth" (Drucker, 1999). Because BI can deliver the business information and analytical tools that managers and knowledge workers need to improve knowledge worker productivity, what can we and should we expect from BI over the next decade? Equally important, what can we and should we expect management to do with BI over the next decade?

Just as the Internet, cell phones, and instant messaging have changed our way of life and enabled us to work smarter, BI holds great potential to revolutionize organizations by enabling them to become smarter about their business, compared with their competitors, to achieve a competitive advantage. Some of the real-world examples have been presented in this book:

- Wal-Mart, a poster child of BI excellence, uses BI capabilities to optimize strategic, tactical, and operational decision making. BI enables Wal-Mart to make smart decisions about everything, ranging from what suppliers will be used to what products will be carried. One can argue that without its BI capabilities, Wal-Mart would not be where it is today.

- First American Corp. avoided financial disaster by reinventing its business model to become customer-centric. BI capabilities enabled and served as a key element of its business strategy. In just eight years, BI enabled First American to go from a $60 million loss to a $211 million profit.
- Whirlpool, a company that competes on its reputation for quality, used BI capabilities to rapidly identify and resolve quality problems, which enabled the company to improve its ability to manufacture quality products and further strengthen its reputation for quality. By improving the quality of supplier components and reducing failures, Whirlpool was also able to reduce manufacturing costs. Suppliers are able to review the quality records of the products they've sold to Whirlpool and are held accountable for product quality. Whirlpool managers can also use BI capabilities to scour the globe for the lowest-cost, highest-quality parts.

Some organizations, such as Wal-Mart, recognized and captured the opportunities presented by BI. Other organizations, such as First American, used BI to help them combat external threats. Finally, some organizations, such as Whirlpool, used BI to further strengthen their positions in the marketplace, based on core competencies. Although many organizations have been slow to exploit BI opportunities, models of BI excellence clearly illustrate opportunities that are there for companies to capture.

It remains to be seen whether businesses in the future will take the lead of BI visionaries to craft BI strategies that enable them to improve their bottom line. Businesses have always looked to information technology (IT) to develop applications to automate and streamline operational processes in order to improve profits, and have been willing to make the business process and organizational changes needed to reap the benefits. In contrast, businesses have been generally slow to recognize the potential that data warehousing approaches afford to put in place BI programs that enable knowledge workers to recognize opportunities to improve business performance. Even in companies that aggressively move to improve operational performance through technology, process, and organizational change, it is not uncommon that their data warehousing investments have amounted to little more than Web-enabled legacy reports and providing databases so that business users can produce ad hoc reports. To reap the true potential of their investments, it will be necessary to move beyond this to craft BI strategies and employ BI programs that have the potential to have bottom line impact. The advantage that BI can bring is there for those who recognize and exploit its potential.

The ideal would be that, similar to the wholesale adoption of the Internet, most organizations recognize and capture the opportunity that BI affords over the next decade. This would markedly change the nature of business, adding a new type of competition—one that relies on companies outsmarting their competitors by coming up with new and innovative ways to use information for competitive advantage. Although hard to imagine, it was not long ago that few companies conducted commerce over the Internet. From a business strategy perspective, the issue that will determine the future of BI is not the lack of BI opportunities for profit improvement or a dearth of the technical and business know-how required to design and deliver BI applications that can improve profits. Rather, we see the strategic issue as a lack of top management recognition that business information and its exploitation by knowledge workers via relevant analytical techniques can be a core strategic competency that can make the difference between success and failure in the marketplace. We will present our ideas about underlying causes of this later in this chapter. Before that, however, we'd like to present our views on where we see BI heading over the next decade. With that as the foundation, we will then return to the reasons we believe management has not yet stepped up to the plate in many cases when it comes to leveraging BI for profit improvement.

9.1   Business Intelligence Moves into the Mainstream

As we noted throughout this book, there are more and more documented cases of BI bottom-line successes and these successes are increasingly being published in business publications. In addition, there is more of a focus on business performance measurement, including the popularization of Balanced Scorecards, dashboards, and the use of key process indicators (KPIs) in the marketplace. Although led by vendors, the need for performance-based management is being increasingly recognized and adopted by businesses. We believe that as business executives increasingly recognize how improved BI capabilities can lead to improved business performance, there will be more business attention paid to BI and an increased willingness to make the changes needed to achieve it. As we discussed throughout this book, business leadership is essential to achieving BI and is currently lacking in many companies.

9.2   Decision Process Engineering: Equipping Knowledge Workers with Information and Instituting Standards and Accountability

At many points in this book, we have stressed the importance of driving the use of BI into business processes that impact profits, be they management processes, revenue-generating processes, or operating processes. This is happening in more and more companies, and we see it continuing as followers and laggards look to catch up with innovators.

Although most companies have well-defined operational processes for line workers and hold these workers to standards of performance, few knowledge workers, who are responsible for strategic and tactical decision making, are held to the same standards of performance. Operational reports that are produced by operational systems have typically provided the information needed to measure and manage the operational performance of workers. In many cases, the information needed to support strategic and tactical decision making by knowledge workers has been of low quality or unavailable. Because strategic and tactical decision making requires historical views and analyzing trends, as well as seeing views of the business that crossed functional areas or lines of business, before data warehousing this information was often unavailable. As a result, managers learned to make do with little information and to make many decisions based on their experience rather than on the numbers. In many organizations, even when the information is available to improve upon knowledge worker performance and to hold knowledge workers accountable for their decisions, ad hoc approaches still prevail. As a result, in many businesses operational processes are defined, measured, and optimized, whereas strategic and tactical decision processes are not. As a result, although a business may have achieved high levels of productivity, optimizing operational performance, they may not be doing the right things. An example is the Whirlpool case study: before their BI initiative, the manufacturing operation may have been producing their quotas of washers, not knowing that they were producing defective washing machines if they had purchased defective parts from suppliers. The management decision to use the "best suppliers" based on quality and price is now possible because this information is available. Now that information is available on both price and quality of supplier parts, how that decision is made can be defined and measured as a knowledge worker decision process. Ensuring that these knowledge worker decisions are optimized will lead to improved business performance.

Looking ahead, we see an opportunity to re-engineer knowledge work by marrying BI, business processes, and structured fact-based decision making—the latter aimed at measuring, managing, and improving the effectiveness of key strategic and tactical decisions that impact profits.

Historically, this type of decision making has been predominantly an ad hoc, idiosyncratic process in many business contexts. That said, there are readily defined business processes for making decisions for recurring, well-structured business problems, that is, problems for which there is a clear consensus on objectives, alternatives, and impacts (Marakas, 1999). For example, pricing decisions in asset-intensive businesses such as commercial aviation and lodging are made dynamically by revenue optimization systems. More broadly, a decision process is simply a specific type of business process and thus is amenable to process specification, standardization, and improvement via business processes re-engineering techniques. In effect, companies can leverage BI and existing technologies and methods to

- Bring structure and consistency to business decision making where feasible and appropriate
- Drive the use of specific business information and analytical techniques into strategic and tactical decision processes to improve the consistency and effectiveness of recurring decisions
- Allow for application of intuition and judgment within a defined decision process
- Ensure that appropriate analytical frameworks and tools are used for key decisions
- Increase the level of transparency, accountability, and traceability of important decisions
- Measure key decision process variables such as cycle time, cost, service level, and quality

Effectively, by blending BI with "decision process engineering," we can re-engineer aspects of knowledge work that can have a substantial profit impact. We can think of this endeavor as expanding the number of business situations within which structured, fact-based decision making can be brought to bear. Technically, decision process engineering employs BI, business process modeling, business rules, and workflow software.

Although many industries have in place highly defined day-to-day operations that are under process control and build in worker accountability, this same standard is not used for management decision making. Too often acquiring business information and analyzing it to improve the effectiveness of business decisions is still an idiosyncratic, ad hoc process. We believe that for every leader in the use of BI there are dozens who have fallen behind or who are stuck in the earlier stages of BI maturity (see Chapter 5). Based on the magnitude of business value that successful BI investments have created, we believe these companies are leaving tens of millions of dollars in profits on the table. That said, evidence suggests that companies are capitalizing on BI, business process engineering, and workflow to automate routine operational decisions, and thus we believe this concept will be extended to a much broader set of decision processes over the next decade. For example

- Antifraud applications in the credit card business use BI in the form of data mining of a customer's transaction patterns to identify potentially fraudulent transactions and decide to disapprove the transaction. This entails using workflow within a transaction approval process that accesses BI before making a decision according to predefined business rules.
- Online sales applications at sites such as Amazon.com use BI in the form of collaborative filtering of customers' transaction patterns to identify additional books or compact discs a customer may wish to purchase and offer those items to the customer. This entails using workflow within a purchasing process that accesses BI before making a decision according to predefined business rules.
- Business credit scoring applications used in different industries use BI in the form of data mining of credit history of a given firm and similar firms to determine whether or not to extend trade credit. This entails using workflow within a credit approval process that accesses BI before making a decision according to predefined business rules.

The above examples show the degree of structured, fact-based decision making that is possible for well-structured operational business processes. By use of the same concepts and technologies, companies can re-engineer decision processes that occur within the context of management processes, revenue-generating processes, and operating processes. An overview of some of the possibilities is provided in Table 9-1, which builds on the examples of BI applications described in Chapter 7.

Table 9-1 is designed to illustrate the concept of decision process engineering and, hopefully, spark your thinking about how the concept can be applied at your company. As a general proposition, the state of the art in business process management (BPM) is advancing to the point at which recurring multi-step business processes such as order processing, claims processing, campaign management, inventory management, materials management, and many other knowledge work processes are being standardized via the use of flexible, configurable BPM applications. BPM applications allow companies to specify reusable process patterns to

Table 9-1

Opportunities for decision process re-engineering

	Examples of Opportunities for Decision Process Engineering		
	The BI Component	The Business Process Engineering Component	The Workflow Component
Management Processes			
Forecasting & Planning	Multi-dimensional information about sales, outputs, performance, and other variables of interest coupled with analytical applications	Define Current State and Target State Processes for the various forecasting and planning activities of the company as input to workflow business rules	Pre-defined rules and routings for who prepares initial forecasts and/or plans, what BI application they use, what decision needs to be made, who reviews the initial forecasts, who makes the approval decision, and what timetable is to be followed
Budgeting	Multi-dimensional information about historical revenues, costs, outputs, and other variables of interest coupled with analytical applications	Define Current State and Target State Processes for the budgeting activities of the company as input to workflow business rules	Pre-defined rules and routings for who prepares initial budgets, what BI application they use, what decisions need to be made, who reviews the initial budgets, who makes the approval decision, and what timetable is to be followed
Performance Management, Process Improvement, Quality Management, Performance Optimization, etc.	Multi-dimensional information about historical revenues, costs, outputs, quality, service, asset utilization, supply chain performance, customer performance, internal operational performance, organizational learning, and other variables of interest coupled with analytical applications	Define Current State and Target State Processes for performance management, process improvement, quality management, performance optimization and other management activities as input to workflow business rules	Pre-defined rules and routings for who develops performance/process/quality baselines or targets, what BI applications are to be used, what variance analysis approach is to be used, what decisions need to be made, who reviews the analyses, who makes the decisions, and what timetables are to be followed

Revenue Generating Processes

Marketing Analysis and Customer Segmentation	Multi-dimensional information about sales, sales trends, products/services, product/service features, prices, promotions, customers, channels, transactions, and other variables of interest coupled with analytical applications	Define Current State and Target State Processes for the marketing analysis and customer segmentation activities of the company as input to workflow business rules	Pre-defined rules and routings for who performs marketing analysis and/or customer segmentation, what BI applications they use, what decisions need to be made, who reviews the initial analyses, who decides to accept the marketing analysis and/or customer segmentation, and what timetable is to be followed
Advertising, Direct Marketing, and Public Relations	Multi-dimensional information about sales, sales trends, products/services, product/service features, prices, promotions, customers, channels, transactions, and other variables of interest coupled with analytical applications	Define Current State and Target State Processes for the message generation activities of the company as input to workflow business rules	Pre-defined rules and routings for who generates research-driven messages, what BI application they use to see market analyses and/or customer segmentations, what decisions need to be made, who reviews the initial messages, who makes the approval decision, and what timetable is to be followed
Channel Management	Multi-dimensional information about sales, sales trends, products/services, product/service features, prices, promotions, customers, channels, transactions, and other variables of interest coupled with analytical applications	Define Current State and Target State Processes for the channel management activities of the company as input to workflow business rules	Pre-defined rules and routings for who conducts channel analyses, what BI application they use, what decisions need to be made, who reviews the initial analyses, who decides what to do as a result of the analyses, and what timetable is to be followed
Category Management	Multi-dimensional information about sales, sales trends, products/services, product/service features, prices, promotions, customers, channels, transactions, and other variables of interest coupled with analytical applications	Define Current State and Target State Processes for the category management activities of the company as input to workflow business rules	Pre-defined rules and routings for who prepares initial category performance analyses, what BI application they use, what decisions need to be made, who reviews the analyses, who makes the category management decisions, and what timetable is to be followed

(Continued)

Table 9-1

Opportunities for decision process re-engineering—Cont'd

	Examples of Opportunities for Decision Process Engineering		
Operating Processes	The BI Component	The Business Process Engineering Component	The Workflow Component
Process Improvement	Multi-dimensional information about cycle-time by process step, asset utilization, process cost, process service level, process quality, and process outputs coupled with analytical applications, benchmark data, and operations research techniques	Define Current State and Target State process improvement methods as input to workflow business rules	Pre-defined rules and routings for who prepares initial process performance assessments, what BI application they use, what decisions need to be made, who reviews the analyses, who makes the process improvement decisions, and what timtable is to be followed
Risk Reduction	Multi-dimensional information about e.g. warranty repairs, obsolete inventory, fraudulent transactions, bad debt, machine down time, supplier performance, and/or other areas of business uncertainty, coupled with analytical applications and operations research techniques	Define Current State and Target State risk management/risk reduction processes as input to workflow business rules	Pre-defined rules and routings for who prepares initial risk assessments, what BI application they use, what decisions need to be made, who reviews the analyses, who makes the decisions, and what timtable is to be followed
Purchasing	Multi-dimensional information about what products and/or services are purchased, from whom, by whom, at what prices, in what quantity, within what product or service category, and during what time period, coupled with reference data about global supply conditions and apropriate analytical applications	Define Current State and Target State purchasing processes as input to workflow business rules	Pre-defined rules and routings for who prepares initial purchase price targets, what BI application they use, what decisions need to be made, who reviews the analyses, who makes the decisions, and what timtable is to be followed

improve the quality and efficiency of recurring processes (Smith, 2003). Our view is that the same technologies and methods will be applied to fact-based decision making, leveraging BI in the context of business processes that impact profits.

9.3 Re-engineering Knowledge Work: Releasing the Power of Business Intelligence

The Peter Drucker quote at the start of this chapter communicates his position that the "most important contribution management needs to make in the 21st century is. . . to increase the productivity of *knowledge work* and the *knowledge worker.*" Our view is that BI know-how is the core competency needed for this crucial management task. BI marries business information, business analysis, and fact-based structured decision making, all of which have the potential to dramatically improve knowledge worker productivity. More broadly, BI provides a systematic way to do knowledge work, and to quote Drucker (1999) again, "productivity of the knowledge worker will almost always require the *work itself* be restructured and be made part of a *system.*"

Building on these thoughts for our view over the horizon, and consistent with the leadership and general management challenges we described in Chapter 5, we can predict that improving knowledge worker productivity will require companies to

- Create a broad vision of how the knowledge work that most impacts profits should be done
- Make specific decisions about what management and analytical frameworks are most appropriate for their core business processes in order to standardize around those frameworks
- Determine what business information is needed to apply the selected frameworks
- Determine how key decisions should be made and by whom
- Infuse accountability and process metrics into business processes and decision processes
- Invest in BI and BPM competencies, methods, and tools
- Actively manage the changes required to redirect knowledge work from an artisan model to a systems model

In effect, management will be pushed by economic circumstances to re-engineer its own work—to do to its own work what it has done to manual work over the past 100 years. Needless to say, this will be a daunting task, and it will demand BI competencies that are not widely distributed among top executives and managers today. To understand the magnitude of the challenge, let us examine some of the tasks that are involved.

9.3.1 Creating a Vision of How Knowledge Work that Impacts Profits Should Be Performed

In factory settings or large-scale service operations, industrial engineers and business process analysts can directly observe business processes, apply automation where appropriate, create specialized jobs and tasks, train individual workers, measure process performance, and continuously improve results. We have a century-long tradition of doing so, the latest manifestations of which are off-shoring and outsourcing. There is no such tradition when it comes to knowledge worker productivity, in which the tasks are less defined, the desired outcomes are less specific, and the optimal means of getting the work done is more a matter of art than science. Recent developments in the field of BPM are starting to change this state of practice, but key management processes, revenue-generating processes, and operating processes that are the core processes of knowledge work remain largely ad hoc and idiosyncratic in many companies. To re-engineer knowledge work and knowledge worker productivity, companies will need to develop a vision of how knowledge work should be done, which presupposes a good understanding of the current state and an informed sense of the possible and desirable future state.

9.3.2 Making Specific Decisions About Management and Analytical Frameworks for Core Business Processes That Impact Profits

Advances in management thinking and technological capabilities drive innovation in management processes, revenue-generating processes, and operating processes. These innovations have an adoption cycle and a useful life, and they are typically marketed to businesses by consulting firms and software vendors. To re-engineer knowledge work and knowledge worker productivity, companies must understand what the actual state of the art is for a given core business process, whether so-called "best practices" are really best practices or only common practices, whether adopting prepackaged "best practices" will actually advance their cause, and whether they would be better served to continuously improve their own practices. Volumes of information about just about any aspect of business are available, and thus, company managements must sift through the information and make choices about how they want their knowledge workers to think about and analyze business information. For example, would the company be well served to adopt a balanced scorecard approach as a key management framework, or would some other management control system approach work better?

9.3.3 Determining What Business Information Is Needed to Apply the Selected Frameworks

The BI opportunity analysis technique we described in Chapter 2 ensures alignment between drivers, business strategies, and core business processes, as well as the business information and business analyses needed to support fact-based decisions in the context of those core business processes. There is an implicit assumption that a given company has mature management and analytical frameworks with which to align BI in the form of business information and analytical applications. To the extent that this assumption holds, the task of determining business information needs is straightforward. On the other hand, the task of re-engineering knowledge work by unleashing the power of BI may require changes to existing management and analytical frameworks. In either case, the business information required for re-engineering knowledge work is a function of the management and analytical frameworks used or to be used by a given company.

9.3.4 Determining How Key Decisions Should Be Made and by Whom

Picking up again on the concept of decision process engineering, the technologies and methods exist to re-engineer the decision-making processes that are a key component of knowledge work. This brings us into the realm of organizational design and decision support systems. Essentially, organizations are designed to meet the needs of their customers and in accordance with structural archetypes, which results in specified spans of control and accountability for organizational units (Simons, 2005). Along with control and accountability come delegated decision rights, which can be implemented in a variety of ways. Some companies have taken a very structured approach to decision rights. For example, Duke Power created a formal decision rights matrix, which describes the role of each manager for various key decisions, specifies the decision maker and who must be consulted before the decision is made, and specifies who receives what information after the decision is made (Hammer et al., 1999). At the other end of the spectrum are companies with decision processes that are less transparent. In general, the possibilities exist for decision-making processes that vary in terms of formality, the number of persons involved, the manner in which those involved participate, the subject matter, and the type of BI (decision support) used to inform decisions. From a BI perspective, the key is to design BI that meets the needs of different decision styles (Marakas, 1999). Once that has been done, the decision process can be engineered such that it enhances knowledge worker productivity and contributes to more effective decisions, that is, decisions that have a positive profit impact.

9.3.5 Infusing Accountability and Process Metrics into Business Processes and Decision Processes

By restructuring knowledge work to leverage BI, we can make such work part of a system, as suggested by Drucker. Specifically, we can leverage BPM technologies, coupled with BI, to create systematic approaches to core management, revenue generation, and operating processes. This in turn will allow greater transparency into key elements of business process and decision process performance. For example, if we know that a business process is supposed to follow steps 1 through 8, we can use BPM software to ascertain that those steps were in fact followed, determine how long each step took, identify who performed the various steps, and measure other aspects of process performance. Just as we can improve manual work by automation and process improvement techniques, we can re-engineer knowledge work in the same way.

9.3.6 Investing in Business Intelligence and Business Process Management Competencies, Methods, and Tools

Much of re-engineering knowledge work can be built around BI. Simply, just making the right business information and analytical tools available to knowledge workers will go a long way toward improved productivity and profits. Today, companies who are at the earlier stage of BI maturity struggle to bring information to bear in support of key business decisions. As they mature in their use of BI, these companies will have the opportunity to take the next step of re-engineering knowledge work by leveraging BPM technologies and methods. To gain the full benefits of increased knowledge worker productivity, companies will need to invest in BI and BPM competencies, methods, and tools.

As noted previously, Wal-Mart is one of the most outstanding examples of how investing in BI can increase the power and productivity of knowledge work. From its headquarters in Bentonville, Arkansas, Wal-Mart uses BI to manage a world-wide supply chain that includes thousands of vendors and millions of products. A non-stop convoy of trucks brings products from all over the world to Wal-Mart's 1.2 million-square-foot distribution center, where real-time BI systems track each product and send it on its way to the shelves of Wal-Mart stores. Inventory management BI systems tell Wal-Mart which stores need which products, when, and in what quantity (Friedman, 2005).

Wal-Mart has not only invested in BI but has also aligned BI with its strategic goals, has aligned its business processes to use the information BI makes available, and has even helped its suppliers align their systems and processes with those of Wal-Mart.

None of that would have been possible without both investing in BI and using it with common sense and business acumen.

9.3.7 Managing the Changes Required to Redirect Knowledge Work from an Artisan Model to a Systems Model

Unlike with manual workers, where the company owns the means of production, knowledge workers own most of the means of doing their work, that is, the education, knowledge, and expertise they have accumulated over some number of years. Accordingly, we believe that they must be enlisted in any effort to re-engineer their work. In addition to possessing the knowledge of how the work is done, knowledge workers value the opportunity to exercise their analytical and problem solving skills. As we re-engineer knowledge work, the case needs to be made that the resulting knowledge work system will not replace individual creativity but rather will augment creativity and individual initiative by providing business information and analytical applications that allow knowledge workers to consider more scenarios, evaluate more options, analyze more specific information, and apply more sophisticated tools. In effect, the combination of BI and business performance management can afford knowledge workers relief from the drudgework of basic data accumulation and manipulation and instead offer opportunities to have a far greater impact on company profitability. To reach this point, companies will have to manage the change from the artisan model to a systems model.

Although the challenges of re-engineering knowledge work—as described above—may be daunting to some, we believe the rewards will be substantial for those who take up the challenge. By making knowledge work more systematic, companies can ensure that the linkage between strategy, process, information, process, and action is explicit. Coupled with BI about results, the ability to determine the effectiveness of core business processes and decision processes will enable managements to ensure that successful processes and practices are consistently and correctly leveraged to increase profits.

9.4   Closing The Loop: Optimizing and Integrating Strategic, Tactical, and Operational Business Performance

As discussed above, BI provides great potential to improve on knowledge worker performance through optimizing both the information available to knowledge workers and the way in which that information is used by knowledge workers to improve profits. Once optimal decisions and actions are taken by the knowledge worker to optimize business performance, those decisions must be followed through operationally to close the loop and achieve the potential that exists for performance improvement. Going back to the Whirlpool case study, assuming that the managers that are charged with selecting suppliers based on price/quality considerations determine how suppliers will be selected and relay this decision to the purchasing department, the workers charged with ordering supplies have to actually place the orders as stipulated to ensure that the benefit is achieved. Similarly, if a company employs a customer segmentation strategy that identifies high-valued customers and determines that these customers have their fees waived, this action must be taken at the operational level when a highly valued customer order is placed. By optimizing strategic and tactical decisions and actions and ensuring that these decisions are operationalized, businesses can then measure the effect of the decisions and actions that were enabled by BI. They can also hold all employees, including knowledge workers, accountable for the decisions and actions that result in business performance.

In addition to aligning, optimizing, and measuring business performance at the strategic, tactical, and operational levels, we believe that there will be a technical alignment and optimization of the systems that are used to support this new business environment. Business users will no longer have to distinguish between business actions and systems and take conscious efforts to logon to BI applications. Rather, technology will improve such that business users can seamlessly do their work, moving between analytical and operational activities with ease.

9.5   Barriers to Realizing the Benefits of Business Intelligence

At the start of this chapter, we asked: what can we and should we expect management to do with BI over the next decade? In our view, we can and should expect management to actively and persistently drive the use of BI to improve profits and business performance. We believe this should take the form of decision process engineering and re-engineering knowledge work. The technologies, business process engineering competencies, and change management techniques are in place, and we see no technical reason why BI cannot be raised to the level where it is integral to how companies do business. That being said, we believe there are identifiable barriers to getting there, not least of which is lack of recognition of the profit and performance impacts of BI. We have attempted to overcome that specific barrier by sharing the information presented in this book. Beyond that, we see five other key barriers, which we will discuss below.

9.5.1 Noise and Confusion in the Business Tools Environment

Executives and managers are bombarded with claims about the merits of various approaches to improving business performance and profits. Strategic Planning, benchmarking, pay-for-performance, outsourcing, customer segmentation, re-engineering, Balanced Scorecard, and total quality management are but a few of the approaches, and there are a host of others that fall into the realm of IT. For example, enterprise requirements planning (ERP), customer relationship management (CRM), and supply chain management (SCM) are three prominent types of enterprise applications that have been sold to businesses over the past decade. All of these approaches are sold by consultants, academics, and software vendors as ways to improve profits and performance, and the results have been mixed. Because of the well-publicized successes and failures and because of the advertising muscle of large software vendors and consulting firms, there is noise and confusion in the business tools environment, and that works against more aggressive adoption of BI and against taking it to the higher level represented by decision process engineering and re-engineering knowledge work.

9.5.2 Skepticism about Information Technology Value Propositions

Simply put, executives and managers are skeptical about IT value propositions, and rightly so. Although major investments in enterprise applications have paid off in some cases, plenty of documented cases indicate where the investments haven't, as well as a few cases in which the applications actually caused major financial and customer relations damage to the companies who made the investments. We believe that the norm is that the investments result in advantages for early movers, parity for later adopters, and massive value transfer from the purchasing companies to the software vendors and consulting companies. As an example, we worked with one company that invested $100 million over the course of a few years to install a well-known ERP system. The major consulting firm that sold the system projected operating margin improvements that would more than cover the investment, whereas a study of the company's Securities and Exchange Commission (SEC) filing shows that the margin improvements have not come anywhere close to paying back the investment. We hear similar stories about CRM and SCM systems, and there are enough published stories to create healthy skepticism in the marketplace. Furthermore, because major consulting companies in effect act as salespersons for enterprise software vendors, executives and managers find it hard to turn to these same consultants for independent, objective advice when it comes to IT, which exacerbates their skepticism about IT value propositions. In this environment, BI is tarred with the same brush.

9.5.3 Executive and Management Challenges Relative to Information Technology

With pervasive cost competition in the global economy and the attendant downsizing, surviving executives and managers are left with significant bandwidth challenges across the board, which often translates into not having the time to really understand IT, its value propositions, and its organizational implications. Compounding this challenge is the fact that many executives and managers are not IT savvy, and so they shy away from the jargon-laden meetings that make them feel uncomfortable. Some of this may be generational, but even today, many top business schools do not emphasize management of IT or essentially ignore the subject. And yet, IT capital spending is a huge proportion of overall business investment. This all manifests itself in the BI arena as a lack of executive and management engagement in BI strategy and the associated organizational changes, and yet it is only these business people who can drive the process changes needed to capture the business value of BI.

9.5.4 Competition for Business and Information Technology Resources

In today's lean business environments, daily and weekly operational requirements typically consume much of the bandwidth of executives, managers, and other knowledge workers. In effect, companies are so busy taking care of today's customers that they have limited time to help evolve the company toward a better way of doing business. This bandwidth issue constrains organizational capacity for improvement. When coupled with actual capital spending constraints and alternative potential investments, this results in internal competition for the business and IT resources needed to make any given initiative successful. One result that we've seen is that companies make a number of small, incremental investments rather than making more substantial investments in a few key initiatives. What this means for BI is that the initiative proceeds more slowly and takes longer to deliver business value, which sometimes results in further skepticism about the business value of BI.

9.5.5 Risk Aversion

The saying used to be that nobody ever got fired for buying IBM. That was business shorthand for saying that sticking to the tried-and-true, accepted ways of doing things is the safest for executives and managers. That fact of business life manifests itself every day in companies around the world. Whether it is a dominant consumer products company or a high-tech manufacturer, companies that regularly compete and innovate in their core products or services become followers when it comes to business tools and IT investments, waiting until they see that others in their industry or value chain have adopted a tool before following along. That said, it has been proven in a range of industries that IT innovation can lead to competitive advantage and superior profits. With innovation, however, comes risk, and thus executives and managers play it conservatively when it comes to IT. Realizing the full profit and performance potential of BI entails risk-taking, and many executives and managers are not prepared to place bets in an area within which they are uncomfortable.

Although there are a host of more tactical, BI specific barriers to realizing the full potential of BI over the next decade, we believe the five barriers discussed above combine to create the most strategic barrier—the reluctance or unwillingness of executives and managers to really go full tilt in the BI arena. This is unfortunate, because there are documented cases in which BI has delivered tens of millions of dollars of incremental profits for those companies who are bold enough to innovate with BI.

9.6 Summary

BI tools and methods have reached a state of maturity where the opportunities for companies to leverage BI are readily grasped. The innovators are already well down the road, and the followers are moving forward to try to catch up. Looking ahead, we believe BI holds the key to meeting the 21st-century management challenges articulated by Drucker, the challenges of leveraging information and improving knowledge worker productivity. Once the strategic and tactical decisions that knowledge workers are charged with are optimized and implemented, this will add to the productivity improvements that business has achieved through operational performance improvements, bringing business performance to new heights in line with Drucker's vision. Although significant barriers exist to achieving this vision, we believe that they can be overcome. These are challenges of enormous economic import, and we would be thrilled to see companies win in the marketplace by being daring and innovative in leveraging BI.

9.7 Key Points to Remember

- BI is not mainly about technology: it's about improving how you manage your organization so you achieve your strategic goals effectively, no matter what those goals are. The ultimate purpose of BI is to help you make your best possible contribution to human welfare and human society.
- You can use BI to incorporate structure, consistency, and analytical techniques into your organization's decision making while still preserving individual intuition and judgment.
- BI is an essential tool in re-engineering knowledge work to align it with the organization's strategic goals and make it more productive. It can help you apply the same productivity insights to knowledge work as businesses have already applied to work whose output is physically measurable.
- By providing information that measures activities' contribution to the organization's strategic goals, BI can incorporate accountability and metrics into business and decision processes.
- In re-engineering knowledge work, seek the help and advice of knowledge workers themselves. Show them how BI, far from replacing the need for their expertise, can help them do their jobs better.
- Healthy skepticism about BI is a good thing. It gives you both the chance and the incentive to think through your BI plans carefully and present them in a solid argument to management.
- Understand that all change involves some risk—even change that ends up conferring a great benefit on the organization. If you are aware of the risks—technological risks, people risks, and business risks—you can plan for them and increase your probability of BI success.

9.8 Think Tank

9.8.1 Seven Questions to Ask About Your Own View Ahead

1. What are your highest-value opportunities to apply BI in the next five years?
2. How is BI already being applied in your industry?
3. How do you expect your industry to apply BI tomorrow?
4. How are your competitors using BI right now?
5. Can you see BI opportunities that your competitors haven't thought of? What are they?
6. How can you use BI to re-engineer decision processes in your own organization?
7. How can you use BI to re-engineer knowledge work in your own organization?

9.8.2 Quiz: How Will You Make the Most of Business Intelligence in the Future?

1. What's holding back your BI efforts right now?
2. How will you overcome that obstacle?
3. How will you use BI to improve service to your customers?
4. How will you use BI to manage your supply chain?
5. How will you use BI to improve management, operating, and revenue-generating processes?
6. How will you forge alliances with your own top management to invest in BI?
7. How do you expect BI to transform your company?

A Business Intelligence Glossary

This appendix defines the most important business intelligence and other technical terms used in this book.

Balanced scorecard: A strategic management system that connects activities to strategic goals and measures how much the activities contribute to achieving those goals. It provides a broader view of the business than merely looking at financial data. Devised by management theorists Robert Kaplan and David Norton.

BI Pathway: A business-centric approach to designing and implementing BI that explicitly connects BI program initiatives with the organization's needs, readiness, strategic goals, and return on investment (however measured).

Business-centric: Methods that design return on investment into BI initiatives from the outset and systematically drive the use of BI into the core business processes and decisions that determine business results. Business-centric methods go beyond traditional approaches by putting rigor into defining the *business value capture mechanism* for each BI project.

Business information: Sets of data presented in a business context that are about a business and its environment.

Business intelligence (BI): Business information and business analyses within the context of key business processes that lead to decisions and actions and which result in improved business performance.

Business question: A question (i.e., a business requirement) that provides details of business users' information needs.

Business value capture mechanism: The manner in which business processes and key decision processes must change in order to leverage BI investments, which are managed as a portfolio. This also includes using process reengineering and process improvement techniques to ensure that BI projects actually deliver the intended ROI.

Customer relationship management (CRM): The tracking and management of all the organization's interactions with its customers in order to provide better service, encourage customer loyalty, and increase the organization's long-term profit per customer.

Data: Facts (such as measurements, statistics, names, categories, etc.) recorded or stored and used as a basis for reasoning, discussion, or calculation.

Data cleansing: The removal of inconsistencies, errors, and gaps in source data prior to its incorporation into data warehouses or data marts to facilitate data integration and improve data quality.

Data mart: A data structure that is optimized for access. It is designed to facilitate end-user analysis of data. It typically supports a single, analytic application used by a distinct set of workers. (Standard definition from The Data Warehousing Institute)

Data warehouse: A data structure that is optimized for distribution. It collects and stores integrated sets of historical data from multiple operational systems and feeds them to one or more data marts. (Standard definition from The Data Warehousing Institute)

Extract, transformation, and loading (ETL): Data Warehouse process that extracts data from source systems, potentially changes it (transformation process), and loads it into target data stores in the BI/DW environment.

Fact/qualifier matrix: A technique to (partially) model target data at a conceptual level. Consists of *facts* (discrete items of business information that users need from the data warehouse), *qualifiers* (criteria or data items needed to group, sequence, select, and access facts for presentation to a data warehouse user), and *associations* (intersecting cells in the matrix that show how qualifiers are related to the facts). (Standard definition from The Data Warehousing Institute)

Information: Sets of data presented in a context. Information about a business and its environment.

OLAP: Online analytical processing. Programmatic analysis of data warehouse or data mart data to yield actionable business intelligence.

OLTP: Online transaction processing. Real-time programmatic processing for operational (rather than analytical) purposes, such as recording a bank customer's deposit at an automated teller machine or tracking a new customer order.

Program: A set of projects pointed toward the same objective.

Project: A formal commitment of resources to deliver known results by a specified time. (Standard definition from The Data Warehousing Institute)

Return on investment (ROI): The full potential business value of an investment.

Supply chain management (SCM): The practice of designing and optimizing supply chain business processes to provide superior service to those customers who drive the bulk of one's profit.

A Business Intelligence Readiness Assessment

This appendix gets you started with a basic assessment of your readiness to implement a business intelligence (BI) program.

B.1 Strategic Alignment

Readiness Factor	Description
1	Company leaders and managers have a keen awareness of the environmental factors that drive our business, e.g., regulations, competition, demand trends, innovations.
2	The relative importance of the environmental factors that drive our business is understood.
3	The relative importance of the environmental factors that drive our business is acted upon.
4	Our company has a clear, actionable strategy for our business.
5	Our company's strategy is appropriate for our business.
6	The key management and business processes the company uses reinforce each other.
7	The key management and business processes the company uses effectively execute our strategy.
8	Everybody in our company understands how we compete.
9	The key management and business processes the company uses help us compete effectively.
10	Our company measures strategically relevant performance factors.
11	Our BI initiatives provide business information and analytical tools to make our management processes more effective.
12	Our BI initiatives provide business information and analytical tools to make our revenue generation processes more effective.
13	Our BI initiatives provide business information and analytical tools to make our operating processes more effective.
14	Our BI initiatives enable fact-based decision making.

B.2   Continuous Improvement Culture

Readiness Factor	Description
1	Our leaders and managers are adept at driving changes to our core business processes.
2	We consistently measure process costs.
3	We consistently measure process cycle times.
4	We consistently measure process quality.
5	We consistently measure customer service levels.
6	We consistently measure asset utilization.
7	We consistently measure process outputs.
8	We are always looking to improve our core business processes.
9	Our process performance information is organized for multidimensional analysis.
10	We use prior period performance information for process improvement initiatives.
11	We apply data-driven improvement techniques such as Six Sigma, Continuous Process Improvement, and/or Total Quality Management (TQM).
12	Our leaders and managers understand that "best practices" mature and are replaced over time.

B.3   Information Usage Culture

Readiness Factor	Description
1	When typical operating decisions are required, we have enough relevant information to make fact-based decisions.
2	When our company develops forecasts, budgets, and plans, we use prior period performance information.
3	Our company is a heavy user of quantitative methods, e.g., linear programming, optimization, modeling and simulation, data mining, and collaborative filtering.
4	Our leaders and managers emphasize the use of analytical frameworks and fact-based decision making.
5	The sharpest analysts in the company are regularly involved in making presentations to our leaders and managers.
6	Our company has institutionalized the use of metrics for performance measurement and improvement.
7	The management information used within our company is timely.
8	The management information used within our company is relevant.
9	Our company rewards the development and use of analytical tools.
10	Our company actively manages the use of information and analysis within our key business processes.

B.4   Business Intelligence Portfolio Management

Readiness Factor	Description
1	We have identified major BI opportunities within our key functions and/or processes.
2	We have prioritized our major BI opportunities based on factors we believe are relevant, e.g., return on investment (ROI) and technical risk.
3	We manage our BI opportunities as a portfolio of projects, i.e., as a program.
4	Management understands that our BI program is a multi-year effort requiring consistent funding/resources and business involvement.
5	We use a BI roadmap or program plan to guide, coordinate, and integrate our BI initiatives.
6	We have strategies and/or methods for ensuring that new BI applications are used to improve business performance.
7	We are investing or have invested in developing core BI competencies.
8	We actively manage the business and technical risks associated with our BI projects.
9	Our BI program is adequately funded to achieve its goals.

B.5   Decision Process Engineering

Readiness Factor	Description
1	For any important operating decision, the relevant managers can tell you how the decision is made.
2	We routinely use information technology (IT)—e.g., groupware or workflow—to formally collaborate in decision making.
3	There is a standard decision-making routine for any well-structured problem situation we face.
4	There is a standard analytical routine for any well-structured problem situation we face.
5	There is a standard approach for any recurring and semi-recurring decisions we face.
6	Our company is data-driven in its key decisions.
7	Our company regularly uses models and/or simulations to support decision making.

B.6   Business Intelligence and Data Warehousing Technical Readiness

Readiness Factor	Description
1	Our company can effectively build and operate a robust BI/data warehousing (DW) technical environment.
2	Our IT function uses an effective, repeatable methodology on all BI/DW projects.
3	We have mature BI/DW operating processes in place.
4	We have a strong, customer-oriented help-desk function.
5	We have a strong program for training business users to use available BI.
6	We have strong source system analysis skills.
7	We have strong data integration skills.
8	We have strong skills in at least one extract, transformation, and loading (ETL) tool.
9	We have strong data quality and stewardship skills.
10	We know how to work with business users to design what they see via BI applications.
11	We know how to manage meta-data.
12	We have strong skills in at least one query and reporting tool.
13	We have strong data architecture skills.
14	We have strong systems integration skills.
15	We have strong BI design skills.
16	The specific needs of BI and DW projects are effectively accommodated within our broader IT environment.

B.7   Business/Information Technology Partnership

Readiness Factor	Description
1	Our leaders and managers spend at least 40 hours a month on IT.
2	Our leaders and managers are IT-savvy.
3	Our IT leaders and managers are business-savvy.
4	The responsibility for capturing the ROI on IT investments resides with the business units.
5	Business managers make the business case for IT investments with inputs from IT.
6	IT is a player at the strategic level of the firm.
7	The chief information officer reports to the chief executive officer.
8	Business people are actively involved in our BI projects.
9	The BI team meets regularly with the business sponsor.
10	Our BI (or IT) governance mechanisms are effective.

Bibliography

Ante, S., "Giving the Boss the Big Picture," *BusinessWeek*, February 13, 2006.

Balanced Scorecard Collaborative, *Balanced Scorecard Functional Release Standards Release 1.0a*, May 5, 2000. Balanced Scorecard Collaborative, Inc., http://www.bscol.com.

Broadbent, M., and Weill, P., *Leveraging the New Infrastructure*. Boston: Harvard Business School Press, 1998.

Cokins, G., *Activity-Based Cost Management: An Executive's Guide*. New York: John Wiley & Sons, 2001.

Cooper, B., Watson, H., Wixom, B., and Goodhue, D., "Data Warehousing Supports Corporate Strategy at First American Corporation," *MIS Quarterly*, December 2000.

Cooper, R., and Kaplan, R., "Profit Priorities from Activity-Based Costing," *Harvard Business Review*, May–June 1991.

D'Aveni, R., *Hypercompetitive Rivalries*. New York: The Free Press, 1994.

Davenport, T., "Competing on Analytics." Keynote Address, New York, NY, January 17, 2006.

Davenport, T., and Short, J., "The New Industrial Engineering: Information Technology and Business Process Redesign," Center for Information Systems Research, Sloan School of Management, Massachusetts Institute of Technology, June 1990.

Davenport, T., et al., "Data to Knowledge to Results: Building an Analytic Capability." *California Management Review*, Winter 2001.

Drucker, P., *Management Challenges for the 21st Century*. New York: HarperBusiness, 1999.

Drucker, P. M., "Be Data-Literate: Know What to Know." *The Wall Street Journal*, December 1, 1992.

Drucker, P. M., *Management Challenges for the 21st Century*. New York: Collins Publishing, 2001.

Dvorak, R., Holen, E., Mark, D., and Meehan III, W., "Six Principles of High Performance IT," *McKinsey Quarterly*, 1997, Number 3.

Executive Office of the President, Office of Management and Budget, *North American Industry Classification System, United States 1997*. Lanham, MD: Bernan Press and National Technical Information Service, 1998.

Hamel, G., and Prahalad, C. K., *Competing for the Future*. Boston: Harvard Business School Press, 1994.

Hammer, M., and Stanton, S., "How Process Enterprises Really Work," *Harvard Business Review*, November–December 1999.

Hayes, R., Wheelwright, S., and Clark, K, *Dynamic Manufacturing*. New York: The Free Press, 1988.

Henderson, J., and Venkatraman, N., "Strategic Alignment: A Model for Organizational Transformation via Information Technology," Center for Information Systems Research, Sloan School of Management, Massachusetts Institute of Technology, CISR WP No. 217, November 1990.

Henderson, J., and Venkatraman, N., "Strategic Alignment: A Model for Organizational Transformation via Information Technology," Center for Information Systems Research, Sloan School of Management, Massachusetts Institute of Technology, 2005.

Johnson, H. T., and Kaplan, R., *Relevance Lost: The Rise and Fall of Management Accounting.* Boston: Harvard Business School Press, 1987.

Kaplan, R., "One Cost System Isn't Enough," *Harvard Business Review,* January–February 1988.

Kempis, R., and Ringbeck, J., "Manufacturing's Use and Abuse of IT," *McKinsey Quarterly,* 1998, Number 1.

Kotter, J., "Leading Change: Why Transformation Efforts Fail," *Harvard Business Review,* March–April 1995.

Marakas, G., *Decision Support Systems in the 21st Century.* New York: Prentice Hall, 1999.

Mintzberg, H., *The Rise and Fall of Strategic Planning.* New York: The Free Press, 1994.

Moore, G., *Living on the Fault Line.* New York: HarperBusiness, 2000.

Morris, H., "The BSC and Analytic Application Integration," *Balanced Scorecard Report,* January–February 2002.

Porter, M., *Competitive Advantage.* New York: The Free Press, 1985.

Porter, M., *Competitive Strategy.* New York: The Free Press, 1980.

Porter, M., and Millar, V., "How Information Gives You Competitive Advantage," *Harvard Business Review,* July–August 1985.

Rigby, D., "Management Tools and Techniques: A Survey," *California Management Review,* Winter 2001.

Ross, J. W., and Beath, C. M. "Beyond the Business Case: Strategic IT Investment." *MIT Sloane Management Review,* Winter 2002, Vol. 43, No. 2, pp. 51-59.

Simons, R., *Levers of Organization Design.* Boston: Harvard Business School Press, 2005.

Slywotsky, A., *Value Migration.* Boston: Harvard Business School Press, 1996.

Smith, H., and Fingar, P., *Business Process Management: The Third Wave.* Tampa, FL: Meghan-Kiffer Press, 2003.

The Data Warehousing Institute (TDWI), "TDWI Business Intelligence Fundamentals, Part II: BI Architectures and DW Methods," Seattle: TDWI, 2004.

Weill, P., and Broadbent, M., *Leveraging the New Infrastructure.* Boston: Harvard Business School Press, 1998.

Williams, S., and Williams, N., "Capturing ROI through Business-Centric BI Development Methods," *DM Review,* August 2004.

Williams, S., and Williams, N., "The Business Value of Business Intelligence," *Business Intelligence Journal,* Fall 2003.

Index

Page numbers followed by *f* indicate figures. Page numbers followed by *t* indicate tables.

About The Authors

Steve Williams, President

Steve Williams founded DecisionPath Consulting in 1999 with the vision of creating maximum business value for clients by using the most innovative, business-driven methods to architect and deliver customized business intelligence (BI) and data warehousing (DW) solutions. This proven, business-oriented approach to leveraging BI is described in the book *The Profit Impact of Business Intelligence* and in several articles in magazines such as *DM Review, Business Intelligence Journal*, and *Strategic Finance*.

At the applied level, Steve and his colleagues at DecisionPath have created an innovative approach to designing, developing, deploying, and leveraging BI to improve business performance. The BI Pathway method has been used at leading organizations in a variety of industries, including financial services, the U.S. federal government, high-tech manufacturing, consumer packaged goods, industrial products, food manufacturing semiconductors, and lodging and leisure. Over the past six years, Steve has had the privilege of applying the BI Pathway method on behalf of the U.S. Social Security Administration, The Principal Financial Group, McCormick & Company, Micron Technologies, the U.S. Environmental Protection Agency, and the U.S. Treasury.

Prior to founding DecisionPath, Steve worked for 20 years in several specialized consulting companies where he developed expertise in program management, systems integration, software engineering, IT strategy, management accounting, and business strategy. He holds an MBA from the Darden School at the University of Virginia and a B.S. in Business Management from the University of Maryland.

Nancy Williams, Vice President — Business Intelligence and Data Warehousing

Nancy Williams is co-founder of DecisionPath Consulting and a recognized leader in the field of business intelligence and data warehousing. In addition to co-authoring *The Profit Impact of Business Intelligence* and several articles in publications such as *DM Review, Business Intelligence Journal*, and *TDWI Flashpoint*, she is a regular instructor at TDWI Conferences and is co-developer (with Jim Thomann and Steve Williams) of the BI Pathway method. Nancy is also a judge for TDWI Best Practices competition.

In addition to providing leadership on BI methods and approaches within DecisionPath, Nancy is substantially involved in many of DecisionPath's consulting engagements. She typically helps clients achieve alignment between business strategies and BI opportunities, define their business requirements for leveraging BI to drive performance, and develop their architectural and program management frameworks for reducing risk and ensuring that BI investments pay off. Over the past six years, Nancy has had the privilege of applying the BI Pathway method on behalf of the U.S. Social Security Administration, McCormick & Company, Legg Mason, Marriott International, the U.S. Treasury, and a number of other organizations.

Prior to co-founding DecisionPath, Nancy worked for 14 years in several specialized consulting companies, where she developed expertise in business process engineering, business intelligence, data warehousing, IT project management and control, program management, financial management, and database systems. She holds an MBA from the Darden School at the University of Virginia and a B.A. in Education, also from the University of Virginia.